State sovereignty is an ir... system is not based on so... the production of a non...... conception which links authority, territory, population (society, nation), and recognition in a unique way, and in a particular place (the state). Attempting to realize this ideal entails a great deal of hard work on the part of statespersons, diplomats, and intellectuals. The ideal of state sovereignty is a product of the actions of powerful agents and the resistances to those actions by those located at the margins of power. The unique contribution of this book is to describe, theorize, and illustrate the practices which have socially constructed, reproduced, reconstructed, and deconstructed various sovereign ideals and resistances to them. The contributors analyze how all the components of state sovereignty – not only recognition, but also territory, population, and authority – are socially constructed and combined in specific historical contexts.

CAMBRIDGE STUDIES IN INTERNATIONAL RELATIONS: 46

State sovereignty as social construct

Cambridge Studies in International Relations is a joint initiative of Cambridge University Press and the British International Studies Association (BISA). The series will include a wide range of material, from undergraduate textbooks and surveys to research-based monographs and collaborative volumes. The aim of the series is to publish the best new scholarship in International Studies from Europe, North America and the rest of the world.

CAMBRIDGE STUDIES IN INTERNATIONAL RELATIONS

State sovereignty as social construct

Edited by

Thomas J. Biersteker and Cynthia Weber

Published by the Press Syndicate of the University of Cambridge
The Pitt Building, Trumpington Street, Cambridge CB2 1RP
40 West 20th Street, Oakleigh, Melbourne 3166, Australia

© Cambridge University Press 1996

First published 1996

Printed in Great Britain at the University Press, Cambridge

A catalogue record for this book is available from the British Library

Library of Congress cataloguing in publication data

State sovereignty as social construct / edited by Thomas J. Biersteker
and Cynthia Weber.
     p.   cm. – (Cambridge studies in international relations: 46)
ISBN 0 521 56252 X (hc). – ISBN 0 521 56599 5 (pb)
1. Sovereignty.   2. Social contract.   3. International relations.
I. Biersteker, Thomas J.   II. Weber, Cynthia.   III. Series.
JX4041.S73   1996
320.1′5 – dc20   95–44523   CIP

ISBN 0 521 56252 X hardback
ISBN 0 521 56599 5 paperback

CE

Contents

Contents

Figures

Contributors

Michael Barnett is associate professor of political science at the University of Wisconsin in Madison. He is the author of *Confronting the Costs of War: Military Power, State, and Society in Egypt and Israel*, and of publications on international relations theory, the United Nations, and Middle Eastern politics. He is currently a MacArthur International Peace and Security Fellow and is completing a book titled *Dialogues in Arab Politics: Negotiations in Regional Order*.

Thomas J. Biersteker is director of the Thomas J. Watson Jr. Institute for International Studies and the Henry R. Luce Professor of International Relations and Political Science at Brown University. His research focuses primarily on international political economy and North–South issues. His most recent books include *Dealing with Debt: International Financial Negotiations and Adjustment Bargaining*.

Daniel Deudney is the Janice and Julian Bers Assistant Professor in the Social Sciences in the Department of Political Science at the University of Pennsylvania. His research focuses on international relations theory, political theory, and environmental politics.

Roxanne Lynn Doty, assistant professor of political science at Arizona State University, is the author of *Imperial Encounters: The Politics of Representation in North/South Relations*. Her articles have been published in *International Studies Quarterly*, *Millennium*, and *Review of International Studies*. She focuses her current research on race and international relations, sovereignty and national identity, and global immigration.

Daniel Friedheim is a visiting instructor in government at Dartmouth

College. His dissertation, "Democratic Transition through Regime Collapse," is on the peaceful East German revolution of 1989. He has published related articles in Shain and Linz's *Between States*, as well as the journals *German Politics* and *East European Politics and Society*.

Naeem Inayatullah is an assistant professor at the Maxwell School of Citizenship and Public Affairs at Syracuse University. His recent publications include articles in *Review of International Studies* and *Alternatives*, as well as numerous book chapters on cultural aspects of international political economy. He is coeditor of *The Global Economy as Political Space*. His current project explores the role of European projections of non-Europeans in the construction of classical and modern political economy.

Alexander B. Murphy is associate professor of geography at the University of Oregon. He is the author of *The Regional Dynamics of Language Differentiation in Belgium* and numerous articles and book chapters on territorial aspects of international relations and on the political and cultural geography of Europe.

David Strang is associate professor and chair of the Department of Sociology at Cornell University. His publications include articles in *International Organization* and *American Sociological Review*.

Cynthia Weber is associate professor of political science at Purdue University. She is the author of *Simulating Sovereignty: Intervention, the State, and Symbolic Exchange*, also published in the Cambridge Studies in International Relations series. Her current research project is a gendered reading of US–Caribbean relations from the 1959 Cuban Revolution to the recent US-led intervention into Haiti.

Alexander Wendt, associate professor of political science at Yale University, has published articles in *International Organization*, *Review of International Studies*, and *American Political Science Review*. He is currently finishing a book manuscript, *Social Theory of International Politics*, forthcoming from Cambridge University Press.

Acknowledgments

Like sovereignty, the construction of this edited book involved extensive consultation, constant negotiation, and a variety of different forms of intervention. Recognition is crucial to the social construction of sovereignty, and at this stage we would like to turn our attention to those who most merit recognition. We would like to begin by thanking the Social Science Research Council for its generous support of the two conferences that produced the papers contained in this volume. The Watson Institute at Brown University and the Jackson School at the University of Washington also made financial and other important logistical contributions that made the two conferences successful.

We benefited from our collaboration with Janice Thomson of the University of Washington, who played an important role in our thinking about sovereignty at the initial stages of the project. She also played a central role in organizing the initial conference at Silverdale, Washington at which the draft memos were produced that eventually became the papers collected in this volume. But we owe a special debt of gratitude to each of the authors included in this collection. Our intense and frequent interactions with each of them over the past three years have contributed significantly to our knowledge and understanding of the social construction of sovereignty. Each of their chapters was strengthened by the comments they received from their colleagues and home institutions, as indicated in their separate acknowledgments. However, their individual contributions and the project as a whole benefited significantly from the insightful and reflective comments provided at the Brown conference by John Agnew, Hayward Alker, Jarat Chopra, James Der Derian, Sohail Hashmi, Yuen Foong Khong, Craig Murphy, Donald Puchala, Richard Smoke, Celeste Wallander, Thomas Weiss, and Albert Yee. The conference planning (and post conference analysis) phase of the project was also strengthened considerably by the suggestions of Lori Gronich and Kent Worcester of the Social Science Research Council staff.

The project as a whole benefited greatly from the comments and suggestions provided by a number of international relations scholars, including Richard Ashley, Peter Katzenstein, Robert Keohane, Stephen Krasner, Friedrich Kratochwil, Timothy Luke, John Odell, and Rob Walker. Steve Smith and an anonymous reviewer for Cambridge University Press also provided extremely helpful advice which both strengthened and de-parochialized yet another North American theoretical enterprise with global pretensions.

A number of individuals on the staff of the Watson Institute for International Studies at Brown University deserve special mention for their assistance with the project in its various stages. Jean Lawlor of the conference staff played a crucial role organizing the Brown University conference. Fred Fullerton, Mary Lhowe, and Amy Langlais of the Institute publications staff worked painstakingly (and extremely effectively) in preparing a consistent and highly readable copy-edited manuscript for John Haslam and his staff at Cambridge University Press. Jennifer Patrick at the early stages and Susan Costa at the final stages played critical and greatly appreciated roles in keeping the project organizers and participants in constant (and almost instantaneous) communication.

Thomas J. Biersteker and Cynthia Weber
Providence, R.I. and West Lafayette, Ind.

1 The social construction of state sovereignty

Thomas J. Biersteker and Cynthia Weber

During the last several years, there has been a virtual explosion of scholarly interest in sovereignty.[1] This interest transcends all of the major divisions within the study of international relations, and it engages scholars across the globe. There has been a comparable increase in the level of attention given to sovereignty within the popular media.[2] Much of this concern with sovereignty can be explained at least in part by the end of the Cold War and the possibilities of a "New World Order," which have raised questions about many old assumptions, including those made about state sovereignty. Moreover, the dramatic fragmentation and dismemberment of major states such as Yugoslavia and the Soviet Union, along with the potential fragmentation of many others, have led to renewed questions about the location of sovereignty – whether it lies in a population, or within a contiguous territorial space – and about the criteria for recognition as a sovereign state. As questions begin to be raised about the criteria for recognizing the modern state, can challenges to the traditional idea of sovereignty be far behind?

Traditionally, sovereignty has been characterized as a basic rule of coexistence within the states system,[3] a concept that transcends both ideological differences and the rise and fall of major powers,[4] and it is frequently invoked as an institution that must be both protected and defended. Sovereignty provides the basis in international law for claims for state actions, and its violation is routinely invoked as a justification for the use of force in international relations.[5] Sovereignty, therefore, is an inherently *social* concept. States' claims to sovereignty construct a social environment in which they can interact as an international society of states, while at the same time the mutual

1

recognition of claims to sovereignty is an important element in the construction of states themselves.

In spite of the agreement on some of these basic issues, sovereignty remains an ambiguous concept. Attention to sovereignty tends to raise more questions about international relations than it answers. Is the relationship between sovereign recognition and political identity always constructed in the same way, or does it change with changing historical contexts from the colonial and postcolonial to the post Cold War international setting? Are the legal criteria for external recognition of a state's legitimate domination equivalent to a practical definition of sovereignty?[6] If so, where does sovereignty ultimately reside: in an apparently homogeneous people (such as the Bosnian Muslim population), among the residents of a territorially bounded entity (called Bosnia-Herzogovina), or elsewhere? Or are de jure claims to sovereignty dependent upon de facto capabilities of states, ranging from a monopoly on legitimate uses of domestic violence to meeting the economic needs of a citizenry?

Consideration of the social construction of state sovereignty should not be limited to analyzing processes of mutual recognition. Highlighting how state sovereignty is enmeshed in systems of social relations is clearer when we separate concepts like state and sovereignty analytically, rather than collapse the two into a single ideal of "state sovereignty."[7] As a starting point, therefore, we provisionally define the "territorial state" as a geographically-contained structure whose agents claim ultimate political authority within their domain.[8] We consider "sovereignty" as a political entity's externally recognized right to exercise final authority over its affairs. Even though we recognize the importance of both the internal and the external dimensions of sovereignty (where "internal" refers to the existence of some ultimate authority over a particular domain and "external" refers to the recognition of that authority by others), we begin our analysis with a focus on the external.[9]

We consider these definitions to be provisional, not because we cannot agree on them, but because we cannot use definitions to capture the essence of a subject we believe is so deeply contested and undergoing change. Disputes over fundamentally contested concepts cannot be brought to closure by means of a definition. We agree with R.B.J. Walker when he writes "the very attempt to treat sovereignty as a matter of definition and legal principle encourages a certain amnesia about its historical and culturally specific character."[10] In his recent book on sovereignty, Jens Bartelson makes a similar point, following Nietzsche, that only that which has no history can be defined. Defining a concept such as sovereignty, Bartelson argues, freezes that concept's meaning in the present, thus neglecting the rich history of the concept, which enabled its particular present meaning to emerge.[11] One of the goals of our research is to understand why the contested nature of the state and sovereignty has been obscured or submerged by an apparent 300-year-old agreement to disagree on definitions in order to get on with the business of diplomacy and theory. By proposing provisional definitions of principal concepts, we are attempting to clarify how international relations theory has narrowed the investigation of the territorial state and sovereignty, thus providing common reference points for ourselves, our readers, and the others included in this volume. But rather than stop there, the project of this volume is to investigate how these present understandings of the territorial state, sovereignty, and their relationships were and continue to be socially constructed.

We agree with other scholars interested in sovereignty, that territory, population, and authority – in addition to recognition – are important aspects of state sovereignty. Unlike most scholars, however, we contend that each of these components of state sovereignty is also socially constructed, as is the modern state system. The modern state system is not based on some timeless principle of sovereignty, but on the production of a normative conception that links authority, territory, population (society, nation), and recognition in a unique way and in a particular place (the state). Attempting to realize this ideal entails a great deal of hard work on the part of statespersons, diplomats, and intellectuals: to establish and police practices consistent with the ideal, its components, and the links between them; to delegitimate and quash challenges or threats; and to paper over persistent anomalies to make them appear to be consistent with the ideal or temporary divergences from the diachronic trajectory toward a pristine Westphalian ideal. The ideal of state sovereignty is a product of the actions of powerful agents and the resistances to those actions by those located at the margins of power.

The unique contribution of this volume is to describe, theorize, and illustrate the practices that have socially constructed, reproduced, reconstructed, and deconstructed various sovereign ideals and resistances to them. This entails analyses of how all of the components of state sovereignty – not only recognition, but also territory, population, and authority – are socially constructed and combined in specific historical contexts.

Recent treatments of sovereignty in the theoretical literature

We are by no means the first to examine this issue. We are, however, the first to place an empirical consideration of the social construction of sovereignty at the center of analysis. In doing so, we are making an effort to build upon the insights of other scholars who have grappled with this difficult subject, and to redirect scholarly attention to an area we regard as fruitful for further research. Although theoretical disagreements over sovereignty did not preoccupy most scholars of international relations writing after World War II and up until very recently, their relative lack of attention to the issue has nevertheless had some important consequences for their research.

Realist accounts

Writing in the middle of the twentieth century, a number of scholars who described themselves as taking a "realist" approach to the scientific study of international relations produced important statements about the meaning of sovereignty. Although he continued the classical practice of reifying the nation-state (and was subsequently criticized for doing so),[12] Hans Morgenthau did not assume the existence of sovereignty and devoted an entire chapter of his classic textbook to the subject.[13] In it, he defined sovereignty in legal terms as "the appearance of a centralized power that exercised its lawmaking and law-enforcing authority within a certain territory."[14] Morgenthau stressed the continuity of the "doctrine" of sovereignty throughout the modern era (since its origins in the late sixteenth century), and suggested that the idea of popular sovereignty legitimized the contemporary national democratic state.[15] One of Morgenthau's principal concerns was whether international law provided a decisive challenge to the principle of state sovereignty by imposing legal restraints on sovereign states. He dismissed the question by arguing that sovereignty is only incompatible with a strong, effective, and centralized system of international law, a system that did not exist. Indeed, for Morgenthau, "national sovereignty is the very source of [international law's] decentralization, weakness and ineffectiveness."[16]

Not all mid-twentieth-century realists shared Morgenthau's confidence about the continuity of state and sovereignty. E.H. Carr concluded his study of the interwar years with the observation that, "Few things are permanent in history; and it would be rash to assume that the territorial unit of power is one of them."[17] He went on to predict that the concept of sovereignty "is likely to become in the future even more blurred and indistinct than it is at present."[18] For Carr, sovereignty was never anything more "than a convenient label" for the independent authority claimed by states after the breakup of the medieval system.[19]

Contemporary neorealists are usually identified as writing in the same realist tradition as Carr and Morgenthau, and can be characterized as clarifying some of the conceptual ambiguity (and attempting to raise the scientific standards) of the postwar realists.[20] In the process, however, most appear to have lost interest in the problematic nature of sovereignty. Neorealists tend to combine population, territory, authority, and recognition – the principal constitutive elements of sovereignty – into a single, unproblematic actor: the sovereign state.[21] This conflation of state and sovereignty enables them to abstract from, or simply ignore, problems in the domestic domain and to leave the assessment of problems of internal sovereignty to others.

Because of their preoccupation with the anarchy of the international system and the ways in which this anarchy influences, socializes, and constrains the behavior of states, most neorealists have relatively little interest in sovereignty and even less interest in its potentially problematic nature. They are concerned with sovereignty principally as it manifests itself as one possible institution for managing anarchy, which they define as the absence of formal governmental authority in the international system.[22] Kenneth Waltz essentially defines sovereignty in terms of this conception of anarchy: "To say that a state is sovereign means that it decides for itself how it will cope with its internal and external problems."[23] That is, states are sovereign because there is no competing (overarching) governmental authority in the international system. What neorealists fail to recognize, however, is how extensively the socially constructed practices of sovereignty – of recognition, of intervention, of the language of justification – contribute to the structures of international society that exist beyond the realm of neorealist analysis. As many recent constructivist critiques of neorealism have argued, there is a great deal of order within anarchy.[24] Perhaps statecraft is not primarily about relations between different state units, but about the construction and reconstruction of the units themselves.[25] By granting and withholding recognition, international society participates in the social construction of sovereign states; we think it is important to investigate precisely how this process takes place.

Although neorealists have provided a parsimonious explanation of how and why the state system has persisted as long as it has, they have not done as good a job explaining how it emerged in the first place, or, for that matter, how it might still be in the process of emerging. Once the system of sovereign states is established, competition and socialization are said to produce similar units. Power balancing preserves the system, with each state striving to assure its own existence, while simultaneously maintaining a system of states. While this explanation might be adequate for an analysis of the maintenance of order, it is not sufficient in times of rupture and potentially radical change, as at present. As John Ruggie has argued, realists and neorealists have a reproductive, but not a transformative logic.[26] We believe that a change of focus toward the social construction of sovereignty would allow a richer analysis of the changing nature of sovereignty over time, and in particular, a greater understanding of whether contemporary changes such as the end of the Cold War, the internationalization of production and finance, the globalization of democracy, and the new activism of the United Nations are compatible with a realist and neorealist conception of state sovereignty, or indicative of its transformation toward something different.

Interdependence and dependence assessments

During the early 1970s, a number of scholars began to challenge what they characterized as the state-centric bias prevailing in international relations theory and to stress the need to incorporate important nonstate actors like multinational corporations and international organizations into the analysis of international phenomena.[27] Although their principal focus was on developments within the international political economy, these critiques emanated as well from scholars interested in the analysis of foreign policy decisionmaking.[28] Their critiques suggested that the state was not the only significant actor in the international arena (or the most appropriate level for analysis of important issues); that states coexisted with transnational actors in situations of complex interdependence; and that state sovereignty was eroded by transnational phenomena. Although it was premature to suggest that the sovereignty of states was at bay,[29] it was increasingly apparent to a number of scholars that the international system might be undergoing significant change and needed to be reconceptualized. At around the same time, scholars writing from the periphery of the world system observed many of the same phenomena (particularly from their dealings with multinational corporations), which they articulated in their analyses of hierarchical dependency relations.[30]

Although scholars from the interdependence and dependence traditions have disagreed strongly on many issues, most notably on the benefits of participation in a world economy conducted according to liberal principles, they have nonetheless shared some significant concerns. First, both have been interested in understanding transnational phenomena as agents that exist independent of the state. Interdependence writers explored the emergence and potential consequences of international regimes. Dependency writers critically examined the complex set of linkages between multinational corporations and local entrepreneurs, identifying them in terms of transnational class alliances, and mourned the loss of national control and the absence of an indigenous bourgeoisie. Second, both have an interest in the potential impact of these transnational phenomena. Although there are important exceptions, interdependence writers have tended to stress the positive potential of transnational phenomena, while dependency writers have tended to condemn their negative consequences. In either case, transnational phenomena illuminate important locations of authority outside the state.

While interdependence and dependence writers have documented many of the ways in which the state centrism of realist and neorealist scholars was inadequate for an understanding of contemporary international relations, they never presented a comprehensive theoretical reevaluation of the concept of sovereignty. They tended to focus instead on a description of the "erosion" of state sovereignty, often confusing it with a reduction in state capabilities for independence and autonomy. Realist scholars countered that transnational relations were not eroding state sovereignty, but that these relations flourished because of state sovereignty, since transnational phenomena expanded under the aegis of a hegemonic state with an interest in allowing and promoting them.[31] However, now that transnational phenomena such as economics, drugs, the environment, and human rights have increased in salience in many parts of the world in the wake of American hegemony, it may be an opportune time to revisit some of these conceptual issues.

In retrospect, by problematizing the state as a unit and identifying so many different actors and competing locations for authority in international relations, interdependence and dependence writers conducted path-breaking conceptual work. Their distinctions between states and a variety of different transnational actors are increasingly relevant today, as questions about agency and identity (regional, state, ethnic, religious, gender, racial) increasingly rise to the top of the policy and theoretical agenda. Once again, by shifting our attention to a focus on the social construction of sovereignty, we can approach these questions by considering not only how sovereignty is constructed, but by what practices and on whose behalf it is constructed. This is the *social* part of social construction.

Recent conceptual analyses of sovereignty

During the past few years, there has been a substantial increase in the number of scholars who are dissatisfied with the realist tendency to assume or ignore sovereignty's existence and who are interested in going beyond interdependence descriptions of the erosion of sovereignty. F.H. Hinsley, Alan James, and Robert Jackson each have recently published or re-published major work that places a conceptual analysis of sovereignty at the center of their inquiry.[32] They are united more by their mutual interest in sovereignty than by method, scope of analysis, or conclusion, yet each provides timely insights for our reconsideration of the concept.

F.H. Hinsley's re-publication of his classic study, *Sovereignty*, provides a sweeping intellectual history of the idea, from its origins in antiquity to its contemporary usage. Hinsley is concerned primarily with the internal dimension of sovereignty, and he defines it as "the idea that there is a final and absolute political authority in the political community" and that "*no final and absolute authority exists elsewhere.*"[33] For Hinsley, the ideas of sovereignty and the state are inextricably linked such that "when a society is ruled by means of the state the concept of sovereignty is sooner or later unavoidable."[34] Hinsley's historical survey of the idea also offers some insight into why interest in sovereignty has recently increased; he suggests that the concept "has been the source of greatest preoccupation and contention when conditions have been producing rapid changes in the scope of government or in the nature of society or in both."[35] Toward the end of his historical review, when he considers the external dimension of sovereignty, Hinsley comments on a growing gap he observes between

8

sovereign authority and the effectiveness of rule in some states. He concludes that "the fiction" that states are sovereign even if they do not rule effectively is "a logical requirement of the fact that when applied in the international context the sovereignty concept has involved no more than the assertion or the justification of the independence of the state."[36] Thus, while he begins to address a potential challenge to the realist ideal of sovereignty, he does not provide an explanation for it. If sovereignty is "no more than an assertion," just how is it made? What role do recognition, intervention, and language play in the construction of sovereignty? These are questions Hinsley leaves for others.

Unlike Hinsley, Alan James is primarily concerned with a conceptual analysis of the external dimension of sovereignty. James defines sovereignty in terms of constitutional independence, an authority derived from a state's constitution, "which exists in its own right."[37] This independent, constitutional authority is not divisible, and it simultaneously defines both the internal and external dimensions of sovereignty. For James, "Sovereignty, meaning the condition which fits a state for international life, is a matter of law and not of stature. It expresses a legal and not a physical reality."[38] James provides an extensive survey of the great variety of forms that exist on the margins of the sovereign state, considering the status of colonial protectorates, secession attempts, annexations, and mergers that entail the renunciation of sovereignty. One of the virtues of his work is how extensively James directs us to examine state practices. Indeed, what distinguishes sovereign states from non-sovereign entities can be ascertained "most authoritatively, from the practices of states."[39] His work, however, suffers somewhat from a lack of attention to the origins and composition of the international community that enforces international law. Like Hinsley, James also observes and addresses a variety of potential challenges to sovereign statehood in the contemporary world (what he terms the "permeated" state), but, again like Hinsley, has difficulty coming up with an approach that can accommodate them. He also has difficulty explaining how an international community is formed to enforce international law.

Robert Jackson has suggested the term "quasi-states" to describe the status of states whose sovereignty is more juridical than empirical.[40] Jackson's principal analytical contribution is his distinction between positive and negative sovereignty, where positive sovereignty refers to freedom to act or deter in the international arena, and negative

9

sovereignty refers to the freedom from the actions of others in that same arena (the principle of nonintervention).[41] The capabilities of states and their societies provide the basis for positive sovereignty, while the external recognition of other states provides the basis for negative sovereignty. Jackson posits a basic dualism in contemporary international relations, a distinction between the world of Great Power balance-of-power politics among states with positive sovereignty, and the world of quasi-states that are the creation of non-competitive international norms. However, by considering self-determination to be an historical and largely completed event, Jackson fails to anticipate the emergence of new forms and locations for sovereignty claims (including Eritrea, Ukraine, and possibly even among peoples within Europe).[42]

Each of these careful, conceptual analyses of sovereignty has struggled with the significance of potential challenges to the ideal of state sovereignty (Hinsley's ineffective states, James's permeable states, and Jackson's quasi-states) and has reached the rather static conclusion that sovereignty's central role as an international organizing principle is essentially unchanged. Although both James and Jackson are explicitly concerned with state practices, neither has considered how the interactive dynamics of contemporary state *and nonstate* practices might have questioned the foundations of sovereignty. For example, the norm of nonintervention in the sovereign affairs of states is subverted by agents located outside the state with a potential stake in the outcome of "internal" affairs. The communicative actions of human rights groups have created new transnational communities that do not respect traditional boundaries between the domestic and the international.[43] This raises the possibility that the emergence of a "global civil society" might have begun to construct an alternative location for authority in the area of human rights, an authority that resides outside of the state. This implies that "the very basis of international society, its criterion of eligibility for membership, may be in the process of modification."[44] Once again, a focus on the social construction of sovereignty enables us to address this as an empirical question, and to consider how sophisticated conceptual analyses like those of Hinsley, James, and Jackson assist in making sovereignty appear to be such a persistent feature of the international system.

In their collective effort to define and pin down the elusive concept of sovereignty, recent investigations of the subject in the theoretical literature have assumed or ignored why sovereignty would persist (realists); confused capabilities for independence and autonomy with the erosion of sovereignty (dependence and interdependence writers); and grappled with and ultimately denied the significance of potential challenges to the ideal (recent conceptual analyses). Unfortunately, none of these theoretical traditions has paid adequate attention to the ways that the practices of states and nonstate agents produce, reform, and redefine sovereignty and its constitutive elements: population, recognition, authority, and territory. Approaching sovereignty in this way allows us to proceed from the point where most traditional international relations theory leaves off. Rather than proceeding from the assumption that all states are sovereign, we are interested in considering the variety of ways in which states are constantly negotiating their sovereignty. Before we can proceed any further, however, it is incumbent upon us to elaborate more fully on what a shift of focus to the social construction of state sovereignty entails.

Toward the social construction of state sovereignty

A focus on the social construction of state sovereignty directs us to a consideration of the constitutive relationship between state and sovereignty; the ways the meaning of sovereignty is negotiated out of interactions within intersubjectively identifiable communities; and the variety of ways in which practices construct, reproduce, reconstruct, and deconstruct both state and sovereignty. We begin our analysis by analytically disentangling the concepts "state" and "sovereignty." There is some danger that by making this distinction we might cause readers to mistake our preliminary analytical differentiation for an assumption about the prior existence of either agency or structure. We are not attempting to depict the state as a fully formed agent or identity that interacts with sovereignty, taken as a fully formed institution or structure. Rather, we consider state, as an identity or agent, and sovereignty, as an institution or discourse, as mutually constitutive and constantly undergoing change and transformation. States can be defined in terms of their claims to sovereignty, while sovereignty can be defined in terms of the interactions and practices of states. Therefore, while we wish to proceed from the assumption that we can distinguish between the two phenomena, neither state nor sovereignty should be assumed or taken as given, fixed, or immutable.

By beginning with this analytical distinction, we are able to address some of the deficiencies of the recent theoretical literature, such as the neorealist tendency to ignore problems and issues in the "domestic" domain, and also the tendency within recent conceptual work on sovereignty to miss important qualitative changes in the meaning of both state and sovereignty. Moreover, observing how state sovereignty is enmeshed in different systems of social relations is more apparent if we make an effort to separate state and sovereignty.

Earlier in the chapter, we provisionally defined sovereignty as a political entity's externally recognized right to exercise final authority over its affairs. We also pointed out that recognition is the one component of state sovereignty that is widely regarded as socially constructed. Precisely what a state has to do to gain sovereign recognition is something that has yet to be specified, however. The authors in this volume suggest that sovereignty provides textual and/or contextual prescriptions for what a state must do to be recognized as sovereign. Whether considered as an institution, a discourse, a principle, a structure, or a context, sovereignty is "about the social terms of individuality, not individuality per se, and in that sense it is an historically contingent social [category] rather than an inherent quality of stateness."[45]

Our understanding of sovereignty links the social construction of agency or identity (in this case the state) to practice, and it highlights how sovereignty itself can be conceptualized as a set of practices. For example, while sovereignty is intimately bound up with the issue of recognition, recognition itself is embedded in an array of different practices. While it is generally regarded as a positive, empowering term in discussion of state sovereignty and international law,[46] recognition may be linked to specific cultural practices, resulting in the delegitimation of claims to authority made on behalf of territories and peoples with non-Western cultural traditions. Similarly, sovereign recognition is embedded in a network of international political economy practices that, in their liberal form, exclude ethical considerations such as a right to wealth, which may ultimately be necessary if sovereignty is ever to be fully realized by Third World states.

Practices of recognition or non-recognition are not only linked to imperialism or to its legacy, neocolonialism, but they also take practical political form during military conflicts. Wars and interventions, as well as the justifications offered by states for these activities, participate in the social construction of which territories, peoples, and authority claims will be accorded sovereign recognition. The refusal of some states to intervene in the "civil" wars of others is one way in which intervention (or non-intervention, in this case) serves to define the meaning of sovereignty. Moreover, an analysis of the justifications given by states for the wars and interventions on which they embark is another way to observe some of the practices that construct and reconstruct sovereignty, as well as how these practices have changed over time.[47]

We suggest that as the prescriptions for sovereign recognition change, so does the meaning of sovereignty. How to identify these changes returns our analysis to the state. The authors in this volume regard the state as an agent or identity that may have specific roles designated to it by sovereignty. Certainly, sovereignty is not the only institution or discourse that makes prescriptions for agents or identities. Sovereignty may, for example, be in conflict with apparently incompatible institutions or discourses like pan-Arabism, socialist internationalism, or heteronomy.[48] Identities or agents like the state, then, are never the product of any one institution or discourse; their meanings arise out of interaction with other states and with the international society they form.

Even so, the authors in this volume focus primarily on sovereignty because the prescriptions for sovereign recognition are very much linked to the components of the state – territory, population, and authority. Furthermore, they suggest that the components of state sovereignty are intimately tied up with the construction, reconstruction, and negotiation of boundaries. Territorial boundaries are the most tangible. Sovereign recognition depends upon states having a territorial basis. Indeed, as we noted earlier, for a state to receive sovereign recognition in the contemporary international system, it must be a territorial state. Our definition of the territorial state as a geographically contained structure whose agents claim ultimate political authority within their domain leaves open to empirical investigation the prescriptions for constructing territorial boundaries at any specific historical and geographical locale.

Boundaries are also drawn around and through populations. We noted earlier how international or regional communities have excluded cultural, ethnic, or racial "others" by denying them sovereign recognition. Such exclusionary practices also are involved in the construction of domestic communities. For example, establishing the criteria for national citizenship – whether in everyday discourse or by legal proclamation – constructs the foundation of a state's identity, the

13

nation. Moreover, promises to provide protection from some foreign "other" reinforce that identify. In the contemporary state system, sovereign recognition is granted to states that are organized (or hold the promise of becoming organized) in accordance with the principles of nationalism.

The range of a state's authority raises yet another boundary issue. Sovereign recognition is traditionally said to depend upon a state's claim to hold a monopoly on the legitimate use of violence within its territory. Yet there have been numerous illustrations throughout history of territorially contained political structures that were granted sovereign recognition either in the absence of making such a claim (i.e., the pre-Civil War United States, where individual members of the states union claimed and exercised legitimate authority to mobilize armies), or as a direct result of their inability to make such a claim (i.e., East Germany, whose incorporation into the informal empire of the former Soviet Union produced hierarchical authority relationships that challenged its juridical sovereignty). These illustrations suggest that the ways that authority claims are demarcated are a core issue for understanding the relationship between states and sovereignty.

The practice of granting or withholding sovereign recognition participates in the social construction of territories, populations, and authority claims. This point is key to our understanding of the relationship between the components of state sovereignty and understandings of change. Throughout the course of history, the meaning of sovereignty has undergone important change and transformation – from the location of the source of its legitimacy (in God, in the monarch, or in a people) – to the scope of activities claimed under its protection. While many recognize the existence of change in the meaning of sovereignty, there has been a great deal of disagreement about how to interpret the significance of the change. Kratochwil has forcefully argued that sovereignty should be considered an institution analogous to private property, which changes in its scope of application and in the range of activities allowed within its domain, but not in its core meaning.[49] Others have contended that the relational identities of state and sovereignty are not fixed in meaning, but are constantly undergoing change and transformation.[50] Moreover, these changes in meaning arise out of the interaction of states with other states and out of the interaction of states and the international society that they form (and that forms them).

The papers in this volume investigate how claims to territory, authority, and national identity consonant with Eurocentric cultural ideals socially construct sovereign and non-sovereign political entities. We also consider how each of these basic components of state sovereignty changes its meaning over time, particularly in relation to the granting or withholding of sovereign recognition.

We begin with an analysis of the component of state sovereignty that is widely regarded as social, that is, recognition. David Strang (Chapter 2) focuses on the way Western perceptions of the sovereignty or lack of sovereignty of non-Western polities enters into the construction of imperialism. This concern takes Strang immediately to the question of how recognition is socially constructed. Rather than investigating recognition as an isolated concept, Strang pairs the concept of recognition with that of legitimacy. He argues that non-Western sovereignty was not so much absent as actively delegitimated in the eyes of the West because non-Western entities were located outside a rich Western framework of political meanings and a community of identities organized around those meanings. Some of the roots of Western perceptions of the legitimacy of non-Western polities are traced, as are some of the ways that these perceptions entered into the real life chances of non-Western states like Siam.

Naeem Inayatullah (Chapter 3) problematizes recognition by placing it in the context of international political economy concerns, especially as they apply to Third World states. Failure to contextualize sovereignty in this way, Inayatullah argues, is to presume that Third World states have somehow overcome their historical status as functional elements within a global division of labor, a status that (as Strang also implies) inhibits Third World states from realizing sovereignty. Like Strang, Inayatullah casts recognition in a critical light by arguing that recognition of sovereignty by other states is a necessary but not sufficient condition for realizing sovereignty because it ignores economic inequality. Through his critical reading of Adam Smith's *Wealth of Nations* and Robert Jackson's *Quasi-States*, Inayatullah develops his argument that realizing sovereignty also requires a right to wealth.

In his chapter on the sovereign state system as a political-territorial ideal, Alexander Murphy (Chapter 4) examines how the modern territorial state has co-opted our spatial imaginations and proceeded to shape everything from policy responses, to international developments, to the theory of international relations itself. Murphy reviews the origins of sovereignty as a political concept and proceeds to consider the social construction of political-territorial conceptions from the seventeenth century through the twentieth. He argues that conceptions of sovereignty have been "thrown into crisis" historically "when social, technological, and economic developments challenged the theoretical and functional bases of particular territorial arrangements." Thus, he raises important questions about the political map of the late twentieth century, which "increasingly fails to reflect or encompass significant economic and social arrangements," and he concludes with a consideration of possibilities for a multilayered approach to governance – such as that emerging in the European Union – that more closely reflects the different spatial structures and scales at which contemporary issues and problems are manifest.

The essays by Roxanne Doty (Chapter 5) and Michael Barnett (Chapter 6) examine the social construction of populations understood as various forms of nations. Doty investigates the constitution of a political community or national identity in Great Britain through the drafting of its immigration policies from 1948 to 1981. Britain might be thought of as a least-likely case, possessing a stable, simply given population that was organized into a nation long ago. It is precisely for this reason that Doty selected Britain for her analysis. She illustrates how even in an "established" state like Britain, the production of a national identity is an ongoing activity. She reads immigration debates of this period as constitutive both of an internal/external boundary that might contain a political community and of a particular understanding of a British citizen located within this boundary who might be referred to as the foundation of British sovereignty.

While Doty focuses primarily on the internal aspects of national identity, Barnett focuses more on nationalism's external aspects. Barnett's essay illustrates how pan-Arab nationalism functioned as an external constraint on state formation in the Arab world. Populations within Arab states, Barnett argues, were forced to grapple with incompatible roles – those prescribed by Pan-Arabism, which raised regional affiliation over state affiliations, and those prescribed by sovereignty, which constitute citizens whose foremost political allegiances are to the state. Arab nationalism constrained the development of both internal sovereignty, with its conception of citizenship and national identity and loyalty, and external sovereignty, with its idea of mutual recognition of boundaries and authority over that territory. Regional order, Barnett claims, resulted from a change in the institutional character of the Arab states system, specifically the development of Arab states with greater internal and external sovereignty and of a definition of Arab nationalism that is consistent with state sovereignty.

The chapters by Daniel Deudney (Chapter 7) and by Alexander Wendt and Daniel Friedheim (Chapter 8) analyze authority as a socially constructed component of state sovereignty. Both chapters investigate cases that are not easily dealt with by realist analysts because these cases involve identities that are not organized exclusively according to either hierarchical or anarchical authority structures. Among the difficult cases for realists are international systems that exist between the modified hierarchy of federal states and the modified hierarchy of confederation, most notably the pre-Civil War American Union. Deudney turns to structural republican theory to analyze this specific historical instance of an organized states union structured as a compound republic. While its generative principle was popular sovereignty and its institutional structure resembled a state, Deudney points out that this "states union" was expressly designed to prevent both the monopolization of authority (including authority over violence) in a single hierarchical structure, and an anarchical system of states. Deudney's work describes in compelling detail an alternative to the Westphalian ideal, which was not a mere imagining but actually existed and persisted for nearly a century. It reveals that the breakdown of this Philadelphian system was not due to pressure emanating from the (European) state system, but from changes within the United States, especially the rapid expansion of the system, which generated regional and sectoral imbalances. Finally, Deudney's analysis provides us with some criteria with which to evaluate the prospects for contemporary or future attempts to construct an alternative to the Westphalian state system as we move into the twenty-first century.

In their chapter on informal empire and the East German state, Alexander Wendt and Daniel Friedheim continue the discussion of how authority relations are socially constructed by arguing that sovereign authority is not an unproblematically given attribute of state identity. They make their case by analyzing informal empires, defined as transnational structures of de facto political authority in which members are juridically sovereign states but in which a tension exists between sovereign and hierarchical authority relations. Focusing on the historical relationship between the USSR and East Germany, Wendt and Friedheim suggest that sovereignty should be seen as one of several various social identities that a state actor can have, and that the theoretical task should be to study the processes of social construction by which such an identity does or does not become dominant.

When we begin to consider sovereignty as a social construct, it emerges as a product of knowledgeable practices by human agents, including citizens, non-citizens, theorists, and diplomats. It is neither natural nor ever fully "completed." It has to be actively propped up and preserved, and its meanings and their referents vary across both time and space. The authors of the chapters that follow provide important insights to our understanding of sovereignty by illustrating empirically the ways in which specific practices – such as authority claims, recognition, intervention, diplomatic justifications, and the drawing of boundaries around populations and space – help us understand both the origins of and changes in the meanings of sovereignty.

Notes

This is a jointly authored essay. The order in which the names appear is alphabetical, since the contribution of both authors is equal. This is a substantially revised version of a paper we previously co-authored with Janice E. Thomson of the University of Washington, and we acknowledge her contribution to our understanding of this issue. We would also like to acknowledge the financial support of the Social Science Research Council, the Jackson School of International Studies at the University of Washington, and the Watson Institute for International Studies at Brown University. Finally, we have benefited enormously from extensive comments on previous drafts of this introduction by each of the participants included in this volume, as well as by John Agnew, Hayward Alker, Richard Ashley, James Caporaso, Jarat Chopra, James Der Derian, Leslie Eliason, Lori Gronich, Peter Katzenstein, Robert Keohane, Stephen Krasner, Friedrich Kratochwil, Timothy Luke, David Martin, Joel Migdal, Craig Murphy, John Odell, Donald Puchala, and Kent Worcester.

[1] Hinsley, F.H. 1986. *Sovereignty*. 2nd ed. Cambridge: Cambridge University Press; James, Alan 1986. *Sovereign Statehood: The Basis of International Society*. London: Allen & Unwin; Ashley, Richard K. 1988. "Untying the Sovereign State: A Double Reading of the Anarchy Problematique," *Millennium: Journal of International Studies* 17: 227–62; Krasner, Stephen D. 1988. "Sovereignty: An Institutional Perspective," *Comparative Political Studies* 21: 66–94; Allot, Philip 1990. *Eunomia: New Order for a New World*. New York: Oxford University Press; Jackson, Robert. 1990. *Quasi-States: Sovereignty, International Relations and the Third World*. Cambridge: Cambridge University Press; Onuf, Nicholas Greenwood 1991. "Sovereignty: Outline of a Conceptual History," *Alternatives* 16: 425–46; Hoffmann, Stanley 9 April 1992. "Delusions of World Order," *The New York Review of Books*: 36–43; Ruggie, John Gerard 1993. "Territoriality and Beyond: Problematizing Modernity in International Relations," *International Organization* 47: 139–74; Walker, R.B.J. 1993. *Inside/Outside: International Rela-*

tions as Political Theory. Cambridge: Cambridge University Press; Krasner, Stephen D. 1995. "Westphalia," in Lyons, Gene M. and Mastanduno, Michael (eds.), *Beyond Westphalia?: State Sovereignty and International Intervention*. Baltimore and London: Johns Hopkins University Press; Bartelson, Jens 1995. *A Genealogy of Sovereignty*. Cambridge: Cambridge University Press.

[2] Pear, Robert 16 April 1995. "Source of State Power is Pulled from Ashes," *The New York Times*: 16; 13 March 1995. 'Scrambling for Sovereignty," *Macleans* 108: 39; 17 February 1995. "The Millennium Bill," *New Statesman and Society* 8: SS30.

[3] Bull, Hedley 1977. *The Anarchical Society*. New York: Columbia University Press, p. 36.

[4] Hinsley, *Sovereignty*, 234.

[5] James, *Sovereign Statehood*, 1. See also, Weber, Cynthia 1995. *Simulating Sovereignty: Intervention, the State, and Symbolic Exchange*. Cambridge: Cambridge University Press.

[6] Higgins, Rosalyn 1984. "Intervention and International Law," in Bull, Hedley (ed.) *Intervention in World Politics*. Oxford: Clarendon Press, pp. 29–44.

[7] Once the two concepts are disentangled, it is possible to consider the theoretical possibility of non-sovereign territorial states (Taiwan), or the existence of sovereign, non-territorial ones (Palestine). Moreover, it enables us to consider whether the salience of territoriality has changed historically such that entities other than territorial states can begin to make legitimate (externally recognized) claims of final authority. Later in the volume we take the further step of separating territoriality, identity, and authority from both the state and sovereignty.

[8] Throughout much of the text that follows, we will refer to the state and the territorial state interchangeably.

[9] Even though we employ the terms "internal" and "external" sovereignty, we do so not to take these terms as given; rather, we wish to include the social construction of both supposedly distinct categories into our analysis of state sovereignty. See Walker, *Inside/Outside*.

[10] See Walker, *Inside/Outside*, 166.

[11] Bartelson, *A Genealogy of Sovereignty*, 13.

[12] Nye, Joseph and Keohane, Robert 1972. *Transnational Relations and World Politics*. Cambridge, Mass.: Harvard University Press, p. 1.

[13] Morgenthau, Hans J. 1967. *Politics Among Nations*. New York: Alfred A. Knopf, pp. 299–317.

[14] Ibid., 299. His definition is very close to that of the classical theorists of sovereignty.

[15] Ibid., 300.

[16] Ibid.

[17] Carr, E.H. 1964. *The Twenty Years Crisis, 1919–1939*. New York: Harper & Row, p. 229. Carr's conclusion can be traced back as much to progressively strong currents of historical materialism in his writings as to a skeptical realism.

[18] Ibid., 230.

[19] Ibid.

[20] We make this statement fully cognizant of the contested nature of the definition of "science."

[21] Halliday, Fred 1987. "State and Society in International Relations: A Second Agenda," *Millennium* 16: 215–29.

[22] Gilpin, Robert 1981. *War and Change in World Politics*. Cambridge: Cambridge University Press, p. 28. See also Waltz, Kenneth 1979. *Theory of International Politics*. Reading, Mass.: Addison-Wesley Publishing Company.

[23] Waltz, *Theory of International Politics*, 96.

[24] Alker, Hayward R. "The Presumption of Anarchy," (unpublished manuscript); Wendt, Alexander E. 1992. "Anarchy is What States Make of It," *International Organization* 46: 391–425; Kratochwil, Friedrich V. 1989. *Rules, Norms and Decisions*. Cambridge: Cambridge University Press; Onuf, Nicholas Greenwood 1989. *World of Our Making*. Columbia, S.C.: University of South Carolina Press.

[25] Ashley, "Untying the Sovereign State"; and Campbell, David 1992. *Writing Security*. Minneapolis: University of Minnesota Press.

[26] Ruggie, John 1983. "Continuity and Transformation in the World Polity: Toward a Neorealist Synthesis," *World Politics* 35: 261–95.

[27] Nye and Keohane, *Transnational Relations*; Nye, Joseph and Keohane, Robert 1977. *Power and Interdependence*. Boston: Little, Brown; Vernon, Raymond 1971. *Sovereignty at Bay: The Multinational Spread of U.S. Enterprises*. New York: Basic Books; Cooper, Richard 1968. *The Economics of Interdependence: Economic Policy in the Atlantic Community*. New York: McGraw-Hill; Rosecrance, Richard 1986. *The Rise of the Trading State*. New York: Basic Books. For a more recent statement of this position, see Zacher, Mark 1991. 'Decaying Pillars', in Rosenau and Czempiel (eds.), *Governance Without Government: Order and Change in World Politics*. Cambridge: Cambridge University Press; and Risse-Kappen, Thomas "Bringing Transnational Relations Back In: A Proposal to Re-Open the Debate," presented at Project on Transnational Relations workshop, Yale University, 8–9 May 1992.

[28] Allison, Graham 1971. *Essence of Decision: Explaining the Cuban Missile Crisis*. Boston: Little, Brown.

[29] The title of Raymond Vernon's 1971 seminal study of the spread of US multinational corporations, *Sovereignty at Bay*, New York: Basic Books, was raised to the status of a school of thought by Robert Gilpin in 1975 in *U.S. Power and the Multinational Corporation*, New York: Basic Books. It is worth noting that Vernon did not intend his title to be taken literally. Vernon, Raymond 1991. "Sovereignty at Bay: Twenty Years After," *Millennium* 20: 191–5.

[30] Cardoso, Fernando and Faletto, Enzo 1979. *Dependency and Development in Latin America*. Berkeley, Calif.: University of California Press.

[31] This was originally argued most forcefully by Robert Gilpin in *U.S. Power and the Multinational Corporation*. For a critique of this argument, see Ruggie, "Territoriality."

[32] Hinsley's *Sovereignty*, James's *Sovereign Statehood*, and Jackson's *Quasi-*

States. Several other important works have paid a considerable, but not exclusive, attention to sovereignty: Walker's *Inside/Outside*, Onuf's *World of Our Making*, and Kratochwil's *Rules, Norms, and Decisions*.

[33] Hinsley, *Sovereignty*, 26; Hinsley's italics.

[34] Ibid., 17.

[35] Ibid., 2.

[36] Ibid., 225.

[37] James, *Sovereign Statehood*, 40.

[38] Ibid.

[39] Ibid., 22.

[40] Jackson, *Quasi-States*, 1.

[41] Ibid., 26–31.

[42] Schmitter, Philippe C. Forthcoming. "The Emerging Europolity and Its Impact Upon Euro-Capitalism," in Hollingsworth, J. Rogers and Boyer, Robert (eds.) *Contemporary Capitalism: The Embeddedness of Institutions*.

[43] Clark, Ann Marie 1995. "Non-Governmental Organizations and Their Influence on International Society," *Journal of International Affairs* 48: 507–25, esp. 509.

[44] Clark, Ian 1988. "Making Sense of Sovereignty," *Review of International Studies* 14: 306.

[45] See Chapter 8 by Wendt and Friedheim in this volume, p. 397.

[46] Lauterpacht, Hersch 1947. *Recognition in International Law*. Cambridge: Cambridge University Press; Oppenheim, L.F.L. 1944. *International Law* 6th ed. London: Longman; Crawford, James 1973. *The Creation of States in International Law*. Oxford: Clarendon Press.

[47] Weber, *Simulating Sovereignty*.

[48] Onuf, Nicholas and Klink, Frank F. 1989. "Anarchy, Authority, Rule," *International Studies Quarterly* 33: 149–73; Onuf, *World of Our Making*.

[49] Kratochwil, Friedrich 1992. "The Concept of Sovereignty: Sovereignty as Property," manuscript.

[50] Ashley, "Untying the Sovereign State" and Walker, *Inside/Outside*.

2   Contested sovereignty: the social construction of colonial imperialism

David Strang

The constitutive interplay between state and sovereignty enters into fundamental debates on the nature of the international system. From a realist or liberal perspective, the state is an independent actor in exchange, competition, and conflict with other states.[1] States emerge as organized powers that demand recognition and are constrained only by a web of voluntary compacts. From this perspective, a theoretical focus on sovereignty is misleading when it directs attention toward a derivative realm of understandings and interpretations, and away from the relations of power and interest that generate behavior.

In institutional and poststructuralist accounts, by contrast, the state is seen as embedded within a larger cultural framework.[2] Sovereignty is viewed here as a social status that enables states as participants within a community of mutual recognition. From this perspective, a focus on the state misleads when it treats political actors as natural or exogenous, while directing attention away from the larger community and culture that construct states with specific capacities and warrants.

International legal theory parallels the opposition between realist and institutional accounts in debates over whether international recognition is declaratory or constitutive of statehood. A declaratory theory holds that states exist independent of recognition and that recognition signals that other states have become aware of a new state; a constitutive theory holds that states have no standing in the absence of recognition, which can be said to construct them as international persons. Metaphysics aside, it is clear that recognition is a self-referential act in which states decide what states are. Consider W.E. Hall's effort at a balanced view, for example:

22

> For though no state has a right to withhold recognition when it has been earned, states must be allowed to judge for themselves whether a community claiming to be recognized does really possess all the necessary marks, and especially whether it is likely to live. Thus although the right to be treated as a state is independent of recognition, recognition is the necessary evidence that the right has been acquired.[3]

It should be noted that the idea of an international order founded on or revealed by recognition is crucial only within the Westphalian conception. Recognition was not a developed institution even in international orders with multiple polities like ancient Greece, while interstate orders like that constructed by imperial China rested not on recognized co-action under international law but on bilateral relations of fealty and patronage.

The process by which state and sovereignty define each other would be virtually impenetrable in a world flawlessly aligned with the Westphalian ideal. Centralized political structures would partition the globe and its human population. Such states would formally recognize each other with unambiguous reference to neutral textbook criteria: a clearly delimited territory, population, and a stable and independent government. The mutually constitutive interplay between understandings and structures would be hard to observe, because cultural codes like recognition and obvious concentrations of power would everywhere coincide, reinforce, and legitimate each other.

Opportunities for analysis expand in messier contexts, where understandings of appropriate form (what should a state look like?) and relations (how should states behave toward each other?) are contested. Analytical opportunities are further expanded where state identities and aims are not obviously shared, so each state's legitimacy is not bound up in that of the others. It is in such situations that the social construction of recognition is most palpable, and where it has the most easily discerned impact on behavior.

Perhaps most strikingly, the political and cultural relations that underpin recognition come to the surface where revolutionary states challenge not only the international but the domestic order. Revolutionary France was invaded rather than recognized by the monarchies of Europe, who rushed to restore their Bourbon cousins to the throne; in turn the Convention issued a call for a universal republic. The scene was replayed more than a century later, when the Russian revolution

23

denounced the bourgeois state and its diplomacy while fending off British and French intervention.

The political and cultural sources of recognition also can be seen where colonial peoples aim at independence. In a world of Western empires (from the sixteenth to the mid-twentieth century) diplomatic recognition of colonial independence was resisted. Metropolitan centers were naturally unwilling to accept their rebellious subjects as sovereign nations, and even competing powers did not want to imperil the principle of imperial legitimacy. Thus, Britain's celebrated recognition of the Latin American states (prompted by the threat of a Franco-Spanish dual monarchy) took place almost two decades after independence had been declared, and a decade after it had been won in most of the continent.

By contrast, states since 1945 have been quick for the most part to recognize national independence. Decolonization, spurred by prevailing conceptions of social justice and popular sovereignty, insists upon recognition even where technical criteria like a stable government are lacking. Conversely, recognition is withheld where stable governments appear but global legitimacy is lacking. For example, while Zairian decolonization was immediately recognized, Southern Rhodesia's declaration of independence as a settler-controlled state was not.

This chapter will examine tensions between the state and sovereignty in a third context: that of the imperial expansion of Europe into Asia and Africa. Imperial relations arose outside a shared moral and political discourse, and outside a structure of mutual recognition. This moral vacuum permitted an opposition between state and sovereignty to develop in direct conflict with conventional international practice within Western international society.

One product of this encounter was the generation of international practices at odds with the notion of a society of formally equal sovereign states. Europeans resuscitated pre-Westphalian forms of divided sovereignty like the protectorate, and compromised the internal authority of nominally sovereign states like China. Western powers received tribute as suzerain states in Asia and Africa, and paid it as well. Settler colonies like the British Dominions developed complex mixtures of formal dependence, internal self-government, and international personality.

But inconsistencies between the forms of imperialism and the model of Westphalian state society are less crucial than the fundamental

24

redivision of political authority that colonial imperialism produces. Colonial imperialism involves conflict over who owns or controls what. Standard explanations of this very real conflict typically point to various realistic principles: simple power differentials, economic or political drives within the imperial power, patterns of collaboration between Westerners and non-Westerners, and rivalries between powers within an anarchic state system.

These often-compelling accounts obscure the social construction of international relations. They attend little to how or why polities are recognized or delegitimated. And standard arguments ignore the distinctive absence of a larger framework of political meanings and a community of identities organized around those meanings.

This chapter explores the social construction of Western understandings of non-Western states, and the way these understandings empowered imperial efforts. I argue that much more than the simple lack of affirmative recognition was involved. Instead, non-Western sovereignty was actively delegitimated within the community of Western states and societies. This delegitimation of non-Western polities was crucial in structuring conventional routes toward colonial domination, and in structuring models of resistance or adaptation that sometimes led toward recognition of non-Western polities as sovereign states.

I build on prior work comparing the life chances of non-Western states before and after formal colonialism. Strang notes the great frequency with which non-European polities outside Western state society are colonized and dependent possessions are exchanged between Western empires.[4] By comparison, post-colonial states and non-Western states that were recognized as sovereign are seldom recolonized, merged, or dissolved. I argue that these differentials in life chances cannot be usefully understood through balance-of-power arguments, and require an institutional analysis of the cultural framework of the state system.[5]

The present focus on the colonial moment permits a more vivid picture to emerge. This chapter reviews conventional arguments about the sources of imperial expansion, and explores the explanatory usefulness of close attention to political meanings and identities. Some of the modalities of the collective delegitimation of non-Western polities are traced. The generation of a vocabulary and logic of sovereignty is analyzed, as are its effects on patterns of imperial activity and the opportunities for non-Western response.

Colonial imperialism

Colonial imperialism is understood here as the expansion of formal empires of foreign domination. The strongest instances involve the annexation of a non-Western state as the colonial possession of a Western polity. Comprehensive controls also arise through protectorate relations, where a non-Western ruler retains internal authority but surrenders direction over foreign affairs and full "international personality" to a protecting power.[6]

The chapter thus focuses mainly on colonial imperialism in the strictest sense, where internal and/or external authority was formally assumed by a Western power. It should be emphasized that for non-Western states in the late nineteenth century, the alternative to formal imperialism was not autonomy accompanied by full participation in international relations. Western states dictated unequal treaties to formally independent non-Western states; divided their territory into exclusive spheres of influence and commercial development; and administered their public finances through international directorates. In today's world these kinds of controls would be seen as assaults on national sovereignty. This chapter seeks not to ignore these arrangements, but to ask why colonial imperialism was sometimes complete and sometimes partial.

The historical backdrop for the period under study is the passing of the first age of Western colonial expansion. Between 1783 and 1830, Britain's continental colonies, Haiti, Spain's Latin American provinces, and Brazil all became independent states recognized as sovereign by European powers. Only Britain and the Netherlands retained substantial colonial possessions: the British in India, the Caribbean, and Canada, and the Netherlands in Indonesia.

Most European expansion of the mid-Victorian period was colonial but not imperial, or imperial but not colonial. Settler colonies were founded in Australia and New Zealand, and expanded in the Canadian west and South Africa. China and Japan were coercively opened to the Western world economy. The British Raj and Dutch paramountcy in Batavia were expanded and intensified. But relatively few new "colonies of foreign domination" were launched.

Western political expansion took on a different character in the last two decades of the nineteenth century. After centuries of trade conducted by small coastal stations, the continent of Africa was partitioned. Egypt, Tunisia, and Morocco were brought under European

26

protectorates. Britain, France, Germany, Portugal, and Belgium all laid claim to sub-Saharan territories many times larger than themselves. In Asia, the British annexed Burma and brought the Malay peninsula under protectorate relations; the French occupied Indochina; and the Japanese took Korea. The Pacific came under the control of Britain, France, Germany, and the United States. Non-Western polities that retained independence (but were generally subjected to pervasive European influence) included the Chinese and Ottoman empires, Afghanistan, Ethiopia, Japan, Persia, and Siam.

Even when we combine the formation of settler colonies, trading enclaves, and colonies of foreign domination, the shift in the rate of colonization is obvious. In the hundred years between 1780 and 1880, new colonies were formed at the rate of five a decade.[7] Between 1880 and 1910, new colonies were formed at four times this rate, or twenty per decade. The pace of colonial formation slowed after 1910, as the number of candidates for colonial imperialism declined.

Implicit in the notion that imperialism exhausted itself is the assumption that Europe's former colonies were not at risk of recolonization. The United States did assume control over the public finance of several Caribbean states in the early twentieth century in a fashion reminiscent of the first stage of Western colonialism in Egypt and Morocco. But these controls did not develop into full-scale protectorates. South American states remained independent, though European countries intermittently used force to protect investments and nationals. The only African polity to entirely avoid colonialism was Liberia, formed under the auspices of the American Colonization Society in 1822 to permit freed slaves to return to Africa. Liberia was quickly recognized by Britain and France, and, after the Civil War, by the United States, her "sponsor" during the age of imperialism.

Classic accounts of colonial imperialism

Theoretical accounts of colonial imperialism generally seek to explain the burst of European political expansion in Africa and Asia in the late nineteenth century. To contemporaries, this explosion was most logically traced to the dynamics of an industrialized, capitalist Europe. Industrialized economies needed sources of raw materials and markets for their products; declining investment opportunities at home led to capital export. Underlying these arguments was a notion of the instability of monopoly capitalism.[8] In this view, governments acted as

27

the agents of big business and big finance, securing markets and investment opportunities with military muscle. John Hobson argued, "If, contemplating the enormous expenditure on armaments, the ruinous wars, the diplomatic audacity of knavery by which modern Governments seek to extend their territorial powers, we put the plain, practical question, *Cui bono?* the first and most obvious answer is, The investor."[9]

This interpretation does not square readily with the fact that Europe traded with and invested in her formal colonies very little, and least of all with colonies acquired after 1875.[10] Most European capital was directed to Europe and the former settler colonies of North and South America, not to Europe's formal empire. This was true both before and after formal colonialism. In 1914, for example, only 12 percent of British foreign investment went to her non-settler empire. Twenty percent went to Latin America. If we exclude India and the Dominions, Britain invested more in non-colonized Asian countries than in her empire. Other Western empires provided even less outlet for investment. Only 5 percent of French foreign investment went to her colonies.

Two lines of argument seek to make economic sense of a history of colonial expansion that was marginal to the main currents of trade and investment. One describes colonialism as a response to the collapse of informal collaboration.[11] Either an expanding Western presence sparked nationalist movements against foreign interests, or traditional polities collapsed in the face of pressures imposed by contact with the West. Formal colonialism is understood here as a second-best solution to be employed when the cheaper tactic of informal influence erodes.

Robinson and Gallagher's analysis of the British occupation of Egypt is paradigmatic.[12] They find its proximate cause not in increasing Western investment, but in the challenge posed by Colonel Arabi's rebellion against a traditional autocracy dependent on the West. Further, Robinson and Gallagher argue that Britain's aim was not so much to preserve trading or investment opportunities in Egypt as to secure the Suez Canal, its lifeline to India. The breakdown of informal collaboration and a larger geo-economic analysis counted for more in the British official mind than the appeals of British traders or financiers.

The notion that formal imperialism was induced by the collapse of informal imperialism does not fit the evidence much better than the Hobson-Lenin formulation does. Non-Western polities that were never colonized were not typically stable or receptive to the West. The Boxer Rebellion was a proto-nationalist revolt against the failing Chinese state and the foreigners, very much in the vein of the Arabist rebellion in Egypt. The Manchus resisted Western intrusion on all fronts. And to the extent that the Chinese empire was too weak to resist, it was hardly able to provide an economic environment facilitating Western trade and investment. Yet China was propped up by the European powers, which came to control treaty ports and dictate tariffs but never substantially penetrated inland markets.

Even more notably, the Latin American states that European trade and investment penetrated so fully were hardly stable and pliable. Nineteenth-century South and Central American countries (with the notable exception of Chile) witnessed endemic rebellion and seizures of authority. Where Latin American states gained effective powers, they practiced many of the same policies that led to colonization in the East. Latin American states defaulted on debt obligations to Western interests, set tariffs to stop foreign imports from flooding their markets, and organized public monopolies to raise prices on exports.

Consider the case of Peru, described effectively by Mathew and by Gootenberg.[13] Like Burma and China, Peru organized a restrictive state monopoly that drove up the price of its chief export. (The export was guano, or bird droppings, the main fertilizer used by British farmers in the nineteenth century.) Peruvian tariffs on textiles and hardware goods, Britain's major exports, ranged from 30 to 90 percent. Peru defaulted twice on major British loans during the first half of the nineteenth century. Rather than imposing the political structures displayed in Asia and Africa, however, the British foreign ministry turned a deaf ear to the cries of the guano lobby and the bondholders.

An alternative analysis of the new political requirements of economic expansion points to the threat posed by European competitors. The mid-Victorian era was marked by the almost complete economic and naval dominance of Great Britain in Asia, Africa, and South America. Britain had the largest and most advanced industrial economy, the lion's share of international trade, and the only navy and army able to project military power on a global basis. This unchallenged hegemony in the world economy permitted the construction of an open global trading regime.[14]

This regime disintegrated as England's industrial leadership was challenged by the United States, Germany, and France. Great Britain intensified political controls over client states in Malaysia to block the feared entry of European rivals. Continental powers lacking a competitive edge in trade employed firepower to carve out a politically controlled place in the sun. Status rivalry magnified the economic advantages to be gained from many of these territories, and the diminishing arena of free trade made lands of little obvious commercial value seem prudent investments for the future.

Again, Gallagher and Robinson[15] provide a paradigmatic analysis of the workings of inter-European imperial rivalry. A French expedition to Fashoda aimed to drive the British from Cairo by seizing control of the Nile. The Egyptians' resentment of the British occupation of Egypt also helped spark French military expansion in West Africa. Other events precipitating the scramble for Africa include Leopold's adventure in the Congo and the entry of Germany into the colonial race. The general dynamic is one where expansion in the number of colonial rivals geometrically increased the opportunities for colonial rivalries.

Brunschwig and Fieldhouse argue that declining free trade cannot explain European imperialism since protectionist tariffs emerged after, rather than at, the high-water mark of colony formation.[16] I would add that intense competition over markets occurred in the non-colonized periphery as well as in colonized territories. China, Japan, and the Ottoman empire were the focus of major trading and investment rivalries, much more so than Africa or Southeast Asia. So were the economies of Central America and South America, where the United States and Germany contested what had been an exclusively British economic sphere. In South America, the disappearance of hegemony increased rather than eliminated the peripheral state's maneuvering room. In the Caribbean, the United States replaced Britain as the dominant commercial force without preemptive or competitive attempts at formal empire.

European powers did employ force against Latin American states. The British used armed coercion at least forty times in the Americas between 1820 and 1914.[17] In 1861, Mexico's default on bonds sold on European markets led France, Britain, and Spain to agree on intervention. A French expeditionary force drove the Mexican president to the Rio Grande and captured Mexico City. Napoleon III made the Hapsburg Archduke Maximilian the emperor of Mexico.

But in Latin America, European power was used in the service of limited political objectives. Force was used to protect nationals and their interests, but not to relocate final authority. British sailors seized customs houses and occupied port cities, but the colonial ministry did not annex territory or demand control over the foreign policy of national governments. And when Napoleon III withdrew his troops, Mexican leaders regained control and executed Maximilian.

Expanding production capacities and escalating national rivalries do appear as the great engines that drove the West's expanding contact with Asia, Africa, and South America. But the strength of these drives did not determine which areas would be constructed as formal colonies, which as spheres of influence, and which as sovereign states. I argue instead that an analysis of political forms generated in the course of expanding interaction must take cultural understandings seriously. The West's military and productive dominance made Western cultural understandings decisive, but power asymmetry did not determine what the outcome of expanded interaction would be.

The deconstruction of sovereignty

Collective delegitimation

As Westerners came into contact with non-Western peoples, they generally perceived them as organized into "states." Early explorers often anticipated not only *terra firma* but *terra nullius*, meaning land that was unclaimed and unoccupied. Elaborate routines existed for recording discoveries and establishing claims over virgin territory.[18] But the political communities that occupied these lands could seldom be ignored. The question Westerners asked themselves was not whether non-Western societies possessed states, but what kinds of recognized rights – what sort of sovereignty – they thought these states possessed.

In the traditions of Western international law, the answer was at best ambiguous. Classical international doctrine did regard the independence of any internally constituted political community as natural and legitimate.[19] But there was much speculation that various non-Western peoples were something less than human. Scholastic justifications for the Spanish conquest of the Indies understood Indians as sinners, pagans, animals, idiots, and natural slaves.[20]

Even those who argued against culturalist or racialist ideas hemmed in non-Western sovereignty with the rights of Europeans. Vitoria dismissed the idea that Indians were natural slaves but argued that Indian efforts to restrict the travel or proselytizing by Spain's "ambassadors" (the Conquistadors) provided grounds for just war and

31

conquest.[21] And colonial imperialism was generally legitimated by more powerful and less sympathetic authorities. Thus the Papal Donation of 1493 granted Ferdinand and Isabella outright sovereignty over land to the West inhabited by non-Christians.

By the early nineteenth century, a positivist analysis had supplanted notions of natural law. Here the rights and duties of international law were viewed not as inherent in the human condition but as concrete historical products. This shift in reasoning, part of a much larger recasting of Western thought, greatly narrowed concern over non-European sovereignty. From the 1830s to the 1920s, international lawyers spoke of a "family of nations" to which non-Western states might at some point be admitted. Non-Westerners were viewed as failing to comprehend the requirements of Western international law, and as constitutionally unable to appeal to it. For example, annexation of an Asian or African state could be legally contested by a rival European power, but not by the annexed state itself.

Gerrit Gong details the Western "standard of civilization" used to evaluate non-Western polities.[22] In its relations with Western nationals, a "civilized" state permitted freedom of trade, guaranteed the life and liberty of foreign nationals, and applied law in an egalitarian fashion. In its interstate relations, civilization implied acceptance of European international law, including the laws of war, and the maintenance of continuous diplomatic relations with other members of the system.

The European standard of civilization also involved internal practices. Asian and African social institutions (personal rights, family relations, social norms) were viewed as uncivilized. States had to possess some degree of administrative efficiency and rule by written law. Of course, European states had only recently attained some of these marks of civilization themselves (for example, most colonial powers had outlawed slavery only in the first half of the nineteenth century). The Western social standard was that of the nineteenth-century social and political reformer, not that of the unreconstructed capitalist or gentry.

As the notion of a standard of civilization suggests, the clash of cultures extended beyond the narrow purview of international law to broader social understandings. Nineteenth-century social thought was fundamentally racialist. When the new science of ethnography defined and ranked the races of man, the features of Orientals and Africans were altered to resemble those of apes.[23] "Childlike" Asians and Africans were seen as lacking the character and intelligence that had generated Western technology.[24] Darwin's analysis of natural selection was translated into a celebration of the inevitable ascendancy of Europeans over less "fit" peoples.

Images of racial superiority, barbaric customs, and supine monarchies resonated with the cultural understandings and social projects of all kinds of Western audiences. Imperial discourse appealed to social reformers as well as the anachronistic warrior class dissected by Joseph Schumpeter.[25] Critics of nineteenth-century industrialization had much less to say about the advisability of exporting these practices to Asia and Africa.[26] Karl Marx celebrated the battering down of Chinese walls with cheap textiles, seeing capital as the only force capable of overcoming a "vegetative" Oriental despotism.

These cultural understandings made it easy to rally public opinion around an imperialist policy. Colonial adventure was used to whip crowds into a nationalist fervor. In soberer moments, imperialism could be understood in the West as Kipling's "White Man's Burden," a noble and self-denying trusteeship. Europe's civilizing influence was seen as drawing barbarous and savage humanity out of slavery, poverty, and ignorance. As A.P. Thornton notes, a colonial *realpolitik* of the mid-nineteenth century was transformed into the "moral" imperialism of the turn of the century.[27]

Arthur Stinchcombe defines a power's legitimacy as "the degree that, by virtue of the doctrines and norms by which it is justified, the power-holder can call upon sufficient other centers of power ... to make his power effective."[28] Here, Stinchcombe beautifully balances structural and cultural effects. Legitimacy is bound up in social relations, either to higher authorities or autonomous equals. But these relations are connected by cultural identity, by the doctrines and norms in which social arrangements are motivated and made meaningful.

It is precisely in Stinchcombe's sense that non-Western polities lacked legitimacy. A disjuncture in political universes meant that non-Western polities could not call on Western actors or opinion for support. They were not members of the Western community of recognition, supported by generalized third parties on the basis of common ethnic and religious identities, shared conceptions of collective purposes, or the needs of an "automatic" balance of power. Colonialism in Asia and Africa did not ramify back into Western national or international society to challenge the aims and nature of the imperialist.

Europe's former settler colonies in the Americas were viewed in a fundamentally different light. In Turgot's maxim, colonies were like fruits that fell from the tree as they grew ripe. By 1820, efforts to regain political control over South America appeared a bankrupt policy. The Spanish and Portuguese creoles (and North American ones) shared in the moral, religious, and racial world of the Great Powers. They were also part of the Great Powers' political universe culturally and relationally, as colonies that Spain sought to recover until the 1840s, and as American republics standing alongside the United States. Policy in the Americas did reflect back into the social, cultural, and political worlds of Europe.

The practice of imperialism

Broad, collective delegitimation of non-Western sovereignty facilitated colonial imperialism in two different contexts. It provided a basis for the parlor statesmanship of the metropolitan official mind, and it opened up opportunities for the restless activity of the colonial man on the spot. Imperial historiography lays out both of these characters in loving detail.

What is most striking about accounts of central decisionmaking is the bland inattention paid to colonial subjects. Robinson and Gallagher's description of Lord Salisbury, the architect of British foreign policy during much of the age of imperial conquest, is characteristic:

> Indeed, to Salisbury the issues of partition were always to remain curiously abstract, and even academic. They were complicated, they gave great opportunities for the use of expertise, and the exercise of solitary long-term planning. Africa remained for him above all an intellectual problem, an elaborate game of bids and counter bids, of delimitations and compensations. With the consequences for Africa, the development of the new territories and the impact of conquest, he was not greatly concerned: for him the partition began and ended on the maps of the Foreign Office.[29]

The sort of unconcern that Salisbury exemplifies seems essential to the ability of Western powers to meet and agree upon guidelines for the acquisition of non-Western territory.

Colonial imperialism formed a parlor game for Western diplomats because it was disconnected from the web of understandings and arrangements within which the Western state was embedded. First, imperialism did not refer back to the identity or purposes of the Western polity, because non-Western states and peoples were seen as fundamentally different from their Western counterparts. One could be a liberal domestically and an imperialist in Asia and Africa. (In fact, this was the position taken by many of the most ardent and self-consistent imperialists.) Second, Western statesmen not only held broadly similar views of the colonial situation, but they knew they shared these views. In 1885, an international conference in Berlin could cooperatively write down rules for the acquisition of African territory.

The visible status and marginal importance of much non-Western territory made it an ideal medium of exchange. To assuage French resentment over the British occupation of Egypt, for example, Bismarck suggested that France might take Tunis, Syria, Greece, or Morocco.[30] In 1912, Germany acceded to a French protectorate over Morocco in return for a slice of French Cameroon.[31]

But the real engine of colonial expansion was formed by the men whose livelihood depended on it: colonial officials, settlers, missionaries, and merchants.[32] These groups actively petitioned and propagandized for imperial projects. As Snyder emphasizes, men on the spot possessed near monopolies of information about African and Asian conditions.[33] The history of colonial imperialism is a history of men who misinformed their superiors and exceeded their instructions.

As a result, colonial expansion was a spatially bound process. While the initial motives for colonialism often appear random, it was this first step that was difficult. Given a colonial investment and the interests and actors it generated, frontier tensions and ensuing expansion were almost inevitable. For example, in 1858, the French temporarily occupied Cochin China to protect Catholic missions. Once there, motives and opportunities for acquiring all of Indochina were not hard to find.

Generalized cultural support was crucial for a process that was initiated in the periphery and that required ratification rather than resources from the center. And since the fate of non-Western polities had little meaning for European statesmen except as statusmarkers, metropolitan governments were not highly motivated to find ways of intelligently controlling men on the spot. Restraints were passive; few resources were committed to the colonial frontier, and imperialism was acceptable as long as it was cheap.

It should be noted that much imperial activity occurred on private initiative, with only formal state sponsorship. Twenty percent of new colonies founded in the nineteenth century were organized by chartered companies or private individuals.[34] Leopold laid claim to the Congo not as the head of the Belgian state, but as the organizer of the bogus *Agence Internationale du Congo*, a putative philanthropical society. Even when the imperialist was an agent of the state, he was generally attuned to colonial conditions and needs rather than to national policy.

If the aim here was to develop a general analysis of imperialism, we would want to consider not only Western statesmen and colonials, but the non-Western peoples who resisted or allied themselves with Western forces. Much recent historiographic research recovers resistance to Western domination. And it is clear that Western rule depended fundamentally upon indigenous support.[35] To gain this support, colonial states reinforced (and sometimes reinvented) the power of traditional authorities. See, for example, David Laitin's discussion of the way British rule in Nigeria employed failing institutions of kingship.[36]

But the narrower aim of this chapter leads attention away from the sources of indigenous action. Imperial propaganda was directed at the colonial official and the metropolitan population, aiming to make the public resources of Western societies available for overseas adventure and administration. Imperial discourse did not explain colonialism to the ruled.

As an example of an Egyptian and Moslem voice unimpressed by Western discourse, consider the beautiful irony of Jamal al-din al-Afghani:

> The English entered India and toyed with the minds of her princes and kings in a way that makes intelligent men both laugh and cry. They penetrated deeply into India's interior and seized her lands piece by piece. Whenever they became lords of the land they took liberties with its inhabitants, saying that the English are occupied only with commercial affairs. As for tending to administration and politics, that is not their business. However, what calls them to bear the burdens of administration and politics is pity for the kings and the princes who are incapable of governing their dominions. When the kings or princes are able to control their land, no Englishman will remain there, they said, because they have other important affairs that they have abandoned out of pure compassion.[37]

Reconstructing sovereignty

Given the power of imperialist discourse in the late nineteenth century, how did some non-Western areas avoid formal colonization? One way was to successfully defend territory by force. Before World War I, Ethiopia and Japan had defeated Western states on the battlefield.

Britain had proved unable to control Afghanistan after several major campaigns; Britain and Russia then aided in the construction of an expanded Afghani state that could stand as a buffer between them. Geographically isolated states like Nepal resisted colonialism by barring their gates to the few explorers and traders who ventured their way.

This chapter's focus on the cultural sources of sovereign recognition leads me to slight cases where sovereignty was preserved by force of arms. Before leaving them, however, it should be noted that even here Western recognition did not follow in a simple way from military success, nor did military action stand outside a cultural context. Ethiopia and Japan carefully observed Western rules of war in their struggles with European powers.[38] By following European conventions and standards, non-Western states lowered the chances that Western third parties might enter the conflict on the side of an "outraged civilization."

But rather than evaluate these combinations of factors, I will focus on cases where sovereignty was constructed in the face of unambiguous opportunities for colonial imperialism. Two main routes to Western recognition of non-Western sovereignty remain. One was the stalemate formed when a local balance of Western power surrounded a non-Western polity. The second involved a strategy of defensive Westernization by a non-Western polity.

Realpolitik *outside state society*

A local balance of power arose where two or more Western states possessed substantial interests in a territory. Direct competition between Western interests impeded formal colonialism. Formal control required unilateral occupation by a single Western power, a condominium held by two or more Western powers, or a partition of territory. These became increasingly difficult to accomplish as the number and scope of competing national interests grew.[39]

Balances based on major national interests of three or more Great Powers underlay the maintenance of sovereignty in the Ottoman and Chinese empires. Two-power balances based on peripheral competition emerged in Afghanistan, Persia, and Siam.[40] I focus here on the two major cases of the Ottoman and Chinese empires, which most fully reflect the working of a local balance. Siam is discussed in a later section.

Both the Ottoman and the Chinese empires were of great intrinsic importance to Western powers. In the case of the Ottoman Empire, key aims included Russia's drive southward for a warm-water port and her pan-Slavic and pan-Orthodox ambitions, France's longstanding economic investments and military ties, Germany's railroad-building initiatives, and Britain's commercial and strategic interest in the Mediterranean. China was the focal point of Western concern in Asia, due to its territorial size and the scale of its market. All the Great Powers – Britain, France, Germany, Japan, Russia, and the United States – sought to trade and invest in China.

The geopolitical value that Western states assigned to the Ottoman and Chinese empires rendered their aims directly rather than diffusely competitive. In Africa and much of Asia, expansion by one power spurred colonization somewhere else by its rivals. However, the Ottoman and Chinese empires could not be abstractly balanced with compensating gains elsewhere. For any one of the powers to seize Constantinople or to enter into an exclusive relationship with China was a larger geopolitical gain than the other Great Powers could readily accept.

Even the division of the Ottoman or Manchu dominions into equal shares could potentially shake the global balance of power. Britain's aim was to keep Russia out of the Mediterranean, not to gain a slice of territory in the Near East. Balancing strategies led to Ottoman losses in Europe and spheres of influence in China, but not to wholesale imperial partition.

The diplomatic history of these states in the second half of the nineteenth century was one of Western powers blocking each other's land grabs.[41] In the Crimean War, France and Britain prevented Russia from organizing a protectorate over the Slavic and Orthodox peoples within the Ottoman Empire. Their victory led to the formal admission of the Ottomans to the European concert and a guarantee of Ottoman independence. The British fleet was ordered to Constantinople to prevent a Russian advance in the Russo-Turkish war of 1877 to 1878. The Great Powers rewrote the peace treaty that ended that conflict by eliminating the proposed construction of a huge Bulgarian state to be occupied by Russian troops.

Chinese diplomatic history reads the same way. After the Sino-Japanese War (1894–5), China ceded Japan the Liaotung Peninsula. A Far Eastern triplice manned by France, Germany, and Russia threatened Japan with war if she did not return the peninsula, which she did. In the wake of the Boxer uprising, Germany, Great Britain, and the

United States successfully opposed Russian occupation of southern Manchuria. The later American Open Door Policy sought to arrest the complete collapse of China while perpetuating the de facto partition into spheres of interest that had arisen over the nineteenth century.

A heavily compromised sovereignty emerged out of these balances of foreign interest. Turkish public finances were run by the Ottoman Public Debt Administration, a body staffed largely by European officials. The *Sublime Porte* traded reform for European guarantees. For example, an unpopular edict providing for religious freedom for Christians was worked out by British, French, and Austrian ambassadors in 1856; its promulgation facilitated Ottoman entry into the Concert of Europe. In China, European states mandated low tariffs and set up militarily protected European settlements that possessed extensive extraterritorial jurisdiction. At the height of the treaty port system, European states even administered public functions like the postal service and some tax collection.

Support for the Ottomans and the Manchus was not based upon their modernizing efforts, nor upon their capacity to provide the political infrastructure for economic penetration. Western diplomatic support often did come at the price of promised institutional reforms. But the Ottomans and Manchus did not proactively open their societies and economies to the West. The "Sick Man of Europe" and the "Sick Man of Asia" were declining empires unable to construct national societies to face the Western challenge. Local balances of power were not formed on the basis of Ottoman or Manchu reforms, but on Western perceptions of the commercial and strategic value of Turkish and Chinese territory.

In fact, it was practically impossible for non-Western polities to engineer a local balance of power to embed themselves within a structure of defensive alliances pitting European rivals against each other. Many non-Western polities sought to play Western states off against each other. But in the absence of grounded Western interests (or grounded participation in the European family of nations), such efforts simply hastened preemptive annexation. For example, King Thibaw of Burma attempted in 1883 to enlist French support to balance British aggression. When Britain demanded that Burma accept a protectorate, the king replied that friendly relations with France, Italy, and other countries were being maintained. The British treated this communication as a *casus belli* and took Mandalay within two weeks.[42]

The inability of non-Western powers to embed themselves in a web of alliances suggests the sense in which imperial *realpolitik* was neither a crude war of all against all, nor an elegant balance-of-power system. Imperialism is not properly conceived as the result of interaction between a set of formally disconnected actors. It is better thought of as interaction between a coalition of aligned states (the West's Great Powers) and an isolated state (the non-Western polity). Imperialism had rules, but these rules pertained to competitive and collaborative behavior within the coalition. The fact that the non-Western state could not penetrate the corridors of Western diplomacy disabled efforts to turn Western rivalry into a sophisticated balance of power.

Defensive Westernization

The prime example of defensive Westernization is of course Japan.[43] Explicit imitation of Western political and administrative institutions[44] led to the abrogation of the restrictive treaties imposed by the West on Japanese juridical authority and tariffs in the Kimberly-Aoki Treaty of 1894. By this time, military buildup along Western lines had already permitted Japan to launch an independent imperial career in the Orient, one that identified Japan with the "civilized" West in opposition to the "barbaric practices" of China and Russia.[45] The Japanese case combines compliance with Western cultural models and development of military capacity sufficient to block Western attempts at annexation.

I thus examine an alternative instance of defensive Westernization. As in Japan, Siamese elites undertook a massive effort to reorganize an Asian state and society along Western lines.[46] But Siam did not develop a military capacity sufficient to give pause to Western powers. This makes it a strong test case for investigating whether a policy of defensive Westernization can construct recognized sovereignty.

Siam's "enlightened monarchs," Mongkut and Chulalongkorn, restructured social and political institutions in a Westernizing project. Functionally differentiated administrative units were introduced into a state that had been shaped to mirror Hindu cosmology.[47] Ministries of education, forests and mines, and foreign affairs were staffed by European and American advisers. A capstone agrarian bureaucracy[48] was reconstructed as an engine for development. Tax incentives were provided to expand the cultivation of rice, and irrigation projects were undertaken to increase productivity.

Defensive Westernization in Siam was not limited to techniques of rule. Social institutions like slavery and polygamy were abolished despite their central position in Thai society. King Mongkut instituted a reformed Buddhism that assimilated Western scientific knowledge and emphasized national service. Brahmanistic rituals and an understanding of the monarch as a living god were replaced by public works and an understanding of the monarch as the defender of the Buddhist church.

Siam acceded to the demands of predatory Westerners on the spot in enlightened fashion. Learning from the successes of gunboat diplomacy elsewhere, in 1855 King Mongkut met the East India Company's representative in person, offered him cigars, and proceeded to expound on the virtues of free trade! Mongkut signed the same treaty forced upon Burma and China, giving British consuls wide extraterritorial powers, banning export monopolies, and fixing tariff duties. But Siam did so without military conflict of the type that often served as the prelude to colonial expansion. Instead, it developed a burgeoning rice trade with Britain.

Siam sought to expand her diplomatic relations with the West. It signed treaties with eleven other Western powers that gave similar rights to those accorded the British. (None established an economic relationship of note with Siam until German commercial interests did so in the twentieth century.) Siamese rulers earned a well-founded reputation for diplomatic aplomb in the face of crisis. For example, in 1893 French ships forced an entrance to Bangkok as the result of a territorial dispute and threatened the capital. Siamese minister of foreign affairs, Prince Devawongse, greeted the French commander and congratulated him on his skill and daring.[49]

Despite an active strategy of Westernization, Siamese sovereignty was barely retained during the imperial period. Siam lost over half her territory to Britain and France, mostly in the form of lost tributary states like Cambodia and the Malay sheikdoms. Siam's foreign policy was to seek British support against French colonial ambitions. Despite good relations with Britain, only modest aid was forthcoming. For example, Siam appealed in 1891 for British assistance in the face of French claims to the Mekong basin. Lord Rosebery, the British foreign minister, adopted a posture of "cautious diplomatic reserve"[50] and counseled Siam to accede to French demands, which it did.

In 1896, Britain and France agreed that neither would encroach on Siamese sovereignty without the consent of the other. A year later, Britain signed a secret accord with Siam promising support in the event of foreign aggression. This agreement strengthened the hand of

Siam vis-à-vis continuing French territorial claims. After the signing of the Entente Cordiale in 1904, however, Anglo-French *rapprochement* led Siam to lose more land to both France and Britain.

While Siam lost much territory in the age of imperialism, she remained an independent state. By the turn of the century, the relevant Western powers (Britain and France) had begun to treat Siamese sovereignty as a viable solution to the tensions posed by their commercial and territorial ambitions. Siam was recognized as a buffer state not merely because it stood between Burma and Indochina, but because it had Westernized.

The stability of realpolitik and defensive Westernization

This review suggests how difficult it was for non-Western polities to avoid colonial imperialism. Neither the existence of a balance of Western interests nor an aggressive policy of defensive Westernization provided a decisive road to Western recognition. In the heyday of imperial expansion, Asian and African polities had few tools with which to respond to Western powers jointly pursuing imperial expansion. Even where non-Western states were well-situated or where they had constructed elaborate strategic responses, they had to overcome the momentum of the larger imperial juggernaut.

The Siamese case suggests the limits of a strategy of cultural isomorphism. Without British support Siam would probably have been annexed by France. And if France had not been in the picture, Siam would probably have become British along the lines of the Indian princely states. Siamese sovereignty was constructed from the juxtaposition of British amity and commercial interest, and French territorial aims.

Stalemates based on simple balances of interest were also fragile. The sovereignty of the Ottomans and Manchus was constantly renegotiated with a circle of predatory powers. Its maintenance depended on perceptions that the indigenous polity was sufficiently vigorous to be able to maintain its integrity despite constant rounds of new concessions. And it depended on Western powers not finding that the territory at issue was less important than their rivalries.

When the "Sick Men" of Europe and Asia were perceived to be dying, or when Great Power politics were substantially realigned, recognition based on a balance of interest counted for little. Thus, during World War I Britain and France agreed upon a plan for partitioning the Turkish Empire, and wrote a secret treaty giving

Constantinople to Russia (as an inducement to remain in the war). The fact that the Ottoman empire had been formally inducted into the Concert of Europe more than a half century earlier[51] does not appear to have entered into their calculations.

In other areas, substantial balances of interest did, in fact, yield. A balance between a Great Power and a power of the second rank could break down through unilateral action by the stronger party. Unequal levels of interest could prompt the more concerned party to attempt annexation despite the risks. Or complex balances of interest could be resolved through negotiation and side payments. For example, France assumed a Tunisian protectorate precisely because Italy (the perennial non-Great Power) was gaining influence. Britain risked French enmity by unilaterally occupying Egypt in the same year.[52] And while a complex combination of European interests in Morocco blocked action until 1912, a French-Spanish partition was eventually accomplished.

In each of these situations, higher levels of Western interest, larger numbers of concerned powers, and greater symmetry of interest would have helped forestall colonization. But a policy of defensive Westernization on the part of the polity at risk might have made a qualitative difference. Tunisia, Morocco, and Egypt were all weak traditional autocracies in substantial debt to Western investors. European states viewed the assumption of formal controls over these states as natural and necessary.

In the heyday of Western imperialism, it appears that neither a simple balance of interest nor defensive Westernization could produce a full measure of Western recognition. A cultural policy had to be buttressed with force: either military strength (as in Japan) or some balance of Western interests (as in Siam). For a temporary stalemate based on a balance of interests to become permanent, the non-Western polity had to imitate Western models in some substantial fashion. Only then did formal declarations of recognition become the positive policy and background assumption of relevant Western powers.

Discussion

Much contemporary discussion of sovereignty revolves around the question: does it matter? This chapter argues that it does. I suggest that the imperial moment took place within and was carried forward by a collective delegitimation of the sovereignty of non-Western polities. Most palpably, this delegitimation permitted forms of naked *realpolitik* in Western colonial imperialism that are at best muted in relations within a state society. The structural conditions most often pointed to as driving colonial imperialism appeared in South America as well as in Asia and Africa in the nineteenth century, but with fundamentally different political consequences.

Two routes to recognized sovereignty appear to have existed during the heyday of Western political expansion. A local balance of Western interests might produce a stalemate, making annexation difficult. Policies of defensive Westernization, where Western institutions were incorporated into the state and diplomatic relations assiduously cultivated, also increased survival chances. But neither a balance of interests nor defensive Westernization provided a secure road to stable independence or recognized sovereignty. Local conditions and strategies could not reverse – but only blunt – the larger imperial project of which non-Western polities and societies *in general* were the object.

Absence of recognition is too passive and narrow a way to describe Western perceptions of Asian and African polities in the late nineteenth century. To adopt Harold Garfinkel's imagery,[53] Western witnesses participated in a status degradation ceremony, where Asian and African polities were publicly denounced as outside and in opposition to a self-referentially valid progress. Colonial imperialism took the form of a social movement, complete with moralizing motives, pragmatic analyses, and more than a touch of crowd hysteria. It took the carnage of World War I to bring this project under scrutiny.

Recognition and the granting of international personality are not well viewed as a narrow, almost technical act by and about states. Technical criteria only appear sufficient where real conflicts over national and governmental legitimacy do not arise. Hostility toward the claims of Asian and African polities was not neutrally about state power in Burma or China any more than dynastic opposition to revolutionary Paris was neutrally about state power. And while the Great Powers were undoubtedly the critical sites where the imperial discourse crystallized and was acted upon, this discourse was deeply rooted in Western society. It is a measurement device to act as though clubs of mutual recognition are an achievement of diplomats.[54]

The way perceptions about sovereignty were informed by a much more general delegitimation of the Asian or African "other" suggests two ideas about sovereignty within contemporary international relations. First, today's global community of mutual recognition is not accurately seen as a narrow diplomatic achievement of its members.

Here, too, recognition depends more upon broad understandings of the cultural features that states share and that national societies share. In the early modern period these commonalities revolved around Christianity and dynastic authority; today they revolve around democracy, markets, and human rights. States are delegitimated within the West when they challenge core shared aims and institutions: France in 1789, when it challenged monarchy; the Soviet Union in 1917, when it challenged markets and property.

Second, sovereignty may be fundamental to the cultural framework of contemporary international society but at the same time contestable. Since recognition summarizes much broader assessments of cultural congruence and worth, the institution of sovereignty itself becomes vulnerable when the nation-state appears to be in conflict with more basic cultural projects. For example, when states violate human rights, questions are raised about whether state sovereignty is an appropriate vehicle for realizing the potential of the human individual. A common discursive field thus links the Westphalian state society as an ideal to contemporary efforts to limit the state and organize at an international rather than a domestic level.

Notes

[1] See, for example, Morgenthau, Hans 1978. *Politics Among Nations.* New York: Alfred A. Knopf; Waltz, Kenneth 1979. *Theory of International Politics.* Reading, Mass.: Addison-Wesley; Gilpin, Robert 1981. *War and Change in World Politics.* Cambridge: Cambridge University Press.

[2] See for example Meyer, John W. 1980. "The World Polity and the Authority of the Nation-State," in Bergeson, A. (ed.) *Studies of the Modern World-System.* New York: Academic Press; Ashley, Richard K. 1984. "The Poverty of Neo-Realism," *International Organization* 38: 225–85; Young, Oran R. 1986. "International Regimes: Toward a New Theory of Institutions," *World Politics* 39: 102–22.

[3] Hall, W.E. 1979. *A Treatise on International Law.* 8th ed. London: Clarendon Press, p. 103. On issues and practices related to international recognition, also see Lauterpacht, Hersch 1947. *Recognition in International Law.* Cambridge: Cambridge University Press; Oppenheim, L. F. L. 1944. *International Law.* 6th ed. London: Longman; Crawford, James 1973. *The Creation of States in International Law.* Oxford: Clarendon Press.

[4] Strang, David 1991. "Anomaly and Commonplace in European Political Expansion: Realist and Institutional Accounts," *International Organization* 45: 143–62.

[5] In a related vein, also see Strang, David 1990. "From Dependency to Sovereignty: An Event History Analysis of Decolonization," *American Socio-*

logical Review 55: 846–60 and 1991. "Global Patterns of Decolonization 1500–1987," *International Studies Quarterly* 35: 429–54 for an analysis of the construction of new states that emphasizes the way actors in colonial dependencies mobilized around Western models of the nation-state.

[6] For a description of forms of international status distinguishing "unrecognized," "dependent," and "sovereign" polities, and a description of data mapping movement across these statuses, see Strang, David 1991. "Anomaly and Commonplace" and "From *Terra Incognita* to Sovereign State: the Instability of Formal Dependency, 1415–1987," paper presented at the annual meetings of the American Political Science Association, Washington D.C.

[7] Strang, "From *Terra Incognita* to Sovereign State."

[8] Key accounts include Hobson, John A. 1902. *Imperialism: A Study*. New York: G. Allen & Unwin; Hilferding, Rudolf 1910. *Finance Capital*. London: Routledge & Kegan Paul; Lenin, Vladimir Ilich 1917. *Imperialism, The Highest Stage of Capitalism*. London: International Publishers. Differences between an "imperialism of trade" and an "imperialism of capital" are not critical for present purposes. Nor do we need to ask whether or not capital export was inevitable in a mature capitalist economy, the issue that most divided Hobson and Lenin.

[9] See Hobson, *Imperialism*, 55.

[10] Detailed accounts of colonial commerce, investment, and expenditure are presented in Clark, Graham 1936. *The Balance Sheets of Imperialism*. New York: Russell & Russell; Feis, H. 1965. *Europe the World's Banker, 1870–1914*. New York: Columbia University Press; Davis, Lance E. and Huttenback, Robert A. 1986. *Mammon and the Pursuit of Empire: The Political Economy of British Imperialism, 1860–1912*. Cambridge: Cambridge University Press.

[11] See especially Robinson, Ronald 1972. "Non-European Foundations of European Imperialism: Sketch for a Theory of Collaboration," in Owen, R. and Sutcliffe, B. (eds.) *Studies in the Theory of Imperialism*. London: Longman.

[12] Robinson, Ronald and Gallagher, John (with Alice Denny) 1961. *Africa and the Victorians*. London: St. Martin's Press.

[13] Mathew, W.M. 1968. "The Imperialism of Free Trade: Peru, 1820–70," *Economic History Review* S21: 562–79; Gootenberg, Paul 1989. *Between Silver and Guano*. Princeton: Princeton University Press.

[14] Krasner, Stephen D. 1976. "State Power and the Structure of International Trade," *World Politics* 28: 317–43.

[15] Gallagher and Robinson, *Africa and the Victorians*.

[16] Brunschwig, Henri 1966. *French Colonialism 1871–1914*. London: Pall Mall Press; Fieldhouse, David K. 1973. *Economics and Empire, 1830–1914*. Ithaca: Cornell University Press.

[17] Platt, D.C.M. 1968. *Finance, Trade, and Politics in British Foreign Policy 1815–1914*. Oxford: Clarendon Press.

[18] Keller, Arthur S., Lissitzyn, Oliver J., and Mann, Frederick J. 1938. *Creation of Rights of Sovereignty through Symbolic Acts 1400–1800*. New York: Columbia University Press.

[19] Alexandrowicz, Charles Henry 1967. *An Introduction to the History of the Law of Nations in the East Indies.* Oxford: Clarendon Press.

[20] Pagden, Anthony 1987. "Dispossessing the Barbarian: The Language of Spanish Thomism and the Debate over the Property Rights of the American Indians," in Pagden, A. (ed.) *The Languages of Political Theory in Early-Modern Europe.* Cambridge: Cambridge University Press, pp. 79–98.

[21] Scholastic discussion of the basis of Spanish sovereignty in the Indies was constrained and in fact motivated by more important debates about sovereignty within Christendom. A main concern of Vitoria and his epigones was to counter Lutheran doctrine that the monarch had to be in a state of grace (see Pagden, "Dispossessing the Barbarian").

[22] Gong, Gerrit W. 1984. *The Standard of "Civilization" in International Society.* Oxford: Clarendon Press.

[23] Gould, Stephen Jay 1981. *The Mismeasure of Man.* New York: W.W. Norton.

[24] Adas, Michael 1989. *Machines as the Measure of Man.* Ithaca: Cornell University Press.

[25] Schumpeter, Joseph 1951. "The Sociology of Imperialism," in Schumpeter, J. (ed.) *Imperialism and Social Classes.* New York: Kelley.

[26] Imperialism was not universally applauded within the West. The "Little England" movement was animated in part by the distaste for imperialism held by men like Richard Cobden. But the popular engine of the movement had to do with tariff reform rather than political principle.

[27] Thornton, A.P. 1959. *The Imperial Idea and its Enemies.* New York: St. Martin's Press.

[28] Stinchcombe, Arthur L. 1968, *Constructing Social Theories.* New York: Harcourt, Brace & World, p. 162.

[29] Gallagher and Robinson, *Africa and the Victorians,* 257.

[30] Fieldhouse, *Economics and Empire,* 255.

[31] In an earlier era, territory and population within Europe had been bartered in a similar fashion. For accounting principles in the transfer of territory at the Congress of Vienna, see Gulick, Edward V. 1955. *Europe's Classical Balance of Power.* Binghamton: Vail-Baillou Press.

[32] Imperialism provided excellent career prospects. For example, see Brunschwig's *French Colonialism* on rapid promotion in the French Colonial Service.

[33] Snyder, Jack 1991. *Myths of Empire: Domestic Politics and International Ambition.* Ithaca: Cornell University Press.

[34] Strang, "From *Terra Incognita* to Sovereign State."

[35] Robinson, "Non-European Foundations."

[36] Laitin, David 1985. "Hegemony and Religious Conflict: British Imperial Control and Political Cleavages in Yorubaland," in Evans, P.B., Rueschemeyer, D., and Skocpol, T. (eds.) *Bringing the State Back In.* Cambridge: Cambridge University Press, pp. 285–316.

[37] Quoted in Hodgkin, Thomas 1972. "Some African and Third World

Theories of Imperialism," in Owen, R. and Sutcliffe, B. (eds.) *Studies in the Theory of Imperialism.* London: Longman.

[38] Gong, *The Standard of "Civilization."*

[39] One index of the difficulties involved is the infrequency of formal partitions or condominiums, especially as the importance of the territory increases. The largest non-Western state to be formally partitioned was Morocco. The only successful Western condominium was in the New Hebrides.

[40] Balances of interest failed to ultimately preserve sovereignty in Tunisia, Morocco, and Egypt.

[41] See Langer, William L. 1931. *European Alliances and Alignments 1871–1890.* New York, Alfred A. Knopf; and 1935. *The Diplomacy of Imperialism.* New York, Alfred A. Knopf.

[42] Dhiravegin, Likhit 2518 BE. *Siam and Colonialism (1855–1909): An Analysis of Diplomatic Relations.* Bangkok: Thai Watana Panich, p. 53.

[43] On the general process of institutional isomorphism through coercive pressure, see the sensitive discussion in DiMaggio, Paul J. and Powell, Walter W. 1983. "The Iron Cage Revisited: Institutional Isomorphism and Collective Rationality in Organizational Fields," *American Sociological Review* 48: 147–60.

[44] Westney, D. Eleanor 1987. *Imitation and Innovation: The Transfer of Western Organizational Patterns to Meiji Japan.* Cambridge, Mass.: Harvard University Press.

[45] Gong, *The Standard of "Civilization."*

[46] Siam is an Indian term for Thailand, adopted during the imperial period and discarded in favor of *Muang Thai* or Thailand in the 1930s. I use "Siam" below to emphasize the nineteenth-century construction of the Thai state on Western terms.

[47] For excellent descriptions of the structure of the Hindu state, see Riggs, Fred W. 1966. *Thailand: The Modernization of a Bureaucratic Polity.* Honolulu: East-West Center Press; and also Clifford Geertz, 1980. *Negara: The Theatre State in Nineteenth-Century Bali.* Princeton: Princeton University Press. My discussion of Siam's response to the West is also based on Vella, Walter F. 1955. *The Impact of the West on Government in Thailand.* Berkeley: University of California Press; Gong, *The Standard of "Civilization"*; and Dhiravegin, *Siam and Colonialism.*

[48] The term is taken from Hall, John 1985. *Powers and Liberties: The Causes and Consequences of the Rise of the West.* London: Penguin.

[49] These sorts of responses to an expansionary West were really very unusual. The more typical case of Burma, Siam's neighbor, helps place Siamese strategy in perspective. Despite some efforts at fiscal and judicial reform, Burma in the nineteenth century remained a capstone empire riven by palace coups. Three Anglo-Burmese wars were sparked by border incidents, conflict between Burmese and British subordinates, and judicial fines levied by Burmese courts on British firms. Diplomatically, Burma was at odds with British India throughout the nineteenth century. In fact, disagreement about whether shoes could be worn at royal audiences cut direct contacts between

Burma and Calcutta after 1875. Unsuccessful efforts to cultivate ties to other Western powers gave Calcutta the rationale (vis-à-vis metropolitan conservatism) it needed to annex Burma entirely.

[50] Riggs, *Thailand*.

[51] See Naff, Thomas 1984. "The Ottoman Empire and the European States System," in Bull, H. and Watson, A. (eds.) *The Expansion of International Society*. Oxford: Clarendon Press, pp. 143–70.

[52] Britain and France both possessed longstanding interests in Egypt and had combined to jointly regulate the country's finances in 1879. The reasons why Britain took Egypt more seriously than Anglo-French amity are the focus of much British imperial history. For contrasting views see Gallagher and Robinson, *Africa and the Victorians*, and Hopkins, A.G. 1986. "The Victorians and Africa: A Reconsideration of the Occupation of Egypt, 1882," *Journal of African History* 27: 363–91.

[53] Garfinkel, Harold 1956. "Conditions of successful degradation ceremonies," *American Journal of Sociology* 61: 420–4.

[54] As I do in Strang, "Anomaly and Commonplace."

3   Beyond the sovereignty dilemma: quasi-states as social construct

Naeem Inayatullah

A critical reflection of the end of the Cold War, the collapse of a number of states, and the subsequent interest in humanitarian intervention suggest the ambiguities surrounding the idea of sovereignty.[1] On the one hand, scholars and policymakers increasingly argue that the principle of sovereignty acts as an impediment toward improving the global condition. Individual states appeal to the principle of nonintervention in their internal politics (one of the central features of sovereignty), thereby constraining global humanitarian movements. Unless permission is granted by individual states, sovereignty limits international action against, for example, human rights violations, persecution or genocide of ethnic or religious minorities, internal colonialism, starvation, and environmental concerns such as the depletion of rain forests. Sovereignty provides individual states with a license to purify their domain of opposition, silence alternative voices, and eliminate dissent. In short, the principle of sovereignty shields states' internal deficiencies and failings against external pressure and action. On the other hand, sovereignty remains a significant value in the context of international society as a whole. Its principle of nonintervention constrains traditional empire building and curbs the use of force by the powerful against the less powerful. Its principle of self-determination allows for a diversity of states to construct their projects according to the resonance of their own meanings. It allows, therefore, for a tolerance of ideological differences. Further, an international society based on the principle of sovereignty may be seen as a type of decentralized democracy where ideological differences can be discussed and debated without degenerating into the habitual use of absolute force.[2]

The conventionally recognized and discussed tension between the

50

dysfunctions and achievements of sovereignty is part of the political setting of what I refer to as the sovereignty dilemma. In this context, the sovereignty dilemma posits the problem of expanding the benefits of sovereignty to the substate level. The expansion requires one of two possibilities. Either we respect the sovereignty principle and seek permission from the very state agents whose purificatory national agenda may have motivated global humanitarian concerns in the first place, or we press our agenda (somehow having made a judgment about its superiority) without the permission of state agents and, consequently, erode and delegitimate sovereignty for all states. Such dichotomous treatments merely sidestep the sovereignty dilemma rather than work through it. One way to come to terms with the sovereignty dilemma is to recognize that in addition to the problem of expanding the benefits of sovereignty to the substate level, the sovereignty dilemma posits a second problem – one more explicitly grounded in political economy.

The introduction to this volume observes that sovereignty changes its meaning as it confronts and adapts to challenges. An important challenge occurs when sovereignty encounters an expanding capitalist division of labor. In the current international society, attaining sovereignty – defined as "a political entity's externally recognized right to exercise final authority over its own affairs" – is embedded within a process of the social recognition of territorial states. I argue in this chapter that such recognition is a necessary but not a sufficient condition for realizing sovereignty. Concretely, sovereignty expresses those actions that move beyond its mere formal assertion and demands that territorial states (henceforth referred to simply as "states") pursue projects that construct their identities as states as well as their differences with other states. Such projects of expression require wealth. In capitalism, wealth is the product of a global division of labor and, therefore, discussions of sovereignty obligate an understanding of a wealth-producing division of labor.

The division of labor has a dual relationship to state sovereignty. On the one hand, acquisition of wealth resulting from the economic practices of the global division of labor enables the specific projects upon which expressions of state sovereignty depend. On the other hand, the wealth-creating division of labor operates as a type of *external* authority that limits and challenges the state. The political-economy inspired addition to the problem presented by the sovereignty dilemma highlights the difficulty of realizing concrete sovereignty

51

when the wealth necessary for such expression is beyond the state's authority.

As I will demonstrate, there are two problems – how to expand the benefits of sovereignty to substate levels and how to realize concrete sovereignty in the face of the external authority of the wealth-producing global division of labor. The problems are related, especially for Third World states, whose state agents may be unable or unwilling to pass the benefits of sovereignty to substate levels if they do not feel secure in their ability to accrue these benefits for the state as a whole. The vulnerability of Third World states to the peculiar manner in which the social practices of sovereignty and the global division of labor interact has the effect of constructing some of these entities as "weak" or "quasi-states." The constructed nature of weak or quasi-states can be revealed by clarifying the separable but not separate workings of both sovereignty and the division of labor, not only as opposing but also complementary principles that contribute to the constitution of a state.

The constructed nature of quasi-states also exposes an under-studied question: How do we, and should we, imagine wealth production and acquisition by states? An implicit answer is that individual states are forced to compete for wealth in the world market. For heuristic purposes, I propose instead that states have a "right to wealth." Whether this right is seen as a fair opportunity to compete for wealth in global markets or as a dividend in the wealth produced by a global division of labor, a discussion of it may clarify matters in the following ways. First, it may move the debate on sovereignty beyond the important but perhaps unavailing assessments concerning its achievements and dysfunctions. Second, it may suggest how to influence problems located in substate arenas without unduly undermining the principle of sovereignty either for a particular state or for international society as a whole. Third, it may create a better conversational posture toward those who regard injustice, inequality, and indignity that has been created by the global political economy as the ordering principles of global social life.

Most contemporary discussions do not incorporate the political economy component of sovereignty. This blind spot leads to ignoring the following ideas: (1) the motives of colonizing European states were intimately related to the dynamic expanding power of capitalism and its need for ever greater resources and larger markets; (2) the attempts of colonizers to turn their colonies into regions of specialized production within an expanding division of labor centered around European states' competitive needs; and (3) Third World states were required to graft their sovereignty on to a productive structure historically constructed to deprive their economies of autonomy, diversity, and robustness. The exclusion of these ideas in contemporary discussions presumes that Third World states have somehow overcome their historical status as functional elements within a global division of labor, and therefore that they can and should compete as equals within a global market while meeting their needs with their own efforts and resources. If, in contrast to this assumption, the majority of Third World states are perceived as not having significantly overcome the specialized role imposed on them by a European and North American controlled division of labor, then asking Third World states to compete as equals in a global market is to subsume them in a process in which they usually cannot compete. In correspondence with dependency and world systems theories, my approach to sovereignty assumes that competition in the global political economy has been and continues to be less than fair.

Nevertheless, my discussion differs from the dependency and the world systems approaches because it remains indifferent to the precise ontological status of the political economy. For my purposes, whether the global political economy is or was fair and whether Third World states had or have the opportunities to overcome their colonial past is not fully relevant. More to the point is that dependency and world systems theories provide an analytic narrative that complements the *felt* injustice and indignity of the less powerful. Neglecting the political economy component can be interpreted, therefore, as a way of ignoring the historical and theoretical apparatus employed by those who deem injustice to be the ordering principle of global social life. If my argument is viable, this conversational closure in contemporary literature registers most emphatically as a theoretical presumption that we have a clear and self-conscious understanding of how states acquire and ought to acquire wealth.

Beyond focusing on this presumption, the strategy of this chapter differs in another way from what might be expected in a dependency or world systems analysis. I do not use the tension between sovereignty and the global division of labor merely to emphasize the negative results created by the capitalist division of labor on the sovereignty of Third World states. Instead, the challenge posed by the division of labor to sovereignty is seen as an opportunity to demonstrate the significance of the following issues for the contemporary theoretical and conversational agenda: (1) What is the relationship between sovereignty and the global division of labor? (2) What are the principles that do and ought to determine global wealth creation and acquisition by states? (3) What is the role of wealth creation and acquisition in the erosion and realization of state sovereignty?

This chapter consists of five sections. First, I explore the tension between the logic of sovereignty and that of a capitalist division of labor. This tension requires us to focus on the largely implicit principles by which states produce and acquire wealth. I suggest that while states participate as functional and dependent parts of a division of labor, they are nevertheless expected to secure the resources to express their sovereignty through their own individual efforts. I trace the conflation of the logic of sovereignty and capitalism to Adam Smith's *Wealth of Nations* and suggest that we have yet to move beyond his formulations. Second, I establish continuities between Smith's conflation and the analysis of Robert H. Jackson, which refers to many Third World states as quasi-states.[3] Like Smith, who thinks individuals are independent of the historical origins of a wealth-creating division of labor, Jackson regards Third World states as independent of the colonial history of a capitalist division of labor. Third, to ground my critique of Jackson (offered in section four) I offer three historical illustrations – eighteenth-century Saint Domingue and nineteenth-century Egypt and India – which suggest how both the colonizer and the colonized are caught and embedded within the tension between sovereignty and the division of labor. Fourth, I offer a critique of Jackson relying on a historically informed political economy approach to sovereignty. Finally, I speculate on how a political economy reconstruction of the sovereignty dilemma provides opportunities to move beyond the current discussions about the dysfunctions and the achievements of state sovereignty.

Between sovereignty and the division of labor[4]

The cosmological change that brings about both the society of states and capitalism also introduces the idea of individuality. Persons become sovereign individuals who are free from ties of fealty to the feudal lord and manor. This freedom is doubled-edged; the individual is finally free to become himself or herself, but only within a system of wealth creation that treats the individual as the bearer of commodities.

That is, while the freedom to express individuality is a gain, it is limited by its dependence upon wealth acquisition. The historical purpose of capitalism is to provide this wealth. It does so, however, at the level of the system as a whole. There is no assurance that what Adam Smith calls the "general plenty" will disperse toward a particular individual. The need to acquire wealth forces individuals to participate in a system of commodity exchange within a wealth-creating division of labor. Marx criticizes this element of liberalism with the idea that it is not sufficient to be recognized as a free or sovereign individual; formal recognition needs to be accompanied by a substantive means (wealth) to express individuality.[5] How individuals acquire and how they ought to acquire wealth is a central problem of classical political economy.

States also need to acquire wealth in order to express their individuality. Perhaps the following questions will help motivate the parallel. Paraphrasing Hinsley,[6] we can accept that sovereignty involves the claim that final authority rests with the state and still ask: Why do states treasure their sovereignty? What is the aspiration of this internal final authority? In other words, what is the purpose of sovereignty? One answer is that the purpose of sovereignty is to express and realize the principles that make each state a particular state. States have and create a changing sense of themselves that involves them in projects to realize their self-images and their ideas of the "good life."[7] Regardless of whether these images are an expression of, or an imposition on, the will of the people, such projects – if they are to go beyond the mere assertion of sovereignty – require wealth. In sum, there would seem to be little point in pursuing sovereignty if there is nothing special that requires expression, such as being a particular type of community, and equally important, there are no available means to realize that expression. Given the above formulation, adequate wealth is a necessary condition for the realization of sovereignty. How states acquire and ought to acquire wealth is a central problem for contemporary international political economy, albeit one that does not receive the attention it merits.

A possible reason wealth production and acquisition remains a central problem is because the differentiable logics of capitalism and international society seem to operate in opposite directions. The logic of sovereignty requires that all people who develop a sense of community or nationhood be allowed the rights and responsibilities of formal equal states. While this logic has not been fully actualized, its acceptance helps to break down world social space into more discrete parts. On the other hand, the logic of capitalism is integrative; wealth, to paraphrase Smith, is limited by the extent of the market. This means that the more intensive and extensive the division of labor, the greater the production of wealth. Appreciating the tension between international society and capitalism requires a closer examination of the central metaphor in theories of capitalism: the division of labor.

The attraction of the term "division of labor" lies in its promise to provide an overarching unity and coherence to the seemingly disparate processes of the world political economy. Indeed, the system of capitalism itself can be seen as an expanding global division of labor.[8] However, on closer inspection, the term "division of labor" makes sense only at the level of the factory.[9] The problematic term is "labor." While labor – thought of as tasks performed by humans within a production process – easily can be seen to be "divided" in manufacturing, it applies only metaphorically to occupations within a community and to communities within a sphere. The metaphorical use of the term is interesting because it structures the way we think about political economy.[10] As a metaphor, division of labor highlights thinking about society in terms of production. Society is seen as a giant factory, each element within society – workers, occupations, regions, states – is seen as part of the production process within the factory. As in the factory, each part of society is functionally differentiated and subordinated both to the logic of the production process and the general purpose of producing wealth.

Framed within F.H. Hinsley's vocabulary, we may say that in a division of labor the final authority for the process of wealth creation is external to each part and that this external authority gives each part its function.[11] In this sense, to be part of the division of labor is to be denied sovereignty. To the degree that states operate as concrete functional parts of a global division of labor, they respond to a logic that is both outside and above them. In international society, the opposite is meant to be the case. Each part is formally equal, function is never at issue, as the function of each part is simply to be and become itself, and final authority rests within the part.

The opposition between capitalism and international society does not necessarily mean that the logic of the division of labor must be incompatible with that of sovereignty. For example, if, like mythical individuals in the state of nature, everyone imagines each state producing wealth with only its own resources (autarky), then wealth acquisition is straightforward: each receives according to its own efforts and resources. In this instance, the tension is mollified. Or, at the other end of the ontological continuum, to the degree that the division of labor incorporates each part (state) as a necessary contributor to wealth creation, one can argue that each part therefore has a "stake," "claim," or "right" to a portion of that wealth. That is, participation in a process warrants a share of the results of that process.

Between these ends of a continuum, however, the tension between the division of labor and sovereignty can create confusions that require clarification and debate. For example, if a state is formally considered sovereign and expected to express its sovereignty by procuring its own wealth, and yet is functionally also a part of the global division of labor, how (that is, according to what principle) is it to acquire the means to fulfill its needs? In this case – often the paradigmatic case for Third World states – the principles of wealth production and acquisition remain implicit, contradictory, and pernicious. This lack of a self-consciously articulated principle on which to base production and acquisition of wealth has a deep lineage that plagues both contemporary and classical political economy. It may be illustrative to examine how Adam Smith faces and evades this problem.

Smith begins the *Wealth of Nations* by comparing two abstract nations. The project is to explain why one is poor and the other wealthy. The answer to this question concerns the labor of nations. If labor is divided, that is, if there is a functional differentiation of tasks and specialization within the community, wealth will be produced. If no such specialization occurs, that is, each person must carry out all tasks individually, the lack of specialization results in poverty. To illustrate the power of the division of labor to produce wealth, Smith uses the famous pin factory example at the beginning of chapter 1:

> A workman not educated to this business ... could scarce, perhaps, with his utmost industry, make one pin in a day, and certainly could not make twenty. But in the way in which this business is now carried on, not only the whole work is peculiar, but is divided into a number of branches, of which the greater part are likewise peculiar trades. One man draws out the wire, another straights it, a third cuts it, a fourth points it, a fifth grinds it at the top for receiving the head ... the important business of making a pin is in this manner, divided into about eighteen distinct operations.[12]

As Marx points out, Smith neglects to mention the social relations involved in the example.[13] These relations include agreement on a contract between those whose only property is their labor power with those who own capital. The neglect of social relations allows Smith to think of workers within the factory as independent artisans and not as they exist in their social context, that is, as individuals with only their labor power to sell, performing specialized tasks within a functionally differentiated structure that is controlled by capitalists. He sees them instead as independent artisans owning their own means of production, with surplus to exchange.

> Every workman has a great quantity of his own work to dispose of beyond what he himself has occasion for; and every other workman being exactly in the same situation, he is enabled to exchange a great quantity of his own goods for a great quantity ... of theirs. He supplies them abundantly with what they have occasion for, and they accommodate him as amply with what he has occasion for, and a general plenty diffuses itself through all the different ranks of society.[14]

As a general plenty, wealth naturally diffuses itself to all members of society because Smith has changed the social conditions of the individuals in the first chapter of the *Wealth of Nations*. The parts that were functionally different, subordinate to the whole, and dependent on the contract with capitalists suddenly become equal and independent. To borrow Hinsley's language, these parts become sovereign.

In other words, within the technical division of labor of the pin factory example, each laborer is subordinate to the logic of the production process and, therefore, to the dictates of the capitalist. Outside of this example, *these very same laborers* are seen as independent artisans with their own means of production. They are functionally dependent on the logic of the production process and *at the same time* independent of that process because, as independent artisans, they own their own means of production. To arrive at the *implicit* trickle down principle of wealth acquisition, Smith combines the requirements of the division of labor with those of independent individuality.

Smith's ambiguity parallels contemporary ambiguity regarding the welfare state. How are we to regard the individual who cannot meet his or her own needs within the liberal capitalist state? Do we emphasize the individual's humanity? If so, do we change the rules of the market or find some other way to protect individuals from the often harsh dictates of the market? Do we emphasize the competitive nature of the market that forces humans to create wealth, in which case we may be willing to sacrifice the social welfare, and perhaps even the biological life of the individual? The logical incoherence of Smith's conflation aside, it speaks to his humanism that he insists on retaining both the market relations that create wealth *and* economically sovereign humans who make independent decisions.[15]

Is this conflation not central to how we think of Third World states within the global context? Similar to the individual in Smith's analysis who is both independent and not independent, such states are, in the global context, both sovereign and not sovereign. An examination of Third World states should reveal that in so far as they are assigned the status of sovereign states, they are expected to be responsible for creating their own wealth through their own resources. This mirrors all those things that First World states supposedly are said to have done. It is as if we imagine each state to be an independent corporate artisan. However, individuals within a wealth-producing division of labor are never independent artisans and, once we consider the social context of independent artisans, they become different ranks of people, namely capitalists and workers. Likewise, states within a global division of labor are not strictly sovereign. Once we consider the social and historical context, states are also functionally and hierarchically differentiated, as "colonizer" and "colonized," or as "developed" and "underdeveloped." The intrusion of the social and historical context into the principle of trickle down distribution – an intrusion powerfully asserted by dependency theory – forces us to be more precise about which principles are used and ought to be used for wealth production and acquisition.

Smith's conflation, which is duplicated as a central conflation of liberalism, invites us to clarify our thinking about states in the international liberal society. Ought we to regard states humanely, as deserving the wealth required to express their sovereignty? Should we, therefore, formulate principles that make explicit how the global production of wealth will be distributed to achieve equality and real sovereignty? Or, conversely, does the weakness of Third World states remind us that they are only formally equal and only formally sovereign, and that we ought to ask them to face reality as well as to compel them to accept a diminished status in international society? Robert Jackson's work is most thorough in exploring these issues, especially in highlighting the latter type of argument.

Continuities between Adam Smith and Robert Jackson

In *Quasi-States: Sovereignty, International Relations and the Third World*, Robert Jackson argues that the combination of formal equality and the real incapacities of Third World states may require us to convince Third World state agents that they do not yet have the requisite experience or skills to participate as full members in international society and, therefore, that they should accept a formally diminished status. My criticism of Jackson's presentation should not obscure the fact that he is one of only a few to pose serious questions about the sovereignty of Third World states in international society. I do not challenge Jackson's observation that there are differences in state capacities within international society. We disagree, however, on two points. First, as I emphasized in the previous section, it is important to introduce economics, and especially the historical effects of the capitalist global division of labor, into a discussion of sovereignty. Second, partly as a result of my emphasis on the division of labor, we differ on what should be done about this observed inequality.

Jackson makes the important point that besides being a competitive order, international society is also a normative order. After World War II, changes in international morality were reflected in changes in the attitudes and practices toward colonization. Jackson argues that these changes allowed for sudden decolonization. Briefly, colonization came into disrepute and sovereignty was transferred to indigenous populations. The problem was that some former colonies were ready for self-rule while others were not. Unlike in previous periods, potential states did not have to demonstrate the capacities for self-government to become members of international state society. The elimination of a test to demonstrate such capacities allowed entities that had "very questionable viability and capacities"[16] to become sovereign states.

Such weak states are recognized as sovereign, formally equal, with all the constitutive rights, including the right to nonintervention in their domestic affairs. However, these states are not really able to deliver the goods. That is, they cannot or do not provide protection of human rights, nor do they ensure the provision of socioeconomic welfare to their populations. Worse, the right of nonintervention allows state agents to commit gross abuses against their own populations while international society helplessly observes. Entities formally recognized as states but which either cannot or do not "provide political goods for its citizens" are quasi-states and possess only "negative sovereignty." Real states have "positive sovereignty" that they demonstrate in the following ways: collaborating with other states in international organizations; participating as robust members in the international economy; conceptualizing, institutionalizing, and enforcing domestic and international policy; and creating and maintaining social order.

Articulated in this way, perhaps the deepest problem in the relationship between negative and positive sovereignty is that the former opposes and limits the latter. That is, in Third World states, the recognition of sovereignty by international society allows corrupt, irresponsible, and incompetent governments to violate the rights and welfare of their population. The fact that negative sovereignty disallows positive sovereignty is at the political core of the sovereignty dilemma. Is the presence of negative sovereignty, then, much of an advance in the normative order?

Before we proceed with how Jackson answers this question, let us recall Smith's desire to perceive the human being as participating both in the process of wealth production within a capitalist division of labor and as being independent or sovereign of that process. This conflation, a core tension of liberalism, also lodges itself firmly in Jackson's work. He asks what has changed in the granting of negative sovereignty to the former colonies and his response resembles Marx's judgment on the status of laborers in capitalism:[17]

> In one respect everything has changed: there are no longer any significant dependencies in the world but only equal sovereign states. In another respect, however, there has been far less change: the world's population remains divided along more or less the same North–South lines as previously.[18]

Little has changed because the shift in status is mostly juridical. Real or substantive sovereignty remains a task for the future. Once negative sovereignty is in place, the principle of nonintervention prevents international society from doing anything to help build positive sovereignty. But Jackson provides another reason why international society can do nothing, a reason in line with echoes of Smithian reasoning:

> International society can enfranchise states that usually require general recognition of a government's independence. But international society cannot empower states to anything like the same extent

> since this for the most part involves internal relationships. *State building is primarily a domestic process* occurring over a long period of time that can only be brought about by the combined wills, efforts, and responsibilities of governments and populations.[19]

In making such a stark distinction between the inside and outside, and the relationship between the two, Jackson, like Smith earlier, severs his analysis from the social and historical context. Illustrations from Saint Domingue (present-day Haiti), nineteenth-century Egypt, and nineteenth-century India are presented to provide this missing sense of history.

"Home" economics with "away" politics: Haiti, Egypt, and India

The purpose of these illustrations is primarily to remind us how difficult it is to overcome a functional, specialized, dependent, colonial structure. Specifically, I hope to demonstrate that: (1) the motives of colonizing European states are related to the dynamic expanding power of capitalism and its need for ever greater resources and larger markets; (2) the attempts of colonizers to turn their colonies into regions of specialized production within an expanding division of labor centered around European state needs; and (3) Third World states were required to graft their sovereignty on to a productive structure historically constructed to deprive their economies of autonomy, diversity, and wholeness. Furthermore, I suggest that the conflated status of colonies – as an integrated part of the colonizing state's domestic economy but separated from its polity or culture – may be seen as a confusion in the categories of political economy. The conflated status of the colony nullified two possibilities. First, it rejected the unfettered operation of the logic of sovereignty. Instead of preparing them for a robust state economy, the colonies were economically incorporated as part of the colonizer's home economy. Second, integration into the home economy did not lead to receiving full benefits from an economic union due to the colonizer's refusal to integrate the colony into its politics and culture.

The decision to focus on Haiti, Egypt, and India is based on their status as former colonies. For the purposes of this chapter, however, any formerly colonized Third World state might serve as an example. The type of holistic historiography favored by this chapter conceptualizes capitalism as an expanding and evolving global division of labor.

The strength of this approach is that no region of the world is treated as an isolated monad. The relatedness and the functional interpenetration of all regions within a systematic whole ensure that case illustrations become relevant only when they provide an account of the specialized role of regions within the development of the whole. Thus, any case should be able to express the dynamic logic of an expanding division of labor.

Saint Domingue and the return to a plantation economy

In the 1780s, after more than a hundred years of French rule, Saint Domingue was one of the wealthiest colonies in the world and accounted for 40 percent of France's foreign trade. More than 7,000 plantations with a population of less than 40,000 whites, less than 40,000 free "coloreds," and more than 500,000 slaves grew two-fifths of the world's sugar and half the world's coffee.[20] Historian David Geggus recounts that little of its wealth remained in Saint Domingue and "no other colony ... contributed so much to its mother country."[21] At the source of this wealth were the slaves, who even in the last years of the *ancien régime*, were "being broken into the rhythm of plantation slavery," at about 40,000 slaves a year. The colony was bound to France by mercantile practices, although smuggling with competitors (such as Britain, Spain, and the United States) was not uncommon.[22]

The precise reason why there was a successful armed revolt in Saint Domingue is a question under serious study and beyond our scope. Among the reasons, however, were the complex and very tense social structure with its overlaps between class, caste, and race; the significant presence of "free coloreds," who were mainly mulattos; and the large ratio between slaves and owners. The influence of the French revolution brought the various conflicts within the social stratification of Saint Domingue to a high pitch. It is important to remember that here as elsewhere such influences are never unidirectional. Historian Carolyn Fick recounts with some irony that it was the material contribution of the slaves that allowed the development of a French bourgeoisie. She cites author Jean Jaures's observation: "Sad irony of human history! The fortunes created at Bordeaux, at Nantes, by the slave trade gave to the bourgeoisie that pride which demanded liberty and so contributed to human emancipation."[23] However, it was not just the influence of the revolutionary ideas of emancipation on the various leaders of the different social segments of Saint Domingue, but also the everyday ordinary and extraordinary armed resistance of the mass of black slaves themselves that constituted the revolts that began in August of 1791 and that led to independence by 1804. The slave leader who eventually came to sole power in Saint Domingue is the famed Toussaint L'Ouverture.

Meanwhile, in France, the Directory had fallen and Napoleon Bonaparte had assumed control. Bonaparte ordered a mission to Saint Domingue on the pretext of confirming Toussaint's rank as commander and governor. The real goal of the mission was to create the conditions for an eventual French takeover followed by a return to slavery. Before the mission arrived in Saint Domingue, however, Toussaint had already consolidated power.

What is interesting for our purposes is the decisions Toussaint made, or rather, was forced to make about what to do with the colonial plantation economy. Protecting the gains of the first successful black revolt against the anticipated arrival of the French was a feat made all the more difficult by the fact that the French were supported by the British and the United States. Both supporters feared the spread of slave emancipation to their domains. Toussaint also could not count on internal support to face the French within Saint Domingue, for as Fick observes, "Saint Domingue was a divided society."[24] Not the least of the reasons for this division was that Toussaint's vision for his newly emancipated society was neither particularly democratic nor participatory.

Whatever his mistakes, Toussaint also was faced with a difficult if not impossible economic reality. The only immediate way to feed and reequip his army, organize defense, and sustain a workable state was to require the colony to continue to do that for which it was designed, namely to produce and sell sugar, coffee, and other staples. According to Fick,

> The plantation system was maintained at all costs. Toussaint's overriding economic objective was to make the colony produce ... for the export market, and to produce enough to place it back on the road to economic prosperity. He believed this could be done only by retaining and reinforcing the existing latifundian system.[25]

In Jackson's language, Toussaint's desire to move from a fragile negative sovereignty to positive sovereignty required him to return Saint Domingue to economic dependence and servitude. Without the wealth to make sovereignty real, Toussaint had to regress to a "slave-type plantation regime" from which workers were emancipated from slavery in only a formal way. Thus, "farm workers were now laboring either for their former masters or for a new segment of the ruling elite with whom they had previously shared a common status under slavery."[26]

Egypt and its destiny as an agricultural producer[27]

After Napoleon Bonaparte's defeat in the Egyptian expedition of 1798, Mohammad Ali was able to consolidate power in Egypt through the elimination of competing parties. Like others before him, Mohammad Ali started by seeking to amass a fortune for himself. However, Mohammad Ali's motives also demonstrated a desire to constitute a sovereign Egypt. His plan was to improve agricultural production, streamline the traditional tax bureaucracy, and use the resulting gains in surplus both to build an industrial structure and to modernize the army. Mohammad Ali operated under the assumption that a sovereign Egypt required an army ready to contest the Europeans and that a proficient army required economic autonomy.

In his efforts to modernize Egypt, Mohammad Ali enlisted the services of European technical experts and businessmen while maintaining control over them. By accident, Louis Alexis Jumel, a French engineer under his retinue, discovered Cairo women spinning and weaving an extraordinary cotton grown for household needs. This new type of cotton was used to restructure the Egyptian economy and resulted in the creation of a state monopoly in cotton production. Cotton became the premier revenue producer and accounted for as much as 80 percent of Egyptian exports before the British occupation.[28] The cotton monopoly, coupled with significant international demand, created profits that were subsequently used to import machinery and technical personnel from Europe. Mohammad Ali's policy of import substitution met with some success. In the 1830s, factories produced a range of items such as textiles, sugar, silk, sulfuric acid, rice, indigo, glass, leather, paper, guns, and gunpowder,[29] and employed approximately 6 to 7 percent of workers.[30] The increased output of the economy was absorbed by his expanding the armed forces.

However, when Mohammad Ali died in 1849, Egypt's plan of forced industrialization, import substitution, and diversification of production (in retrospect, similar to the efforts of many Third World economies in the 1960s) ultimately had failed. An explanation of this failure is due in part to internal reasons, and would echo Jackson's sentiment that state-building is a domestic process.

There were at least three domestic reasons for his failure. First was the very low level of literacy and education among Egyptians. L.S. Stavrianos claims, "Egypt not only had learned nothing from Europe, and was quite uninterested in doing so, but also, even worse, had forgotten much of what it had known in the past. The library of the famous al-Azhar University, for example, was only a fraction of what it had been in the Middle Ages."[31] Second, while Mohammad Ali was clear about his vision for Egyptian sovereignty, and despite his outstanding political and business acumen, he was unfamiliar with European technology and susceptible to advice from foreign and domestic experts who may not have shared his vision. Third and most important of all, the burden of Mohammad Ali's entire plan rested on the efforts of the masses. Peasants and artisans often responded to governmental decrees with resistance, sabotage, and flight.

While the internal obstacles to development were severe, external impediments proved insurmountable and resulted in Egypt's becoming a nonmanufacturing, dependent, occupied quasi-colony. British economic intelligence, like John Bowring's 1837 report to Foreign Minister Palmerston declared that, "A manufacturing country Egypt never can become – or at least for ages; a country giving perpetual cause of anxiety to the European Powers by the restlessness of her Rulers, she cannot be allowed to continue – but by the peaceful development of her agricultural aptitude she may interest and benefit all."[32] The idea that Europeans specialized in manufacturing and industrial production while non-Europeans specialized in the production of raw materials was typical of British economic liberalism of the time. Such theoretical truths were confirmed by force when necessary.

During Mohammad Ali's reign, the modernizing process was managed strictly – especially regarding its financing, which remained free of foreign dependence. Later, Egypt permitted and encouraged foreign investment. Under the rule of Ismail (1863–79), there was a remarkable influx and growth in foreign investment. However, little of this vast foreign capital was allocated to industrial projects. The Europeans, it seems, did not want Egyptian industry to compete with European manufactured products. Instead, Egypt was used as a source of raw materials for European industry. In addition, the Egyptian government borrowed heavily from European financiers. It was not long before this credit ran dry and the Egyptian economy neared bankruptcy.[33] A British invasion designed to protect the interests of its private investors was considered to be "in the offing." Robert Tignor reminds us that Hobson's study of imperialism uses Egypt as a key example.[34]

Regardless of whether the British occupation eventually helped to modernize Egypt as some writers claim,[35] or whether it remained an impediment to the development of Egyptian sovereignty, it is important to note the presence of a tension between the goal of sovereignty and that of wealth creation. More than a hundred years earlier than the 1960s policy of import substitution attempted by many Third World states, we can see in Egypt's case an attempt to modernize rapidly to gain both political and economic sovereignty.

We see also the external reasons for failure. Even if Egypt had managed to overcome some of its more onerous domestic and foreign obstacles, its policy of modernization through import substitution still required a dependence on foreign technology and expertise. There was at least one instance in its nineteenth-century history, when in response to Mohammad Ali's edicts, Egypt tried to avoid dependence on foreign loans. However, much like the predicament Toussaint L'Ouverture faced, avoiding foreign dependence required turning Egypt into a monocultural economy specializing in cotton and placing an enormous burden on its population, whose impoverishment was required as a means to gain the surplus for state projects. After Mohammad Ali's death, the burden on the population was somewhat eased under Ismail, who financed projects with foreign capital. However, the interest of foreign financiers configured in such a way that Egypt was relegated to providing raw materials within the world economy.

British India: between laissez-faire and mercantilism

The effect of British colonialism on India was dramatic, long lasting, and remains controversial. Few doubt that the British brought to India elements of the modern spirit as well as significant material structures. The debate lingers over the net effect of British colonialism. In one interpretation of the political economic history of contact between the two cultures, Britain created law and order that ended a long period of anarchy in India. Britain provided India with an efficient administration, an honest bureaucracy, the railway system, the expansion of commerce, improved irrigation systems, and the enhancement of agriculture.[36] India's lack of economic success, despite these gifts, is explained by its continued cultural backwardness. The opposite view, referred to by Bipan Chandra as the "anti-imperialist" school, interprets British rule as exploitative. The British are seen as the major impediment whose removal is necessary before the prerequisites for development can be put in place.

In other, less polarized, interpretations, there are those who argue that while a certain limited type and amount of economic growth was made possible by British rule, the important question is not one of growth, but of development. They concede economic growth but as a by-product of narrow British interests. They judge the British performance, however, on the type of effort that was or was not made in allowing India to compete for its economic and political sovereignty.[37]

As this last interpretation suggests, the question of the net effect of the British in India can be read to support the contention that British thinking and policy was caught between the imperatives of sovereignty and the wealth-creating division of labor. On the one hand, there was an interest in using India as a source of wealth and power, treating India in terms set by liberal economic theory and forcing it to specialize in the production of raw materials consistent with British needs. On the other hand, there was a desire to bring India into the fold of modern civilization by teaching it to live and compete within the modern world of sovereign states. In this latter view, the exploitation of India, while real, is not seen as a straightforward and deliberate British aim. Instead, British policies, sometimes based in laissez-faire economics and other times in selective state intervention, may be seen as the result of an ambiguity in the categories of political economy. While some British believed that helping eventually to create an economic and political Indian sovereignty was in India's best interest, others saw Indian interest as "agricultural rather than manufacturing and mechanical."[38]

The interpretation of the introduction of railways in India's economic history follows the polarized lines of thinking mentioned at the beginning of this section. Some perceive it as the most exploitative tool of imperialism, while others see it as a powerful engine of economic and cultural advancement provided by the British for the Indians. Again, it is possible to make the case for a less polarized argument that suggests that the net effect of railways on India depends upon determining how Britain put the railways into place.

Frederick Lehmann's analysis focuses on the provision of materials for the production of railways. He argues that had materials been purchased in India, the railway industry might have acted to stimulate Indian industry.[39] Lehmann explains that in the early history of railways the British were aware of India's capacity to produce quality iron. A Major James Franklin recommended that the East Indian Company encourage the production of "axeltrees, bridge and arrenal components," which he considered to be of low cost and high quality. Further, William P. Andres, a one-time chairman of the Punjab and Delhi Railway wrote a book that advocated railway manufacture in India.[40] Despite these recommendations, it is not surprising that British interests were decisively opposed to the Indian production of railways.

Nevertheless, it took some time before British interests were effectively marshaled. A consequence of this lag was the initiation of locomotive production in India in the 1880s. But this "healthy" development was arrested from 1898 onwards due to the following events. The heavy demand for locomotives in both India and Britain forced the British Indian government to purchase locomotives from competitors of Britain, namely Germany and the United States. In fact, 66 locomotives from US firms and 99 from Germany were imported to India.[41] The British response was to apply pressure on the Secretary of State of India to ensure that all future locomotives be purchased from Britain. Not only was local production essentially halted, but the government and railway firms also colluded to keep prices high and force India to buy British locomotives, even though the German and US firms consistently underbid British prices by 20 percent.[42]

Lehmann speculates that had political conditions allowed Indian industry to develop, "it would appear that an Indian manufacturer would have enjoyed a large market at home, and if he was established ... might well have broken into the export market during the peak years 1900–1910 and 1918–1922."[43] With the British elimination of such possibilities in mind, Fredrick Clairmonte cites Leland Jenk: "railroad building in India did not give rise to a flood of satellite innovations, and it destroyed more occupational opportunities than it opened up."[44] Moreover, Bipan Chandra can claim that

> Railway ... construction was not coordinated with the economic needs of India, that they were built at the cost of other social overheads and industries, that their "backward and forward linkages" had their positive effects in Britain, that their "demonstration effect" was severely limited, that their impact on economic development was far less than it should have been, that they created an "enclave" economy, and that they were, therefore, not so much a means of developing India as of exploiting it.[45]

Both Chandra and Clairmonte point to the existing link between the ideology of laissez-faire and imperialism.[46] Both give numerous additional examples of how the British resorted to state intervention to secure profits that were not attainable with a free trade ideology.

Lessons from the historical illustrations

While such examples of British duality can be multiplied in India and elsewhere, it is important not to suggest that the British used what R. Pares calls "free trade imperialism" in a systematic and deliberate manner.[47] It is significant to keep in mind that conceptual ambiguity, for example between the imperatives of sovereignty and those of a dynamic division of labor, can make victims out of apparent victimizers. The process of overcoming the dictates of both sovereignty and the division of labor appears difficult.

J.S. Mill could not imagine exploitation occurring if a country followed liberal economic policy. He could claim that "England's trade with the colonial territories is hardly to be considered as external trade, but more resembles the traffic between town and country, and is amenable to the principles of the *home* trade."[48] If the division of labor was allowed to work out its own logic, Mill's assertion might have contained an insight. In our illustrations, British and French racism, their paternalism, and their sense of inherent superiority did not allow the division of labor to extend its logic. Communities specializing in coffee, sugar, cotton, and opium were, in Mill's sense, part of "home trade" but were nevertheless denied recognition by and participation within the "home state." Economically, each was integrated into "home" economics while denied the rights of home on a political and cultural basis. Nor was the idea of sovereignty allowed to work on its own terms without the influence of a division of labor. Far from helping their colonies acquire the basis for economic and political sovereignty, France and Britain used their colonies as a means toward expressing their own positive sovereignty.

In Jackson's terminology, this means that negative sovereignty is not necessarily an obstacle to positive sovereignty as he claims, but rather that colonial communities had an implicit negative sovereignty – a recognition of political and cultural difference from Europeans – which was a way of denying them positive sovereignty. The recognition of their difference, coupled with the belief of their inferiority, created the presumption that the colonizer could speak for, and know what was best for, the non-Europeans. This type of paternalistic thinking resulted in policies that economically and politically undermined the non-European "others," and denied them a chance to express or realize their cultural projects.

Robert Jackson's sense of resignation

By severing his analysis from the social history of an expanding capitalist division of labor, Jackson asks us to regard Third World states as the equivalent of autonomous artisans able to create their own wealth. I sympathize with Jackson's rationale that a serious contemplation of sovereignty may require moving beyond some of the economic determinism of dependency and world systems theories. Nevertheless, there is a cost to ignoring the political and economical insights of these theories. Given our historical illustrations, it becomes difficult to accept Jackson's thesis that state-building is primarily an internal process. How can the inside of any Third World state be seen as disconnected from the outside of the world system? Given the long and penetrating influence exerted on every aspect of the life of the colony and the uneven and questionable inheritance of colonial powers, is it possible to claim that state-building – even after recognition of formal sovereignty – is an internal process?

It seems that the question is different. Instead of *"Can* international society influence state-building and the construction of positive sovereignty?"* (which it certainly can), the question is "How *ought* it to influence this process?" Jackson addresses this question cautiously. He comes very close to suggesting the following scenario. States ought to be left to their own devices and resources to support themselves, and if they are unable to do so without aid from international society, then they must either suffer the consequences or admit that they are not ready to hold the right and responsibility of sovereignty. This implication of Jackson's argument surfaces in the way Jackson favors a return to a past (pre-World War II era) when, besides sovereignty, there were other statuses available, such as colonies, protectorates, mandates, and condominia.[49]

Jackson admits that the past was not absent of quasi-states, but what he calls "small and weak states" had to survive as a result of their own efforts. In a competitive balance-of-power system, "some survived, some succumbed."[50] The post-World War II change in international norms and institutions tampers with this competitive system so that

71

the freedom or positive sovereignty of states expressed by the
traditional balance of power system has been interfered with and
subjected to new normative regulations: weak, marginal, or insubstantial states are now exempted from the power contest at least in
part and treated as international protectorates.[51]

Not only are "weak, marginal and insubstantial" (also referred to by
Jackson as "ramshackle") states protected from international political
and military competition, but also their underdevelopment is used by
weak states as moral grounds for international assistance. Hence his
complaint that "real incapacities and inequalities" have turned into
"positive international rights."[52] Jackson's lament suggests that the
classical balance-of-power system ensured that only fit states survived,
whereas the current norms of the international society permit this
privilege even to the unfit.[53] Jackson echoes the continued importance
of this theme in his conclusion, where he suggests, "In a post-colonial
but highly unequal world such as ours, there ought to be various
international statuses ranging from outright independence to associate
statehood to international trusteeship which are determined by the
circumstances and needs of particular populations."[54]

In taking a principled stand for promoting formal inequality,
Jackson recognizes that he has risked accusations of being an apologist
for colonialism, and that he can be accused of arguing a return to
paternalism and even racism.[55] He deems the risk worth taking
because his overriding concern is for the citizens of Third World states
whose freedom and welfare are denied by quasi-state governments.[56]
Such concern is praiseworthy. Yet Jackson does not believe that the
international community will follow his prescriptions as he concludes
his book not on a note of hope but one of resignation. In the end, he
recognizes that the central problem with his proposal of creating a
system of differential statuses – deciding which communities should
get what status – is "insurmountable." He is correct to assume that the
problem is insurmountable, but perhaps not for the reasons he
provides.

The issue is not merely that of determining which status should be
delegated to which community within a status hierarchy. There is also
the problem of ascertaining what process and which decisionmakers
would make such judgments. In turn, the creation of such a decisionmaking process is not simply a matter of finding a method on which
all appropriate agents would agree – a difficult, if not impossible task
in itself. Rather, the problem of returning to a formally differentiated

hierarchy is insurmountable because it presupposes the deeper question of "who may speak for or represent whom?" In the past, colonialism has answered this question with the pretense that the colonizing power could speak for and know what was best for those whom it subjugated. Presently, many governments in Third World states – but not only Third World states – indulge in a symmetrical pretense for populations who often do not agree that the state speaks for or represents them in any way. The moral and psychological power of independence, something to which Jackson pays little attention, lies in understanding and exposing this pretense.

Because Jackson is not attentive to the psychological significance of independence, he entertains the idea that populations currently subjugated by Third World state agents will allow the return of an international paternalism on the promise of improved living conditions. Jackson speculates that "having experienced the bitter harvest of independence some would now choose a reduced status if it promised improved living conditions through greater international involvement and supervision."[57] While I have no way of ascertaining how most people living in the conditions Jackson describes would respond to this proposition, I have difficulty accepting that it might be seriously considered an option by most.

Jackson has failed to consider the *meaning* of independence to those who value it above all else. Sovereignty means more than just having access to resources on a territory and being juridically recognized as an equal among equals. In the context of colonialism, it means speaking for and representing oneself. It means further that no external force, no matter how correct its prescriptions, determines what is best for oneself. It means, above all, having fought for and won the right to make one's own mistakes. This sense of self-determination allows for a pride and dignity that were among the greatest losses under colonialism and the greatest victory of independence.

One might speculate that even Third World peoples suffering from internal colonialism at the hands of official Third World state agents would view Jackson as having misunderstood the situation. While it is true that those under an internal colonialism are resisting state agents, it is also true that their collective memory of external colonialism is likely to be sharp. One suspects that they would reject greater material and civil prosperity bought at the price of a return to a politically diminished and psychologically enslaved status. Instead, it seems easy to see that they would hope and fight for a further

73

development in their self-determination. Substate groups fight for their own sovereignty.

Jackson has some sense of the irony of this predicament because he resigns himself to the idea that there is nothing much that international society can do for substate groups, and that it is up to the citizenry under the control of Third World states to liberate themselves.[58] This seems correct – even a well-intentioned intervention by international society must be seen in the context of a few centuries of paternalism, colonialism, and racism. If most Third World people regard coloni-alism as having arrested or deformed their natural evolution toward positive sovereignty,[59] then asking them to accept a diminished status as the former colonial powers intervene on their behalf is to ask Third World citizens to shed their fears prior to establishing the conditions that would alleviate those fears. It is to ask for the impossible.

Conclusion: the right to wealth as a form of altercasting

Jackson's sense of resignation in the face of the political aspect of the sovereignty dilemma is due partly to the absence of political economy in his analysis. Much as Smith ignores the stratified social relations of his pin factory example, Jackson's analysis lacks a sense of how the quasi-state nature of Third World states might be a social construct resulting from the political economy aspect of the sovereignty dilemma. Incorporating this aspect might have two effects on Jackson's sense of resignation. On the one hand, it might intensify it. Taking seriously the historical context of the world political economy grounds the quasi-state aspects of Third World states in deeper soil than Jackson's own analysis. It reveals the historical construction of the incapacities and weaknesses of Third World states. Yet, as Karl Polanyi reminds us, profound resignation can open our minds to great oppor-tunities.[60] On the other hand, the historical evolution of the division of labor suggests the social interpenetration and co-construction of all peoples and states on all others. It begins to make concrete for us the idea that "self" and "other" are internal relations within a larger social totality that challenge us to think about the relationship between parts and wholes beyond the stark and mythical atomism of liberalism. An analysis of the division of labor forces us to take the individualism of liberal thought seriously by grounding individualism, and sovereignty in the case of states, in the thoroughly social context of recognition.

This reveals that beyond its mere assertion, the concrete expression of individuality requires wealth and forces us to focus on the question of how individuals participate in the production and acquisition of wealth.

The logic of the division of labor may push us to critically inspect liberalism, but that logic does not provide ready-made technical answers to the question of how we ought to conceive of wealth production and acquisition. Many answers to the question of how individuals and states should be related to the production and acquisition of wealth may accommodate both sovereignty and the logic of capital. After debate, one answer might revolve around the continued treatment of states as independent artisans who are responsible for generating their wealth through their own efforts and resources within their boundaries. Concurrently, the answer also might deal with the treatment of states as parts of a larger social whole that has some minimal responsibilities for state survival. Indeed, this seems to be the solution that some liberal welfare states have provided for their citizens.

Another way to conceive of the relationship between individuals and states and the production and acquisition of wealth is to conclude that the acquisition of wealth is a right. While such a right merely may mean guaranteeing competition for wealth so that it occurs increasingly on a level playing field, I consider it as a claim to a portion of the overall wealth produced by a global division of labor. There are at least two arguments that support a right to wealth. First, because all parts of the division of labor participate in the creation of wealth, they can be perceived to have a claim in the acquisition of wealth more fairly and more humanely than through current historically and structurally skewed market relations. Second, and more importantly, the expression of sovereignty requires wealth. A formal recognition of states as equals, without adequate means to realize the projects specific to a state, equates the rudimentary beginning of sovereignty with its full flowering. Such a truncated understanding of sovereignty suggests a deficiency both in logical rigor and practical resolve. Obviously, these are speculations that require extended treatment beyond the scope of this chapter.[61] However, let me suggest what wealth as a right might mean for the political aspects of the sovereignty dilemma.

An obvious objection to the right to wealth for states is that citizens will never acquire that wealth because state agents will use it to line their pockets as they further subjugate dissenting voices. This objection puts us squarely back in the conventionally recognized understanding of the sovereignty dilemma. I think this is as it should be; as long as international society continues to accept negative sovereignty as the basis of moving to positive sovereignty, it must continue to seek the permission of state agents to accomplish goals within state boundaries. That is, the recognition of social entities as sovereign states requires that we continue to observe the principle of nonintervention.

The right to wealth, however, may create some potentially positive conditions that may move us beyond this intractable understanding of the sovereignty dilemma. First, as Jackson and Rosberg point out, African statesmen feel vulnerable and insecure about the survival of their states, a feeling easily generalizable to most Third World state agents.[62] If much of their subjugation of local populations results from feeling this insecurity, then state agents perceive threats both internally and externally and take large, perhaps extreme, measures to maintain the coherence of the state. In this context, a right to wealth may serve as a tangible indicator of international society's commitment to the future coherence of a particular state and this may decrease a sense of *external* vulnerability. Of course, a decrease in the sense of external vulnerability need not always lead to a decrease of violence against substate groups. Second, a right to wealth might have two effects that decrease violence against internal groups. One reason (although perhaps not the main reason) that state agents subjugate parts of their populations is to wrest away control of resources from local cities to generate wealth for state projects. To the degree that a right to wealth underwrites state projects, it carries with it the possibility of releasing state agents from the need to coerce and oppress their populations. Further, a right to income as an international practice entitles both international and subnational groups to pressure state agents into making a right to income a state practice for both substate groups and individuals. Whether such pressure is effective obviously depends on the sense of responsibility of state agents. Third, and perhaps most important, a right to income can become a self-fulfilling prophecy for generating a sense of responsibility in state actors. Accepting negative sovereignty without question, backing up that acceptance with a right to income, and thereby treating state agents as if they were both responsible citizens of international society and responsible to their citizenry, might have the combined effect of generating responsibility. Although he does not use it in this context, Alexander Wendt refers to such a process as "altercasting."[63]

I have evaded all the practical issues associated with the implementation of a right to wealth because my aim is merely to place such ideas on the theoretical agenda. I have, however, reconceptualized the sovereignty dilemma within the context of a capitalist division of labor and speculated on what this may mean. In the process, I believe I have uncovered a presumption in our theorizing that we have a clear and self-conscious understanding of how states do and ought to create and acquire wealth within the global political economy. This is simply not so. Our current thinking on this crucial issue separates politics from economics and both of these from colonial history. This severed analysis stands as a barrier to understanding injustice felt by states and individuals, constructing conversation, and creating a more just and dignified world. As a response to this oversight we may need to redirect our research so it explicitly confronts the following questions: What role do wealth creation and acquisition play in constructing and challenging sovereignty? Which tacit principles have determined wealth creation and acquisition within the systems of sovereignty and capitalism? And, which principles ought to govern such wealth creation and acquisition? A fuller consideration of these questions may prepare us to converse with those who deem injustice, inequality, and indignity as the ordering principles of global social life.

Notes

I wish to thank John Agnew, Tom Biersteker, David Blaney, Sorayya Khan, Craig Murphy, Jan Thomson, and Cindy Weber for their helpful comments on earlier drafts of this chapter.

[1] See Biersteker, Thomas J. and Weber, Cynthia "The Social Construction of State Sovereignty," this volume, p. 1.

[2] See Stankiewicz, W.J. 1969. "In Defense of Sovereignty: A Critique and Interpretation," in Stankiewicz, W.J. (ed.) *In Defense of Sovereignty*. New York: Oxford University Press; Wight, Martin 1967. "Western Values in International Relations," in Wight, M. and Butterfield, H. (eds.) *Diplomatic Investigations*. London: Allen & Unwin; Gross, Leo 1968. "The Peace of Westphalia, 1648–1948," in Falk, R. and Hanrieden W. (eds.) *International Law and Organization*. New York: Lippincott; Bull, Hedley 1977. *The Anarchical Society*. New York: Columbia University Press; Wight, Martin 1977. "The Origins of the State System," and "International Legitimacy," in *System of States*. Leicester, England: Leicester University Press; Hinsley, F.H. 1986. *Sovereignty* 2nd ed. Cambridge: Cambridge University Press; Blaney, David and Inayatullah, Naeem Forthcoming. "The Third World and a Problem of Borders," in Denham, Mark and Lombardi, Mark (eds.) *Problems Without Borders: Perspectives on Third World Sovereignty*. New York: Macmillan Press.

[3] Jackson, Robert H. 1990. *Quasi-States: Sovereignty, International Relations and the Third World.* New York: Cambridge University Press.

[4] This section draws from Inayatullah, Naeem and Blaney, David 1995. "Realizing Sovereignty," *Review of International Studies* 21: 3–20.

[5] Inayatullah and Blaney, "Realizing Sovereignty," pp. 5–11.

[6] Hinsley, *Sovereignty*, p. 26.

[7] Jackson, Robert 1990. "Martin Wight, International Theory and the Good Life," *Millennium* 19: 261–72, p. 266.

[8] Wallerstein, Immanuel 1974. *The Modern World-System: Capitalist Agriculture and the Origins of the European World Economy, 1600–1750.* New York: Academic Press; Smith, Adam 1976 [1776]. *Wealth of Nations.* Chicago: Chicago University Press; Marx, Karl 1977 [1887]. *Capital*; vol. I. New York: Vintage; Stavrianos, L.S. 1981. *Global Rift: The Third World Comes of Age.* New York: William Morrow; Wolf, Eric 1982. *Europe and the People Without History.* Berkeley: University of California Press.

[9] Inayatullah, Naeem 1988. "Labor and Division of Labor: Conceptual Ambiguities in Political Economy," Ph.D. thesis, University of Denver.

[10] Lakoff, George and Johnson, Frank 1980. *Metaphors We Live By.* Chicago: University of Chicago Press.

[11] See Levine, David P. 1978. *Economic Theory* Vol. I. Boston: Routledge & Kegan Paul, pp. 168–81.

[12] Smith, *Wealth*, p. 8.

[13] For Smith's conflation of the social and technical division of labor, see *Wealth*, p.9. For a detailed commentary on the significance of this conflation, see Levine, David P. 1977. *Contribution to the Critique of Political Economy.* London: Routledge & Kegan Paul, chap. 2. Part of Marx's commentary on the two senses of the "division of labor" can be found in *Capital*, vol. 1, section 4, chap. 14.

[14] Smith, *Wealth*, p. 15.

[15] See Hirschman, Albert O. 1977. *The Passion and the Interests: Political Arguments for Capitalism Before Its Triumph.* Princeton: Princeton University Press, pp. 108–10; Viner, Jacob 1927. "Adam Smith and Laissez Faire," *Journal of Political Economy* 35: 198–232.

[16] Jackson, *Quasi-States*, p. 202; Jackson, Robert H. and Rosberg, Carl G. 1982. "Why Africa's Weak States Persist: The Empirical and Juridical in Statehood," *World Politics* 35: 1–24. p. 16.

[17] Marx, Karl 1973 [1859]. *Grundrisse.* New York: Vintage, p. 488.

[18] Jackson, *Quasi-States*, p. 21.

[19] Ibid., emphasis added. See also p. 30.

[20] Geggus, David Patrick 1982. *Slavery, War, and Revolution.* Oxford: Clarendon Press, pp. 1–6.

[21] Ibid., p. 7.

[22] Fick, Carolyn E. 1990. *The Making of Haiti: The Saint Domingue Revolution from Below.* Knoxville: The University of Tennessee Press, pp. 24–5.

[23] Ibid., p. 23.

[24] Ibid., p. 207.

[25] Ibid.

[26] Ibid.

[27] In this section I rely heavily on Stavrianos, *Global Rift*, and Owen, Roger 1969. *Cotton and the Egyptian Economy 1820–1914*. Oxford: Clarendon Press.

[28] Tignor, Robert L. 1966. *Modernization and British Colonial Rule in Egypt, 1882–1914*. New Jersey, Princeton: Princeton University Press, p. 39.

[29] Owen, *Cotton and the Egyptian Economy*, p. 55.

[30] Stavrainos, *Global Rift*, p. 215.

[31] Ibid., p. 216.

[32] Cited in *ibid.*, p. 218.

[33] Tignor, *Modernization and British Colonial Rule*, p. 41.

[34] Ibid., p. 23.

[35] Owen, *Cotton and the Egyptian Economy*, pp. 352–75.

[36] Chandra, Bipan 1968. "Reinterpretation of Nineteenth Century Indian Economic History," *Indian Economic and Social History Review* 5: 35–75.

[37] Thorner, Daniel and Thorner, Alice 1962. *Land and Labour India*. New York: Asia Publishing House, p. 83.

[38] Thomas Bazley, President of Manchester Chamber of Commerce. Cited in Stavrianos, *Global Rift*, p. 230.

[39] Lehmann, Frederick 1965. "Great Britain and the Supply of Railway Locomotives of India: A Case Study of 'Economic Imperialism,'" *The Indian Economic and Social History Review* 2: 297–306.

[40] Andres, William P. 1857. *Tramroads in Connection with Iron Mines: Cheap Railways in India*. London: E. Wilson.

[41] Lehmann, "Great Britain," pp. 299–300.

[42] Ibid., p. 301.

[43] Ibid., p. 302.

[44] Clairmonte, Fredrick 1960. *Economic Liberalism and Underdevelopment*. New York: Asia Press, p. 119.

[45] Chandra, "Reinterpretation," p. 47.

[46] Clairmonte, *Economic Liberalism*, pp. 70–1 and 93–7; Chandra, "Reinterpretation," pp. 64–5 and 69. E.H. Carr explores this link in chapter 4 of his 1969. *The Twenty Years Crisis, 1919–1939*. New York: Harper Torchbooks.

[47] Cited in Clairmonte, *Economic Liberalism*, p. 93.

[48] Cited in *ibid.*, p. 71, emphasis added.

[49] Jackson, *Quasi-States*, p. 33.

[50] Ibid., p. 23.

[51] Ibid.

[52] Ibid., p. 30.

[53] Ibid., p. 25.

[54] Ibid., p. 200.

[55] Ibid., p. 191.

[56] Ibid., p. 10–11.

[57] Ibid., p. 200.

[58] Ibid., p. 201.

[59] Memmi, Albert 1957. *The Colonizer and the Colonized*. Boston: Beacon Press, pp. 112–14. See also, Chaudhuri, K.N. 1990. *Asia Before Europe: Economy and Civilization of the Indian Ocean from the Rise of Islam to 1750*. New York: Cambridge University Press, pp. 305–6; and Abu-Lughod, Janet 1989. *Before European Hegemony: The World System, A.D. 1250–1350*. New York: Oxford University Press.

[60] "Resignation was ever the fount of man's strength and new hope. Man accepted the reality of death and built the meaning of his bodily life upon it. He resigned himself to the truth that he had a soul to lose and there was worse than death, and founded his freedom upon it. He resigns himself, in our time, to the reality of society which means the end of that freedom. But again life springs from ultimate resignation. Uncomplaining acceptance of reality of society gives man indomitable courage and strength to remove all removable injustice and unfreedom." Polanyi, Karl 1944. *The Great Transformation*. New York: Beacon Press, p. 258B.

[61] Inayatullah and Blaney, "Realizing Sovereignty," pp. 16–20.

[62] Jackson and Rosberg, "Why African States Persist," p. 18.

[63] Wendt, Alexander 1992. "Anarchy is What States Make of It," *International Organization* 46: 391–425, p. 421.

4 The sovereign state system as political-territorial ideal: historical and contemporary considerations

Alexander B. Murphy

> A whole history remains to be written of spaces – which would at the
> same time be the history of powers (both of these terms in the plural)
> – from the great strategies of geopolitics to the little tactics of the
> habitat.
>
> Michel Foucault[1]

From the perspective of the late twentieth century, the territorial
structure of the international state system appears to be one of the
great constants in human affairs. Faith in the stability of the system has
been shaken somewhat by the breakup of the Soviet Union and
Yugoslavia, but few observers seriously question the system itself.
People generally accept the assumption that the land surface of the
earth should be divided up into discrete territorial units, each with a
government that exercises substantial authority within its own territory. There may be disagreement over how much authority state
leaders should have, but it is generally assumed that the political map
of the future will look much like that of today, aside from some
adjustments in certain unstable areas.

Assumptions about the constancy of the dominant political-territorial
order are not the sole province of more casual analysts of the political
world; they pervade the academic literature on politics and government as well. It is true that some scholars are raising questions about
the implications for the sovereign authority of state leaders of growing
economic interdependence and the internationalization of environmental protection and human rights.[2] But in most instances the
existence of a system of more or less distinct territorial units as the
foundation for human governance is not even questioned.[3]

The general acceptance of the current political-territorial order is a reflection of one particular and highly significant effect of the modern state system, that is, its role in shaping peoples' thinking about the geographical structure and organization of their world. The modern state system is the latest incarnation of a political-territorial order that has its roots in late-medieval Europe. That order is associated with the emergence of a group of at least semi-autonomous territorial states. The system began to take shape during an era when individual rulers were increasingly able to consolidate control over discrete territories. As the system developed and grew, so did understandings of its organizing principles. One of the most important of these was the idea that final authority over most if not all social, economic, and political matters should rest with those in control of the territorial units that make up the system. Sovereignty is the term that is generally used to denote this idea. Consequently, the system itself is often called the sovereign state system.

Explanations of the rise of the sovereign state system usually focus on the importance of changing material, economic, technological, and ideological circumstances for the organization of political life.[4] States within the system are seen as logical outgrowths of the spread of capitalism; of technological innovations that facilitated coercion, communication, and combat; and of the genesis of modern nationalism and colonialism. Yet these developments did not simply promote a particular territorial order; the existence of that order itself affected social, economic, and political arrangements and shaped people's geographical imaginations.[5] If we are to gain a better understanding of the modern state system, it is important to consider the territorial structures and understandings that developed along with it.[6]

Toward that end, this chapter focuses on the role of territorial structures and ideas in the development and diffusion of the sovereign state system. After a brief review of the origins of sovereignty as a political concept, the chapter considers the relationship between territorial structure and ideology in Europe from the seventeenth century through the beginning of the twentieth century. The discussion shows that the spatial organization of society in west-central Europe after the Peace of Westphalia fostered a world view in which discrete, quasi-independent territorial units were seen as the principal building blocks for social and political life. This political-geographic understanding is referred to as the sovereign territorial ideal. During the succeeding centuries, sovereignty as a systemic notion was repeatedly thrown into crisis when social, technological, and economic developments challenged the theoretical and functional bases of particular territorial arrangements. Understandings of the meaning of sovereignty as a principle of international relations changed with each of these crises. Yet the inertia of the sovereign territorial ideal was great enough to prevent an enduring alternative from taking root. Instead, efforts were made to create new – and in the minds of the winners, better – political maps in keeping with the sovereign territorial ideal. To the extent that the resulting territorial units emerged as significant functional regions, the sovereign territorial ideal was reinforced.

The process moved forward until, by the beginning of the twentieth century, the idea that the earth's surface should be organized for governance into discrete territorial units dominated throughout much of Europe and beyond. The next section of the chapter considers the implications of World Wars I and II for this mind-set. The political principles that undergirded postwar settlements in 1918, and especially in 1945, show a heightened commitment to preserving a fixed territorial order. Even though the political pattern was increasingly dysfunctional with respect to how most political leaders and theorists understood the geographical structure of society, most of them rejected the legitimacy of attempts to alter the territorial status quo. The World War I order was too unstable for the territorial status quo to endure, and the system disintegrated into chaos only two decades after its founding. The extraordinary devastation and social upheaval of World War II, however, led to the establishment of a political-territorial order whose stability was assumed to be the *sine qua non* for global stability.

The analysis then turns to the nature and significance of dominant territorial understandings that accompanied the post-World War II territorial order. A series of examples shows that the map of independent states that emerged after 1945 is so thoroughly accepted that we rarely even stop to consider its impact on our thinking.[7] Yet it affects everything from our ideas about social groupings to the spatial frameworks we use in scientific studies.[8] At the same time, the dominant spatial structures and ideas of the late twentieth century are not uncontested, nor are they unchanged inheritances from the distant past.[9] Rather, they exist in a world in which the political map increasingly fails to reflect or encompass significant economic and social arrangements. The chapter concludes by considering the significance of this state of affairs for understandings of the link between politics and territory. I argue that traditional territorial assumptions are changing, but that the general failure to analyze those assumptions clouds our view of alternative possibilities. Since no set of discrete territorial units – no matter how configured – can accommodate existing social, political, and economic arrangements, we need to consider the possibility of a multilayered and not strictly hierarchical approach to governance in which the territorial notions that undergird decisionmaking more closely reflect the different spatial structures in which issues and problems arise.

Given the range of issues covered in this chapter, the treatment of individual points is necessarily general in scope and selective in area. Since the territorial dimensions of sovereignty have received relatively little explicit attention,[10] however, there is a need for some preliminary explorations of the terrain of inquiry. By laying out the beginnings of an analytical framework that links ideology, territory, and sovereignty, this chapter seeks to shed some light on the rich rewards that can be gained from analyses of the social construction of the political-geographic universe in which we live.

Historical introduction: Europe before Westphalia

As Stephen Krasner has shown, the concept of sovereignty did not emerge suddenly in 1648 with the signing of the Peace of Westphalia.[11] Rather, the treaties that ended the Thirty Years' War were merely an important early formalization of a political-territorial order with roots in the free cities of late medieval Europe, in the emergent absolutist states of the West, and in the principle of *cuius regio, eius religio* in the Holy Roman Empire.[12] The period leading up to the Peace of Westphalia was one in which the territorial structures and spatial understandings in Europe were undergoing profound transition. The medieval was giving way to the modern.

In the Middle Ages, European territorial structures were complex and overlapping, and no one particular hierarchy of governance dominated throughout.[13] Highly variable senses of territory and space were associated with these territorial structures. The frame of reference for most was the local commune or fief, but the ruling elite thought in terms of (often non-contiguous) royal and/or ecclesiastical territories with fluid boundaries that could easily be changed through inheritance, warfare, or partition.[14] Superimposed on these spatial sensibilities was a larger-scale conception of Christendom as a distinct, religiously constituted realm.[15]

By the late Middle Ages, the emergence of increasingly autonomous cities in northern Italy and in Flanders gave rise to an understanding among a numerically small urban elite that certain places could be more or less immune from the authority structures that dominated elsewhere.[16] A different but related challenge to the feudal order of the Middle Ages came with the gradual consolidation of greater power and territory under a single ruler in the emergent English and French states. The growing capacity of the rulers in early France and England to exercise control over their territories came at the expense of other claimants to power, both inside and outside of these countries.[17] Thus, by the fourteenth century, two models in Europe were distinct from the feudal order: the free city and the proto-absolutist state. In each case, a territorial entity was associated with a government that exercised substantial control over political, social, and economic matters within the territory. The church continued to play a substantial role in the affairs of these early political-territorial entities, and nobles' challenges to the kings' authority continued for some time. Yet the free cities and early independent states of the West, galvanized by an ever more effective ability to accumulate wealth and to develop an expanding group of loyal citizens, offered an increasingly commanding model for the relationship between territory and governance.

The writings of Jean Bodin in the second half of the sixteenth century indicate the new ways of thinking about political territory that these developments helped to produce.[18] Concerned with promoting peace by validating the power of the French king against rival claimants, Bodin championed the idea that a state's ruler had absolute authority within his own realm, subject only to the divinely inspired laws of nature. This idea infused the work of many scholars and theorists in the generation after Bodin, including Hugo Grotius (1583–1645), the Dutch jurist, theologian, and historian who is widely regarded as one of the most important of the early modern Western international legal theorists.[19] Drawing on concepts of property rights developed in ancient Greece and Rome, Grotius and his followers presupposed a territorial order in which states were free from outside control.[20]

Sixteenth- and seventeenth-century central Europe did not offer the same political-territorial models as did the West. Nonetheless, as the fault lines of religious difference deepened with the Protestant Reformation, some change was inevitable in the overlapping layers of authority exercised by the Church, the Holy Roman Emperor, and the kings, princes, and nobles. The change initially took the form of an agreement set forth in the Peace of Augsburg (1555) to allow the prince of any realm to determine the religion of that realm (the principle of *cuius regio, eius religio*).[21] This did not amount to a grant of sovereign authority to the rulers of the German states, but it did establish those rulers' absolute authority in one extremely important matter. In doing so, it enhanced the powers of state rulers within the Holy Roman Empire and directed growing attention to those states as discrete territorial units.

With the rise of absolutism in the West and the emergence of increasingly autonomous states within the Holy Roman Empire, the independent territorial state had become an important part of people's conceptualizations of Europe by the time of the Peace of Westphalia. Indeed, Quentin Skinner argues that by the early seventeenth century the territorial state was "the most important object of analysis in European political thought."[22] It was a central concern of the major political philosophers of the seventeenth century, including Hobbes, Spinoza, Locke, von Pufendorf, and Bossuet, and it undergirded the body of international legal principles that developed in the aftermath of the Thirty Years' War.[23] The independent state was not the only territorial model that existed in seventeenth-century Europe, however, nor was it the exclusive object of analysis. The Church continued to exercise great power in many areas; the Holy Roman Empire was far from gone; and a variety of political-territorial arrangements coexisted with early states, including confederations, republics, principalities, duchies, imperial cities, and free cities. Few thought in terms of a world order or even a European order in which territorial sovereignty was the guiding principle everywhere.

Sovereignty and territory in the emergent sovereign state system

The Thirty Years' War was an unusually bloody period in Europe's history and the treaties that were drawn up at the end, collectively known as the Peace of Westphalia, grew out of the failure of all sides to win a decisive victory.[24] Included within the treaties was an agreement to recognize the political autonomy of many of the different corporate entities that made up the Holy Roman Empire.[25] Despite the limitations that were imposed on the absolute autonomy of rulers in parts of the treaties, many political theorists came to look back on the Peace of Westphalia as the first formal step toward the establishment of a sovereign state system. Taken literally, such a system has never come into being. There have always been external challenges to the autonomy of territorial states, and empires of one form or another have not entirely disappeared.[26] To conclude that sovereignty does not matter, or that it is simply a concept that has been employed when it is politically expedient, however, is to ignore the extraordinary power of the dissemination and widespread acceptance of sovereignty as a political-territorial ideal. In a more philosophical vein, ignoring the significance of sovereignty assumes that ideas and beliefs are simply the outcome of circumstance, not also shapers of circumstance.[27]

Acknowledging the historical importance of sovereignty as an ideal does not suggest that sovereignty is, or has been, a static concept. Rather, understandings of sovereignty have evolved and changed over the past several centuries.[28] To understand those changes, it is useful to distinguish between two different but related aspects of sovereignty: sovereignty as a principle governing relations among states and sovereignty as a territorial ideal. The former is concerned with the role of sovereignty in defining the international obligations and activities of states; its central focus is what states are, or are not, allowed to do in the international arena. The latter is concerned with the relationship between territory and power in a sovereign state system; its central focus is the degree to which the map of individual states is also a map of effective authority. The difference between these two dimensions of sovereignty can be seen in the different ways each dimension has been treated in the past. There have been times of considerable de facto state autonomy, when sovereignty has been understood as a principle that permits state rulers to do anything in their own self-interest, including attacking the territory of a neighboring state. At other times, even though individual states have been no less autonomous, sovereignty has been widely understood as a principle limiting the right of states to pursue territorial claims.

Looking historically at the relationship between these two dimensions of sovereignty helps to clarify the role of territorial arrangements and ideology in the development of the sovereign state system. To see this, it is instructive to think about historical fluctuations in understandings of each dimension of sovereignty. Turning first to sovereignty as a principle governing relations among states, the foregoing discussion suggests that sovereignty can be treated as everything from a systemic commitment to the integrity of an existing territorial order to an exemption from any such commitment. Commitment to the existing order might be thought of as a systemic view of sovereignty,

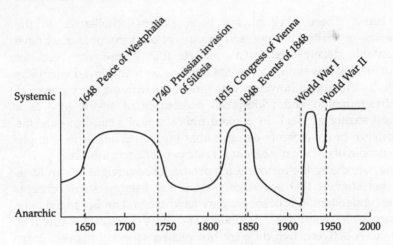

Figure 4.1: Dominant views of the nature of sovereignty as a principle governing relations between states, as seen from the core of the sovereign state system

whereas exemption from commitment might be labeled an anarchic view. As the ensuing discussion will show, Europe has seen wide fluctuations between a systemic and an anarchic view of sovereignty over the past several centuries. To encourage thinking about these fluctuations, it is possible to schematically diagram dominant views of sovereignty as a principle governing relations among states, situating those views in a spectrum running from the complete acceptance of a systemic order to an entirely anarchic understanding of sovereignty (Figure 4.1). Such a diagram is nothing more than a generalized interpretive tool, of course, but it suggests the significant changes that have taken place in the way this dimension of sovereignty has been viewed.

The volatility in historical understandings of sovereignty as a principle governing relations among states is not matched in the history of dominant understandings of the territorial organization of power. In the abstract, a political geographic arrangement can take the form of a multilayered, overlapping set of political spaces (a hetero-nomous system), a set of discrete territorial units in which the exercise of power is circumscribed by territorial boundaries, or something in between. Using the same interpretive device as that employed above, evolving understandings of the link between territory and governance

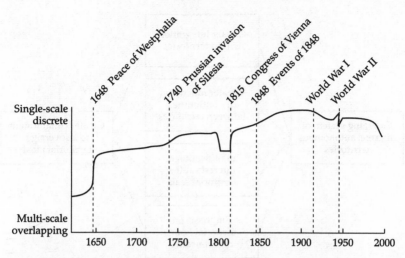

Figure 4.2: Dominant views of the appropriate political-territorial structure for international society, as seen from the core of the sovereign state system

in Europe can be situated along a spectrum between a heteronomous political system and a system conforming to the sovereign territorial ideal. Figure 4.2 presents this spectrum graphically for the period 1600 to 2000, with those understandings that tend toward a political order with power displayed at multiple scales in overlapping territorial structures on the lower end of the vertical axis, and those that tend toward a single-scale sovereign territorial arrangement at the upper end of the vertical axis. As this figure and the ensuing discussion show, the clear trend – at least through the beginning of the twentieth century – has been toward acceptance of a political order in which most power is vested in discrete territorial units. Once again, the figure is nothing more than an interpretive device, but it focuses attention on differences between understandings of the territorial dimension of sovereignty and its role in governing relations among states.

The relatively consistent growth in commitment to the sovereign territorial ideal, particularly compared to the fluctuations highlighted in Figure 4.1, raises two important, interrelated questions: why has the trend generally been toward wider acceptance of the sovereign territorial ideal, at least through the end of the nineteenth century, and what are the political and social consequences of its acceptance? To answer the first question, we must consider the nature of what Robert

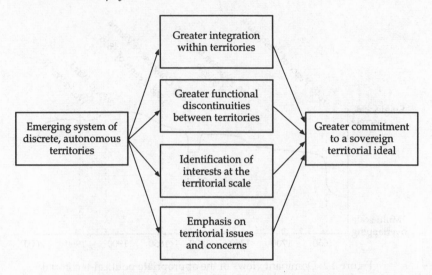

Figure 4.3: Tendencies in a territorial system that has a substantial degree of legitimacy

Sack calls human territoriality.[29] According to Sack, the successful pursuit of a territorial strategy in human affairs has several potential advantages: it is an efficient way of communicating the authority of the controller of territory over people and things; it simplifies the task of enforcing control over those people or things; and it reifies power. To the extent that these advantages can be exploited – and that is only possible under circumstances in which a given territorial order enjoys substantial legitimacy – the spatial units that are the product of territoriality can assume great importance in the way individuals intellectually organize the world. Figure 4.3 outlines some of the processes by which this can occur.[30]

The idea behind Figure 4.3 is that an effective territorial order embodies the potential to change patterns of interaction and shape issues in ways that promote particular spatial ontologies.[31] Those changes come about through a complex set of circumstances. As power is consolidated in discrete, autonomous territories, networks of interaction and communication are built that can enhance the social significance of territorial units. At the same time, as rulers in different territories exercise power in distinctive ways, the boundaries between territories can become increasingly meaningful dividers between social, economic, and cultural systems. In the process, interests can become focused on arrangements geographically structured along territorial lines, and this, in turn, can promote the identification of social concerns with maintaining the existing territorial order. As these tendencies play out, it becomes increasingly likely that political, social, and economic issues will be understood in territorial terms, and ultimately that the logic of the sovereign territorial ideal will be reinforced. By the same reasoning, at whatever point the tendencies identified in the middle of Figure 4.3 are undermined, there is a greater likelihood that the logic of the sovereign territorial ideal will be brought into question.

Applying these ideas to the development of the sovereign state system, the ability of leaders in the early post-Westphalian states to consolidate control over their territories was not just a consequence of a particular set of historical events. It set in motion a conceptual redefinition of the spatial order of life.[32] That process might well have collapsed if the territorial order that emerged from Westphalia had not enjoyed a substantial degree of legitimacy for a time, or if the territorial configuration of the system had not eventually evolved in response to changing notions of legitimacy. Under those circumstances individual states might well have gradually lost their significance as perceptual and functional entities. But that did not happen. Instead, the post-Westphalian period was characterized by a substantial period of stability; when disruptions eventually came they were precipitated by the dysfunctional character of the existing pattern of states in relation to evolving economic, cultural, or security arrangements.[33] Disruptions were not spurred by a challenge to the sovereign territorial ideal itself. Instead, at least until the early twentieth century, they led to territorial readjustments that the winners often could exploit to advance the sovereign territorial ideal.

To return to the two questions posed above, then, the trend toward wider acceptance of the sovereign territorial ideal was a product of the emergence of political territories that were meaningful perceptual and functional regions, and the subsequent symbiotic relationship that developed between changing political arrangements and the sovereign territorial ideal. The political geographic importance of the ideal was no less than to crowd out competing conceptions of how power might be organized to the point where the sovereign territorial ideal became the only imaginable spatial framework for political life. To see how these processes worked in greater detail, we must turn to the specifics of history.

The century after Westphalia

The treaties ending the Thirty Years' War did not sweep aside the old political-territorial order; they did not abolish the Holy Roman Empire nor did they eliminate all sorts of quasi-sovereign polities. But they did embody an early formalization of the idea that sovereignty was not simply a characteristic of individual states, but was also a principle that should govern relations between states.[34] They also created an environment in which individual rulers could more easily consolidate control over their domains, and many proceeded to do just that.[35]

The quasi-sovereign state system that emerged from the Peace of Westphalia was one more step toward an order that Alexander Wendt has described as "spatially rather than functionally differentiated."[36] In keeping with the tendencies of territoriality noted above, the creation of more integrated, self-sufficient territories had important social and political ramifications. Most notably, the states themselves became increasingly significant foci of identity for rulers and subjects alike. Social structures and individual rights became more strongly linked to the state in which they were situated, and the attention of rulers was directed away from their status in relation to quasi-feudal or imperial hierarchies and toward the development of territorial resources and the protection of state boundaries.[37]

Given the political environment in the Holy Roman Empire after the Thirty Years' War, one of the primary concerns was to maintain a balance of power among the different states.[38] As a concrete manifestation of that concern, during the late seventeenth and early eighteenth centuries states sought to develop diplomatic relations with other states; when attempts were made to elaborate formal international legal principles governing such matters as warfare; and when the international conference came to be seen as an appropriate mechanism for solving disputes among states.[39] These developments were not confined to the Holy Roman Empire. The Treaty of Ryswick (1697) between France and Britain bound the French king to "on no account whatsoever disturb the said King of Great Britain, in the free possession of the Kingdoms, Countrys, Lands or Dominions which he now enjoys."[40] Throughout Europe an international society was coming into being, and a commitment to the right of individual rulers to control matters within their own territories lay at its core.

The emergence of the sovereign state system was gradual, however, and for some time it coexisted with other political-territorial forms.[41]

Most strikingly, the Holy Roman Empire in central Europe lasted until the beginning of the nineteenth century, and within the empire were free cities and ecclesiastical states that were at odds with the sovereign territorial ideal. The empire survived for so long in the face of the ascendant Westphalian order because it served a purpose in the context of the political-territorial realities of the age. It provided a framework within which a balance of power among German states could be preserved, and an organizational structure that could keep the German states from being swallowed up by the expanding Turkish empire to the east and the larger absolutist states to the west.[42]

Despite the continued vitality of the Holy Roman Empire, albeit in weakened form, the growing ability of state rulers in western and central Europe to exert control over their realms was the principal political-geographic story of the seventeenth and early eighteenth centuries. As time went on, the larger of the early Westphalian states became the dominant centers of power in the region. The rulers of these states were able to bring the resources and peoples of their territories under their effective control, and this, in turn, enabled them to raise and sustain substantial armies.

From 1740 to the fall of Napoleon

The balance of power that had undergirded the Central European territorial order began to unravel in the middle of the eighteenth century. The Prussian invasion of Silesia in 1740 set in motion a series of territorial wars that would fundamentally recast the political geography of the region over the succeeding twenty-five years. Many smaller states were swallowed up – as were polities that did not fit within the emerging sovereign state system – and the conflict between Austria and Prussia undermined what was left of the imperial order.[43] The details of individual conflicts are less important for this chapter than what this period represents in the development of political-territorial arrangements and understandings. These were rapidly changing in response to shifting territorial ideas and processes that had been set in motion during the preceding century.

In keeping with the tendencies of territoriality described above (Figure 4.3), by the early eighteenth century a functional order based on discrete territorial structures had made territory an increasingly significant basis for power. Hence, sovereignty and territory had become more closely linked. The balance of power that prevailed after the Peace of Westphalia had helped to bring this situation into being. As rulers began to consolidate control over their territories, however, inevitable imbalances emerged. The German princes and kings in the larger territories came to acquire powers that were greatly disproportionate to those of the smaller territorial rulers. They developed substantial armies, sophisticated civil administrations, and well-integrated economies.[44] Further complicating the political-territorial equation was the multitude of small units that did not fit the sovereign territorial ideal. Few of these had evolved into significant, well-integrated functional units, and they therefore were at odds with the developing political-territorial order in the region. At the same time, the importance of the Holy Roman Empire itself was being undermined by the subsiding of the Turkish threat. Hence, by the middle of the eighteenth century, many of the foundations on which the post-Westphalian order had been built were crumbling, and the system was ripe for change.

The direction that change took was fundamentally influenced by the territorial ideas and processes that already had been set in motion. The political and military elite in the larger, more successful states had benefited enormously from the freedom from outside influence that the Westphalian system had afforded. Once the empire lost its *raison d'être*, these elites were looking to enhance their autonomy. Moreover, with a balance of power no longer a factor in political relations, a systemic commitment to sovereignty lost its significance as an organizing principle for political life. Sovereignty thus came to be seen increasingly as a doctrine granting state leaders the right to do whatever was necessary to ensure the territorial viability of their domains, including launching an attack on a neighboring state.

Under the circumstances, it is not surprising that territory was the *leitmotif* of European political affairs during the second half of the eighteenth century. In the French and German realms, elaborate arguments were developed to justify claims to one another's territories; the Hapsburgs maneuvered to consolidate their territorial possessions; and Enlightenment political thinkers from Rousseau to Kant saw the territorial integrity of states as a foundational social principle.[45] At the same time, great pains were taken to establish the precise territorial rights of rulers. The 1797 peace treaty concluded at Campo-Formio between the Republic of France and the Kingdoms of Hungary and Bohemia, for example, included an extended statement of the expanded territorial boundaries of France that the emperor of

Hungary and king of Bohemia agreed to accept.[46] There were minority voices who saw territory in a different light, of course; Johann H.G. van Justi (1705–71) argued that governmental efficiency was more important to state strength than territorial extent.[47] But the need even to make such an argument shows the strong link between territory and power that permeated the political imaginations of eighteenth-century Europeans.

The late eighteenth century is not only a time when territorial considerations occupied a dominant position in political thought; it is also the period when the philosophical basis for absolutist rule was being challenged by the rise of nationalist thinking. The integrative territorial practices of the absolutist monarchs had brought people together. By establishing strong centralized bureaucracies and standing armies, and by encouraging the use of standardized variants of indigenous languages, the more successful absolutist monarchs succeeded in reducing regional differences within their territories.[48] In the process, differences between peoples living within states were reduced while those between peoples living in separate states widened.[49] The territorial order of early modern Europe thus served as an incubator for the rise of nationalism. And in keeping with the dominant territorial concerns of the day, nationalism was fundamentally concerned with the rights of a nation – a group of people who saw themselves as a cultural-historical unit – to control its own territory.[50] Thus, nationalism also helped to solidify commitment to the sovereign territorial ideal.

Although nationalism took on heightened political significance in the French revolution of 1789, its primary impact on the political geography of Europe was not felt until well into the nineteenth century. Instead, as revolutionary France gave way to Napoleonic France, the very idea of a system of sovereign states was brought into question. Napoleon set out to create an empire and, in the process, brought a significant portion of Europe under his control. He completely abolished the Holy Roman Empire, seeking instead to establish a series of vassal states that would be able to resist Austria without threatening France.[51] Even at the height of Napoleon's success, however, certain territorial principles associated with the sovereign territorial ideal retained their vitality. France itself was cast in the image of a sovereign state, and the territorial units within the empire were treated as discrete units, each with its own particular problems and needs.[52]

The Congress of Vienna and the age of nationalism

The Napoleonic period proved to be a short detour from the construction of a sovereign state system. Indeed, reaction to Napoleonic incursions arguably helped to solidify support for that ideal throughout much of Europe. Hence, at the Congress of Vienna following Napoleon's defeat, the sovereign territorial ideal infused the deliberations.[53] The participants declined to reestablish the Holy Roman Empire, instead opting for a system of juridically sovereign states. In an effort to avoid further destructive conflict, however, the congress gave new life to a systemic notion of sovereignty that could help sustain a balance of power between states. Their central concern in redrawing the political map of Europe was to check French power, but not to such a degree that a rebellion would ensue in France, or that France would be too weak to ensure a balance of power on the continent. With an increasingly strong Russia looming to the east, the latter issue was of particular concern to the Great Western Powers.

The powers that redrew the map of Europe at Vienna regarded the new European states as enduring spatial frameworks within which a peaceful order could be forged.[54] The post-Vienna political-territorial framework was so sacrosanct for a time that, at least from the perspective of the Great Powers working together in the Concert of Europe, governmental sovereignty was conditioned on the maintenance of the existing territorial order. Indeed, with the sole exception of the British, the Great Powers saw it as within their rights to intervene in the affairs of any state where internal disruption threatened the existing order.[55] A few changes were accepted in the political map of Europe, such as the emergence of Greece as an independent state in 1820 and the Belgian rejection of Dutch control in 1830. But the first forty years after the Congress of Vienna saw remarkably few changes in the European political map. Even in cases where territorial claims were pursued, they were justified as efforts to recover land that had been wrongfully taken away.[56] France made this type of claim in defending its acquisition of Nice and Savoy, as did Spain in pressing its claim to the Chincha Islands.[57] Territorial adjustments were thus cast as a reaffirmation of the historically ordained territorial order, not a departure from it. With the legitimacy of the existing territorial order elevated to such heights, processes of territorial integration could proceed apace and the functional significance of many European states could be enhanced.

By the middle of the nineteenth century, the stability of the post-

Congress of Vienna political order was being shaken by the explosive combination of liberal political ideas and Romantic nationalism that was sweeping Europe at the time. In some places – notably Spain, France, and The Netherlands – that combination served to reinforce the notion of the existing state as a discrete sovereign entity. In many other places, however, the political order that had emerged from the Congress of Vienna proved inadequate to accommodate the rising tide of new political and social ideals. The Great Powers were helpless to control challenges that were being made to the legitimacy of particular territorial units.[58] Powerful unification movements emerged in the Italian and German states; authoritarian rulers in other states succumbed or adapted to nationalism; and the remaining European empires came under intense pressure from within. Hence, the second half of the century once again saw significant changes in the political geography of Europe.

The territorial significance of nineteenth-century nationalism was not limited to changes in boundaries. Nationalism as an ideology was premised on the link between people and territory. The histories, songs, poetry, and paintings of Romantic nationalists were replete with territorial imagery. Building on territorial ideas that had developed over the preceding centuries, nationalism embodied a reconceptualization of the state as an entity providing identity, autonomy, security, and opportunity for national betterment.[59] As such, nationalism fed directly into the sovereign territorial ideal, and at the same time it gave states that approximated the nation-state ideal a powerful new basis of legitimacy.

Defining political legitimacy in nationalist terms introduced a new source of potential volatility into the system as well. Before the age of nationalism, sovereignty was vested in the ruler; power was circumscribed by whatever territory a ruler controlled as a consequence of the vicissitudes of history. With the rise of nationalism, however, sovereignty came to be understood as resting with the nation. By extension, it became important to see political territories as reflections of nations.[60] The actual territorial extent of states thus took on added significance, a development that ultimately was to lead to a world war.

Before turning to the war, it is important to note that the flowering of European nationalism in the late nineteenth century developed in association with two other important nineteenth-century intellectual currents that were to shape views of sovereignty and territory. These were positivist ideas about law and Darwinian social theory. Positivist legal ideas grew out of a gradual rejection of natural law as the juridical foundation for society.[61] Positivists looked to human-created institutions as the basis for law. In the international political geographic context of the time, this meant sovereign territorial states. Since positivists saw rights in individual terms, they rejected a systemic notion of sovereignty; instead, they treated states as entirely autonomous entities whose rulers could do whatever they saw fit, including wage war on other states. As we have seen, this anarchic view of international society had its roots in the eighteenth century. But in the nineteenth century it emerged as an increasingly powerful doctrine in international law, providing a philosophical basis on which nationalist territorial ambitions could be grafted. Moreover, just as happened in the earlier swing toward an anarchic view of international relations, it developed at a time when the historical underpinnings of a prior order were coming apart. Hence, it once again provided a justification for altering the existing configuration of states to bring them more closely into line with changing social and political circumstances.

The publication of Charles Darwin's *On The Origin of Species* in 1859 also helped to shape the world views of late nineteenth-century Europeans. Among the concepts that came out of the revolution in scientific thinking associated with Darwin's work was the idea that organisms are in a constant struggle for survival and that only those most able to adapt to changing environments can endure. This idea had a tremendous impact outside of the biological sciences; one of the domains in which its influence was strongly felt was the nascent field of political geography.[62] The founder of German political geography, Fredrich Ratzel (1844–1904), drew an analogy between the state and an organism that is born, matures, decays, and dies.[63] Thinking in terms of the state system in Europe and drawing ideas from the territorial history of the United States, Ratzel saw states' frontiers as "changing zone[s] of assimilation" and territorial conflict as endemic to international political life.

The convergence of nationalism, positivism, and Darwinian political geographic thought in late nineteenth- and early twentieth-century Europe helps explain the anarchic view of sovereignty that dominated the period, as well as the upheavals that accompanied that view. It also sheds light on the reasons behind the continued commitment to the sovereign territorial ideal in the face of considerable territorial conflict. If anything, the three intellectual currents took acceptance of the ideal to new heights. Building a strong, competitive national state meant establishing firm control over national territory and doing whatever was necessary to sustain, or even expand, that control. When the Austrians went to war with the Prussians in 1866 and the French with the Germans in 1870, economics was not at the heart of the conflict.[64] Instead, both sides went to war over politics and territory. The paramount importance of territory is enshrined in the treaties that ended these conflicts; the first provision in the Treaty of Versailles ending the Franco-German War, for example, requires the French to renounce all "Rights and Titles" in lands to the east of the newly forged French/German boundary.[65] With territory such a central theme in the political struggles of the time, it is not surprising that geopolitics emerged as a fundamental academic and pragmatic concern in late nineteenth- and early twentieth-century Europe.

The preeminent geopoliticians of the era, Alfred Mahan (1840–1914), Sir Halford Mackinder (1861–1947), Rudolf Kjellén (1864–1922), and Karl Haushofer (1869–1946), were all concerned with the relationship between control of some part of the earth's surface and power.[66] In their attempts to analyze this relationship, they emphasized the importance of geographical position and the physical character of state territory, especially the availability of resources and the configuration of coastlines. The existence of discrete sovereign territorial states was taken for granted in all of their conceptualizations; the central problem was how to ensure state security. Control over particular territories was at the heart of each of their answers.

During the late nineteenth century, the territorial route to national aggrandizement manifested itself most strikingly in Europe's colonial undertakings. The colonial ventures of Europeans since the fifteenth century had played an important role in the rise of certain states to positions of power. However, the colonies were treated as something separate and apart from the sovereign state system that developed in Europe, since they were valued primarily for the economic advantages that they afforded.[67] By the late nineteenth century, the age of Romantic nationalism had ushered in a new phase in the colonial enterprise, one in which the mere acquisition of territory was seen as integral to national power and prestige. The result was the "scramble for Africa" and efforts elsewhere to control as much territory as possible.[68] The primary goal in building these "nationalist empires"[69] was to acquire control over far-flung domains; even economic considerations took a back seat to simple territorial acquisition. There could be no more stark evidence than this of the importance of territory in the late nineteenth-century political imagination.

To summarize, by raising the prospect of a territorial order that could reflect and accommodate nationalist ambitions, the upheavals of the second half of the nineteenth century had, if anything, pushed acceptance of the sovereign territorial ideal to new heights. Strengthened by the rise of national states and the retreat from a systemic notion of sovereignty, that ideal had become the very foundation on which notions of security and identity were built. Acceptance of the sovereign territorial ideal, however, did not translate into agreement over a particular territorial configuration for the European continent. Rather, as the nineteenth century gave way to the twentieth, the question of what the political map of Europe should look like became increasingly contentious.

The impacts of World Wars I and II

Chaos broke out in Europe with the assassination of the Austrian Archduke Ferdinand in Sarajevo on 28 June 1914. Competitive nationalist territorial ambitions legitimated by positivist views of sovereignty and Darwinian notions of competition led to a war of unprecedented destruction. The horror and futility of the war prompted many in its aftermath to embrace a systemic notion of sovereignty, one in which aggressive warfare was deemed entirely illegitimate.[70] In constructing a political-territorial order for post-World War I Europe, however, the great powers continued to think in terms of the sovereign territorial ideal; no other alternative was imaginable in an environment in which territory was equated with power and nations were seen as discrete social units whose members had a right to control their own affairs.[71] Hence, the political blueprint set forth in the Treaty of Versailles called for the establishment of a group of juridically sovereign territorial states. The postwar League of Nations represented the only significant departure from a system in which power was vested in discrete, autonomous territorial entities, but the League itself had a very limited scope of authority and no enforcement capabilities.

The political map of Europe that emerged from Versailles was ostensibly based on the principle of national self-determination. In creating new states in central and southeastern Europe, however, political and pragmatic circumstances caused the principle to be applied inconsistently.[72] Hence, from the outset there was a significant functional discontinuity between the actual territorial configuration of Europe and its ideological base. Nonetheless, the signatories to the

Covenant of the League of Nations in 1919 envisioned the newly partitioned Europe as an inviolable territorial framework. They agreed "to respect and preserve as against external aggression the territorial integrity and existing political independence of all Members of the League."[73] In theory, each of the states in the new order was equal in status, and any questions of regime legitimacy were to be resolved within the confines of the existing territorial order.[74]

Resentment over the territorial decisions made at Versailles soon surfaced, of course, and an explosive mix of nationalism and Darwinian territorial ideas brought the system down within two decades. There were fundamental differences between the collapse of the Versailles system and the disintegration of the Westphalian system in the mid-eighteenth century and the Vienna system in the latter half of the nineteenth century. Coming out of a conflict of extraordinary magnitude, the Versailles system came into being in an environment in which awareness of the human and material costs of territorial adjustment had reached unprecedented levels. At the same time, the Versailles system embodied an unusually significant spatial disjunction between the territorial order and many peoples' conceptions of the social order. This was because the Versailles system was explicitly based on the self-determination of peoples, yet patterns of ethnonational identity rarely corresponded to state boundaries. Under these different circumstances pressures for change in the territorial order were unusually great, but acting on these pressures also required appeals to extremism because of the heightened emphasis on territorial stability that had emerged after World War I.

Nationalism provided the foundation on which extremism could be built, and Nazi Germany ultimately directed that extremism toward an effort to remake the political map of Europe. During the conflict that followed, the Germans established occupation governments in conquered states, thus undermining the political-territorial basis for the prewar system. Yet the sovereign territorial ideal continued to hang over the conflict. The European powers opposing Germany fought to maintain the territorial integrity of the prewar state system, and the German challenge to the sovereign territorial ideal was an important catalyst for extra-European involvement in the war. By the end of World War II, Europe's society, economy, and environment had been devastated by a conflict that had cost millions of lives and had highlighted the dark side of nationalism. From a political-geographic perspective, the war could be seen as a product of egregious violations of both a systemic notion of sovereignty and the sovereign territorial ideal. Under the circumstances, it is not surprising that the postwar order was built around a renewed commitment to the territorial inviolability of states.[75]

The two major conflicts of the twentieth century had made clear that a stable world order could not be constructed on a foundation of unrestrained ethnonationalist territorial ambition or a completely anarchic approach to state sovereignty. What was left was the territorial state itself, and the reconstituted political map of the late 1940s became the structure around which human society was to be understood and organized. What mattered in this new order was existing states. Nations, in the classical sense, were seen as derivative of states, and sovereignty itself became little more than a synonym for a territorial state, irrespective of its true level of autonomy.[76] This order did not come about overnight, however, nor did it represent a major break with the past; an international political system in which most power was exercised at the state level had deep historical roots, and the inertia of the sovereign territorial ideal continually shaped the evolution of the system.

Before World War I, when a particular territorial order lost perceptual and functional legitimacy, the upheavals that followed eventually produced a degree of consensus in favor of a new territorial order. The sovereign territorial ideal was thus preserved and sustained. With the extraordinary destructiveness of the two world wars, however, the act of challenging the territorial status quo itself increasingly lost legitimacy. Thus, even in the face of great functional and perceptual challenges to existing territorial structures, the sovereign territorial ideal came to be conceptually circumscribed by the lines that appear on maps of the world's states. It was into this world that the former colonial territories of the 1950s and 1960s emerged, and they necessarily adapted to its norms.[77] Thus, by the late 1960s most of the habitable land surface of the earth was neatly compartmentalized into units that were seen as proper – even inevitable – building blocks for human social organization.

Modern political-territorial assumptions

It is difficult to exaggerate the impact of the territorial assumptions that have developed in association with the post-World War II political order. In general terms, they have made the territorial state the privileged unit for analyzing most phenomena while discouraging consideration of the nature of the territorial state itself.[78] In the political sphere they have directed overwhelming attention to state government and governmental leaders at the expense of extrastate or substate actors and arrangements. In the economic sphere they have prompted us to frame our most basic theories of development in state terms. In the cultural sphere they have encouraged us to limit our understandings of diversity into state-based categories; for every reference to the Quechua, Aymara, and Guaraní peoples there are thousands of references to Bolivians. In the environmental sphere they have prompted us to conceptualize issues that do not correspond to state boundaries as "transnational" (read "trans-state") or "transboundary" issues, not Upper Rhine or Southeast Asian lowland issues.

Structural features of the modern world encourage such state-oriented thinking. The modern territorial state is a profoundly important entity in contemporary human society. In many respects, whether one lives in a humid subtropical or a semi-arid climate is less important than whether one lives in the United States or Mexico.[79] Moreover, the modern territorial state plays a dominant role in the generation and dissemination of information. It is virtually impossible to address many issues and problems without employing data gathered on a state-by-state basis. Yet every analysis that turns to such data compartmentalizes information and ideas in a manner that promotes the reification of the territorial state. Discussions of matters as diverse as population growth, environmental changes, and trade focus attention on similarities and differences among and between states. In the process, it becomes increasingly difficult to think in terms of a geographical order that is not state-based.

The tendency to conceptualize social, cultural, economic, and even environmental processes in state terms would seem to demand some sort of critical scrutiny. Yet the modern territorial order pervades so much of our lives that we rarely even think about its role in shaping our spatial imaginations.[80] Nowhere is this more evident than in the international relations literature, which has been dominated in recent decades by theories that treat the world's states as taken-for-granted analytical units. The most widely discussed theories of international relations, whether realist, neo-realist, or idealist, start with states as a given and work forward from that point.[81] Modernization theory proceeds from the assumption that individual societies undergoing development surrender their local, ethnic loyalties in favor of state identities as they pursue the project of "nation-building."[82] This view, which permeated all of Western social science for a time, has come under increasing attack, but still continues to influence most conceptualizations of political, economic, and social developments.[83] In the economic realm, "[w]e normally model countries as dimensionless points within which factors of production can be instantly and costlessly moved from one activity to another, and even trade among countries is usually given a sort of spaceless representation."[84] And in more general terms, the state is the unquestioned geographical framework within which we consider issues ranging from ethnicity to migration to water quality.

One significant consequence of this state of affairs is that the concept of sovereignty is generally treated as if it were unproblematic.[85] Studies are legion that treat states as theoretical equals; others recognize that stronger states often interfere in the affairs of weaker states, and therefore treat the concept as if it were essentially meaningless. In neither case is the meaning or significance of sovereignty really examined. This is truly remarkable given that in the past forty years there has been simultaneously an overt commitment to the sovereign state as the basis for an international political order, and uncontested violations of that principle. Although sovereignty is finally receiving more attention in the literature, the long silence on the issue provides clear evidence of how unquestioning the acceptance of the modern political-territorial order has been.

The ubiquitous use of the term "nation-state" underscores the extent to which questions about the underlying territorial character of the modern state system are marginalized. A "nation-state" was understood historically to be a sovereign state inhabited by a group of people who saw themselves as one.[86] By the 1950s, however, most Western social scientists were using the term to refer to any so-called sovereign state, no matter how ethnically or nationally heterogeneous that state might be.[87] Czechoslovakia, Yugoslavia, the Soviet Union, and India were all called "nation-states." Nation and state citizenry were thought of as one. The United Nations itself embodies this idea; the "nations" of the world that meet together in New York do not fit Konstantin Symmons-Symonolewicz's classic definition of a nation as a "territorially based community of human beings sharing a distinct variant of modern culture, bound together by a strong sentiment of unity and solidarity, marked by a clear historically-rooted consciousness of national identity, and possessing, or striving to possess, a genuine political self-government."[88] Instead, they are the world's recognized "sovereign states."

There are innumerable concrete legal and political ramifications of conflating nationality with the territorial state. Many United Nations resolutions refer to the right of self-determination, but in practice this right has essentially been limited to peoples in overseas colonies seeking independence.[89] Moreover, in international law a refugee is defined solely in state terms. The Geneva Convention and other international legal agreements limit refugee status to those who have left their state of origin because of persecution or violence and who are unable to return for the same reason.[90] In practice this means that an Ibo woman who is forced to leave her homeland in Nigeria can claim refugee status if she moves across the border into the Ibo part of Cameroon, but not if she moves to a culturally alien part of Nigeria.

In the foreign policy realm, the treatment of the state as a territorial given shapes governmental policy in fundamental ways. Take US foreign policy over the past two decades as an example. Policymakers have focused primarily on other territorial states, and within those states overwhelming attention has been given to the head of state, who is seen as the personification of the territory.[91] Thus, during the 1970s and 1980s US foreign policy toward Iran was influenced much more by the actions of the Shah, and then by the Ayatollah Khomeini, than it was by anything else that was going on in that country.[92] In a somewhat different vein, so deeply rooted are assumptions about the inviolability of the current territorial order that the US government has frequently been slow to accept impending changes, even when those changes seem consistent with larger foreign policy objectives. Well after the breakup of Yugoslavia was underway, the US Department of State was affirming its commitment to the "territorial integrity of Yugoslavia," even though Slovenia and Croatia had moved quickly to embrace democratic principles and Serbia had not.[93] More strikingly, the United States was framing the issue of independence for Estonia, Latvia, and Lithuania as a Soviet problem for many weeks after those Baltic states had declared independence, even though the US had never recognized the incorporation of these states into the Soviet Union. Indeed, in response to a question about Baltic independence on 4 September 1991, former Secretary of State James Baker declared, "The future of the Soviet Union is for the Soviet people to determine themselves."[94]

The privileged status we have accorded the state is also evident when we divide up the world into large-scale cultural, economic, or environmental regions for purposes of discussion and analysis. In a recent book on the Middle Eastern Arab World, for example, William Polk points to culture and climate as the defining characteristics of the region.[95] Yet he goes on to describe his study area as the region "encompassing Egypt, Libya, the Sudan, the Arabian peninsula, Jordan, Lebanon, Syria, and Iraq."[96] Others point to the vagueness of the term "Middle East," but then proceed to analyze developments in the region on a state-by-state basis.[97] One consequence of treating the Middle East in this way is that territories lying within the former Soviet Union invariably are omitted from consideration. Yet this makes little sense from a historical, cultural, or physical geographic perspective.

The power of the territorial assumptions associated with the modern state system is even evident in our efforts to understand developments that directly challenge the system. Analyses of the prospects for further integration in the European Union provide a case in point. The European Union of the 1990s does not fit easily within the post-World War II state-territorial model since the member states have ceded important aspects of their sovereignty to the central institutions of the Union.[98] Nevertheless, most analyses of the European Union continue to treat it either as a puppet of the member states or as a superstate in its own right. In the former case, the continuation of the territorial status quo is assumed. In the latter, some adjustment in the current political map is contemplated, but not in the nature of the system itself.

The tendency to think about the European Union in traditional state-based terms is evident in many recent assessments of the integration process. Most commentators evaluate the success or failure of the process in terms of the degree to which powers are being transferred from state governmental and economic institutions to the central decisionmaking bodies of the European Union. Transfers that promote the concentration of power in Brussels are interpreted as signs of successful integration, whereas those that challenge centralized decisionmaking are seen in opposite terms. What lies behind this approach is the assumption that the political leaders of the European Union are, or should be, engaged in "state building." The critical question for the Union is assumed to be whether the member states are willing to surrender increasing sovereignty to centralized European Union institutions. Such an approach necessarily posits the European Union as a superstate rather than as a new type of political framework, in which issues can be addressed on a variety of scales and in regional contexts that make sense in terms of the geographical character of the issues themselves. Yet it is the latter conception that arguably demands attention as Europeans increasingly question the further concentration of powers in Brussels, Luxembourg, and Strasbourg.

Taken together, all of these examples illustrate the extent to which the modern territorial state has co-opted our spatial imaginations. And the co-opting has been so far-reaching that we accept it unproblematically. Small wonder, then, that society at large has lost a sense of geography as being much more than the memorization of the location and capital cities of the states of the world. The regions that frame our studies are seen simply as stages on which social and political processes are played out, not as themselves integral to those processes.[99] In Michel Foucault's words, space has come to be treated as "the dead, the fixed, the undialectic, the immobile."[100]

Contemporary challenges to the political-territorial order

Despite the tendency to cast most issues in state terms, developments at a variety of scales are challenging both the power of the state and its conceptual integrity.[101] Most obviously, the spatial structure of the international economy is to some degree at odds with the modern state system.[102] Technological developments have facilitated the establishment of financial and business networks between "world cities" in different countries, and multinational corporations are often able to escape state regulations by carefully assigning facets of their enterprises to the different states in which they operate.[103] As a result, the effective authority of states has been reduced and significant functional spaces have emerged that bear little resemblance to the political map.[104] In some respects the connections between New York, London, and Tokyo are more extensive than the connections between any of these cities and the more distant parts of their national hinterlands.

Beyond the purely economic realm, many social and environmental developments are not easily confronted within the current political-territorial order, and in some cases are directly challenging that order. Ethnic nationalism has been on the rise all over the world; ethnonational groups that at one time sought recognition and access to the political system are now demanding separation, autonomy, or independence.[105] Even the European countries that gave birth to the idea of the nation-state have confronted a surge of regionalism in recent decades. Moreover, a steady stream of reports about global warming, holes in the ozone layer, endangered water supplies, acid rain, oil spills, deforestation, and species extinction have focused unprecedented attention on the need to curtail environmentally deleterious practices. These problems rarely correspond with state boundaries, prompting many to point to the political fragmentation of the planet as one of the primary obstacles to an effective response to the environmental crisis.[106] Indeed, efforts are being made to frame international and regional environmental compacts in a manner that challenges the traditional sovereign rights of states to control activities within their territories.[107]

In a somewhat different vein, developments in the human rights arena have raised questions about the viability of the post-World War II state system as it is traditionally understood.[108] Beginning with the adoption of a Universal Declaration of Human Rights by the United Nations in 1948,[109] challenges have grown to the assumption that states have ultimate authority when it comes to human rights. High-profile international conventions on human rights were signed in the 1960s and 1970s, and in the 1980s economic sanctions came to be seen as an appropriate tool for protesting South Africa's apartheid regime. Lung-Chu Chen argues that, taken en masse, developments in the human rights field now amount to an affirmative obligation on the part of states to guarantee their citizens' basic social and economic rights.[110] Such a guarantee is hardly a reality in many cases, but the increasing willingness of the United Nations to sanction intervention on human rights grounds shows the erosion that has occurred in the assumption that the state is the proper territorial unit within which all social issues should be addressed.[111]

In light of developments on all of these fronts, it is, in Stephen Krasner's terms, "no longer obvious that the state system is the optimal way to organize political life."[112] But if the state system as currently configured is not optimal, what can or will be its replacement? Is it possible that the challenges to the territorial state are so great that a non-territorial state system might emerge? And if so, what would that look like? The pertinence of such questions was highlighted recently in an article by Timothy Luke on the changing environment for national security.[113] Luke argued that the significance of territory for national security has changed in response to shifts in production, consumption, and administrative decisionmaking brought about by the computer revolution and the elaboration of global telecommunications networks. In Luke's words, "the cyberspaces of interoperational coding in global flows now seem to define social purpose and performance as much as the more traditional geographics of organizational and national boundaries."[114]

Luke makes his case by reference to the situation in Kuwait before and during the 1990 to 1991 occupation by the armies of Saddam Hussein. He argues that before the invasion Kuwait's status as a state was as strongly tied to its foreign stockholdings, bank accounts, real estate holdings, and financial networks as it was to its territorial base. Hence, when the Kuwaiti government went into exile, it was able to continue to perform many of its usual functions and to sustain the essential essence of the Kuwaiti state simply by redirecting the focus of its economic and financial networks to Washington, DC, and Taif, Saudi Arabia. Luke recognizes that the existence of a concrete territorial base was symbolically necessary for this to occur, but he argues that the entire scenario exposes the declining importance of territory for statehood in the late twentieth century.

Kuwait, of course, is hardly a typical state, but Luke's overview, when considered along with the dysfunctional character of the current order, does raise important questions about the long-term viability of the state system in its current form. Little can be said with certainty on this subject. Since challenges to the system are mounting in intensity, however, and since the functional meaning of territory is in flux, it is reasonable to conclude that we are at the beginning of a period of significant change. It is doubtful that this change will lead us to a world of non-territorial states. If the history of state-territorial ideas and practices tells us anything, it is that changes in arrangements and understandings occur, but that no one era represents a radical break with the preceding era. Moreover, attachments to territory are as old as human society, and there is little to suggest that the powerful ideological bonds that link identity, politics, and territory will be loosened.[115] To assume otherwise is to perpetuate the error of social theories that fail to address the links between society and the concrete material/ environmental settings in which they are embedded.[116] Indeed, the recent rise of ethnonationalist movements with specific territorial agendas provides clear evidence that territory remains a vital component of identity. And as Luke himself acknowledges, the existence of a Kuwaiti territorial state provided the ideological cement on which the

Kuwaiti government constructed its operations before and during the Iraqi invasion.[117]

Territory is so important to political governance in part because it provides a locus for the exercise of political authority over a range of interests and initiatives. Despite the dramatic changes that have occurred in the conceptualization, management, and defense of territory over the past several hundred years, the notion of territorial control has been at the heart of political life since before the Peace of Westphalia. Political authority can be exerted over sets of issues or institutions, but it is difficult to construct an enduring system without a territorial base.[118] Indeed, as the foregoing discussion suggests, the survival and success of sovereignty as an organizing principle of the modern state system has much to do with its territorial underpinnings.[119]

To conclude from all of this that we are indefinitely imprisoned within the current political-territorial order, however, is as dubious as to assume that territory and politics are about to be entirely uncoupled. Increasingly obvious disjunctions between the political organization of territory and the geography of economic, social, and political life are shaking the territorial assumptions of the post-World War II era at their very foundations. New questions are being asked about the scale of political-territorial organization, about the role of substate and superstate regional formations, and about the nature of the territorial state itself. In the process, it is becoming increasingly difficult simply to treat the current political map as an unproblematic, untransmutable given.[120]

As the earlier discussion suggests, this is not the first time that the legitimacy of a particular territorial order has been called into question. Can we therefore expect a period of political upheaval as occurred in Europe in the mid-eighteenth century and again in the latter half of the nineteenth century? Perhaps. But two fundamental differences characterize the present situation. One is an awareness that large-scale upheaval carries with it the potential for death and destruction on a previously unheard-of scale. Hence, forceful alterations of the territorial status quo – at least in the form of one state seeking to take over the territory of another – are seen as even more problematic than in prior eras. The second is that the challenges to the existing order are manifest at different scales and in overlapping spaces. Demands for ethnoregional autonomy coexist with state nationalism, with regional economic concerns, and with environmental problems of variable spatial character. Hence, it is not at all clear that any particular redrawing of the political map based on the sovereign territorial ideal could provide a stable, less dysfunctional social order. Instead, the nature of the challenges to the existing pattern of states seems to point to the need for a more flexible, multilayered approach to political-territorial governance in the twenty-first century.

Given the ideological hold of the post-World War II political order, it is difficult even to imagine what such a system might look like. Since issues and problems manifest themselves at different scales and in ways that are not necessarily spatially coextensive, a multi-scale, not completely hierarchical set of political-territorial structures might be indicated. Political institutions at the scale of world regions (e.g., South Asia or the Middle East/North Africa) might set overarching standards and guidelines in limited jurisdictional arenas and might be responsible for the coordination of approaches to problems in smaller-scale political units. Strategies for dealing with these standards or guidelines – as well as power over issues beyond the competence of world-regional authorities – might be dealt with in a variety of different smaller-scale political territories, each with a specific range of governmental mandates. Many existing states would probably continue to function as one type of political territory in such a system, but they would coexist with political territories organized along ecological lines with competence over specific environmental matters; political territories organized along ethnocultural lines (e.g., Basques or Tibetans) with competence over certain cultural, social, and educational issues; and political territories organized on the basis of socioeconomic patterns with competence over aspects of economic development and social welfare.

This is all highly speculative, of course, and the potential for bureaucratic excess in such a system would be great. Moreover, developments in various parts of the world point more to a descent into chaos than to a carefully constructed new order.[121] Even the European Union – the political framework that seems to offer the most promise for a multi-tiered approach to governance – continues to be mired in power struggles between constituent states and centralized decisionmaking authorities.[122] Yet some recent, little discussed, developments within the European Union suggest the possibilities that are inherent in a multi-tiered, not strictly hierarchical, political-territorial system. By reducing the economic, social, and psychological importance of boundaries in some places, the Union has provided a framework within which new kinds of regional linkages have been able to emerge.[123] Some of these are developing directly across international boundaries, whereas others involve geographically dispersed regions.[124] Moreover, in a departure from past practice, over the past few years European Union officials have even made modest efforts to facilitate cross-border regional cooperation schemes.[125] At the same time, policy planning groups are beginning to take into consideration regions that are organized along state lines; a recent study of regional development problems in the Union, for example, focused on areas that shared common socioeconomic characteristics without reference to state boundaries.[126] In a variety of different ways, then, seeds are being planted in Europe that could lead to a new phase in the evolution of the political-territorial structure of society. It is far from sure that they will be nurtured, but if they are, the part of the world that gave birth to the sovereign state system could well be the place that forges the basis for an order that transcends that system.

Notes

An earlier version of this article was presented at a workshop sponsored by the Social Science Research Council at Brown University, Providence, Rhode Island, 27–9 February 1993. I am grateful to all participants for their comments on the paper, in particular John Agnew and Tom Biersteker. I am also grateful to George White for research assistance, to Tom Fogarty and Cindy Newman for comments on earlier drafts, and to Sarah Shafer and Nancy Leeper for drafting the figures. Research for this article was supported in part by the National Science Foundation under grant number SBR-9157667.

[1] From "L'Oeil de Pouvoir," a preface to Bentham, Jeremy 1977. *La Panoptique*. Paris: Belfound, as translated and reprinted in Gordon, Colin (ed.) 1980. *Power/Knowledge: Selected Interviews and Other Writings 1972–1977*. New York: Pantheon Books, p. 189.

[2] See, for example, Keohane, Robert O. and Nye, Joseph S. (eds.) 1972. *Transnational Relations and World Politics*. Cambridge, Mass.: Harvard University Press.

[3] Ruggie, John G. 1993. "Territoriality and Beyond: Problematizing Modernity in International Relations," *International Organization* 47: 2–3.

[4] For a recent general overview, see Axtmann, Roland 1993. "The Formation of the Modern State: The Debate in the Social Sciences," in Fulbrook, Mary (ed.) *National Histories and European History*. Boulder, Colo.: Westview Press, pp. 21–45. Among the most important recent works on the subject are Poggi, Gianfranco 1990. *The State: Its Nature, Development, and Prospects*. Oxford: Oxford University Press; Wallerstein, Immanuel 1974–88. *The Modern World System*. 3 vols. New York: Academic Press; Mann, Michael 1988. *States, War and*

Capitalism. Oxford: Blackwell; and Tilly, Charles 1992. *Coercion, Capital, and European States, AD 990–1992.* Oxford: Blackwell.

[5] The term "spatiality" is sometimes used to refer to the complex of territorial arrangements and spatial understanding associated with different eras. See, e.g., Soja, Edward W. 1989. *Postmodern Geographies: The Reassertion of Space in Critical Social Theory.* London: Verso. The importance of examining the "representations of space" associated with the modern state system is highlighted in Agnew, John A. 1994. "Timeless Space and State-Centrism: The Geographical Assumptions of International Relations Theory," in Rosow, S.J., Inayatullah, N. and Mark, R. (eds.) *The Global Economy as Political Space.* Boulder, Colo.: Lynne Reinner, pp. 87–106.

[6] Such a concern is at the core of political geography. See Gottmann, Jean 1973. *The Significance of Territory.* Charlottesville: University of Virginia Press. It is also emerging rapidly in the international relations literature. See Kratochwil, Friedrich 1986. "Of Systems, Boundaries, and Territoriality: An Inquiry into the Formation of the State System," *World Politics* 34: 27–52; and Ruggie, "Territoriality." These contributions treat territoriality as an historical and social process. The political and social dimensions of territoriality are explored at some length in Sack, Robert D. 1986. *Human Territoriality: Its Theory and History.* Cambridge Studies in Historical Geography. Cambridge: Cambridge University Press; and in Soja, Edward W. 1971. *The Political Organization of Space.* Commission on College Geography Resource Paper No. 8. Washington, D.C.: Association of American Geographers.

[7] Taylor, Peter J. 1993. "Contra Political Geography," *Tijdschrift voor Economische en Politische Geografie* 84: 82–90.

[8] For good discussions of the notion of place and its importance in the contemporary world, see Agnew, John A. 1989. "The Devaluation of Place in Social Science," in Agnew, John A. and Duncan, James S. (eds.) *The Power of Place: Bringing Together Geographical and Sociological Imaginations.* Boston: Unwin, Hyman; Johnston, R.J. 1991. *A Question of Place: Exploring the Practice of Human Geography.* Oxford: Blackwell; and Johnston, R.J. 1986. "Placing Politics," *Political Geography Quarterly* 5: 63–78.

[9] An excellent discussion of the contextual nature of territorial arrangements and understandings can be found in Sack, *Human Territoriality.*

[10] J. Samuel Barkin and Bruce Cronin argue that "international relations scholars rarely examine how definitions of populations and territories change throughout history and how this change alters the notion of legitimate authority." Barkin, J. Samuel and Cronin, Bruce 1994. "The State and the Nation: Changing Norms and the Rules of Sovereignty in International Relations," *International Organization* 48: 107.

[11] Krasner, Stephen D. 1991. "Westphalia." Unpublished manuscript, November.

[12] The Latin phrase refers to the right of the ruler of a realm to determine the religion of the realm.

[13] See Ruggie, John 1983. "Continuity and Transformation in the World

Polity: Toward a Neorealist Synthesis," *World Politics* 35: 274–5; and Fischer, Markus 1992. "Feudal Europe, 800–1300: Communal Discourse and Conflictual Practice," *International Organization* 46: 427–66.

14 See generally, Treasure, Geoffrey 1985. *The Making of Modern Europe, 1648–1780*. London and New York: Methuen, pp. 376–7.

15 Krasner, "Westphalia," p. 33.

16 Hohenberg, Paul M. and Lees, Lynn Hollen 1985. *The Making of Urban Europe, 1000–1950*. Cambridge, Mass.: Harvard University Press.

17 Anderson, James 1985. "Nationalism and Geography," in Anderson, James (ed.) *The Rise of the Modern State*. Brighton, Sussex: Wheatsheaf, p. 125.

18 See Friedman, Wolfgang 1967. *Legal Theory*. 5th ed. New York: Columbia University Press, p. 574.

19 Edwards, Charles S. 1981. *Hugo Grotius and the Miracle of Holland: A Study in Political and Legal Thought*. Chicago: Nelson-Hall.

20 Watson, Adam 1992. *The Evolution of International Society: A Comparative Historical Analysis*. London and New York: Routledge.

21 See generally, Strayer, Joseph R. 1970. *On the Medieval Origins of the Modern State*. Princeton: Princeton University Press.

22 Skinner, Quentin 1978. *The Foundation of Modern Political Thought*. Vol. II. Cambridge: Cambridge University Press, p. 349.

23 Treasure, *The Making of Modern Europe*, p. 183.

24 See generally McKay, Derek and Scott, H.M. 1983. *The Rise of the Great Powers, 1648–1815*. London and New York: Longman.

25 Among the more important of these were Bavaria, Saxony, Hanover, and Brandenberg, but the empire also encompassed many small principalities, bishoprics, cities, and the like.

26 See Thomson, Janice E. and Krasner, Stephen D. 1989. "Global Transactions and the Consolidation of Sovereignty," in Czempiel, Ernst-Otto and Rosenau, James N. (eds.) *Global Changes and Theoretical Challenges: Approaches to World Politics for the 1990s*. Lexington, Mass.: Lexington Books.

27 The problems with such assumptions are discussed in Manning, D.J. and Robinson, T.J. 1985. *The Place of Ideology in Political Life*. London: Croom Helm. See also Giddens, Anthony 1987. *Social Theory and Modern Sociology*. Cambridge: Polity Press; Stanford: Stanford University Press, pp. 4–21.

28 Barkin and Cronin, "The State and the Nation," pp. 109–10.

29 Sack, *Human Territoriality*.

30 For a case study that shows these tendencies of a territorial system in an environment in which the territorial arrangements enjoy a substantial degree of legitimacy, see Murphy, Alexander B. 1988. *The Regional Dynamics of Language Differentiation in Belgium: A Study in Cultural-Political Geography*. Geography Research Paper no. 227. Chicago: University of Chicago Press.

31 On the issue of spatial ontology more generally, see Sack, Robert D. 1980. *Conceptions of Space in Social Thought*. Minneapolis: University of Minnesota Press.

32 R.B.J. Walker describes this process as one in which "the principle of hierarchical subordination gradually gave way to the principle of spatial

exclusion." 1990. "Security, Sovereignty, and the Challenge of World Politics," *Alternatives* 15: 10. For a case study of this process, see Sahlins, Peter 1989. *Boundaries: The Making of France and Spain in the Pyrenees.* Berkeley: University of California Press.

[33] See generally Mann, *States, War and Capitalism*; Tilly, *Coercion, Capital, and European States*; and Treasure, *The Making of Modern Europe.*

[34] Gross, Leo 1969. "The Peace of Westphalia, 1648–1948," in Gross, Leo (ed.) *International Law in the Twentieth Century.* New York: Appleton-Century-Crofts, p. 25.

[35] The Prussian case provides a good example of this. See Treasure, *Making of Modern Europe*, pp. 432–41.

[36] Wendt, Alexander 1992. "Anarchy is What States Make of It: The Social Construction of Power Politics," *International Organization* 46: 412.

[37] Taylor, Peter J. 1994. "The State as Container: Territoriality in the Modern World-System," *Progress in Human Geography* 18: 151–62. These distinct territorial boundaries differed from the frontiers of prior eras, which were loosely defined zones of transition between different polities. See Kristof, Ladis 1959. "The Nature of Frontiers and Boundaries," *Annals of the Association of American Geographers* 49: 269–82; and Kratochwil, "Of Systems, Boundaries, and Territoriality."

[38] Gagliardo, John G. 1980. *Reich and Nation: The Holy Roman Empire as Idea and Reality, 1763–1806.* Bloomington, Ind.: Indiana University Press, pp. 43–4.

[39] Watson, Adam 1984."European International Society and Its Expansion," in Bull, Hedley and Watson, Adam (eds.) *The Expansion of International Society.* New York: Oxford University Press, pp. 23–5.

[40] Israel, Fred L. (ed.) 1967. *Major Peace Treaties of Modern History: 1648–1967.* Vol. I. New York and London: McGraw-Hill, p. 146. A similar commitment was made in the Treaty of Utrecht, which was entered into by the British, French, and Irish monarchs in 1713. Ibid., p. 180.

[41] Krasner, "Westphalia," pp. 20–2.

[42] Treasure, *The Making of Modern Europe*, pp. 374–409.

[43] Gagliardo, *Reich and Nation.*

[44] Treasure, *The Making of Modern Europe*, pp. 385–6.

[45] Pounds, Norman J.G. 1954. "France and 'Les Limites Naturelles' from the Seventeenth to the Twentieth Centuries," *Annals of the Association of American Geographers* 44: 51–62.

[46] Israel, *Major Peace Treaties*, p. 440.

[47] Anchor, Robert 1967. *The Enlightenment Tradition.* New York: Harper & Row, p. 18.

[48] Pounds, Norman J.G. and Ball, Sue Simons 1964. "Core Areas and the Development of the European States System," *Annals of the Association of American Geographers* 54: 24–40.

[49] Anderson, "Nationalism and Geography," p. 126.

[50] Van Dyke, Vernon 1974. "Human Rights and the Rights of Groups," *American Journal of Political Science* 18: 726–7.

[51] Gagliardo, *Reich and Nation*, pp. 194–5.

[52] See, for example, the instructions given by Napoleon to his brother Jerome before his brother took control of the Kingdom of Westphalia, in a letter reprinted in Hutt, Maurice (ed.) 1972. *Napoleon*. Englewood Cliffs, N.J.: Prentice-Hall, p. 34.

[53] Fox, Edward Whiting 1991. *The Emergence of the Modern European World*. Oxford: Blackwell, pp. 107–12.

[54] Barkin and Cronin, "The State and the Nation."

[55] Ibid., pp. 112–13.

[56] Murphy, Alexander B. 1990. "Historical Justifications for Territorial Claims," *Annals of the Association of American Geographers* 80: 536. For a discussion of the importance of discourse in political affairs, see Ó Tuathail, Gearóid and Agnew, John A. 1992. "Geopolitics and Discourse: Practical Geopolitical Reasoning in American Foreign Policy," *Political Geography* 11: 190–204.

[57] Hill, Norman 1976. *Claims to Territory in International Law and Relations*. Westport, Conn.: Greenwood Press, pp. 41–3 (originally published in 1945 by Oxford University Press).

[58] See, e.g., Breuilly, John 1993. "Sovereignty and Boundaries: Modern State Formation and National Identity in Germany," in Fulbrook, Mary (ed.) *National Histories and European History*. Boulder, Colo.: Westview Press, pp. 94–140.

[59] See Paasi, Anssi 1986. "The Institutionalization of Regions: A Theoretical Framework for Understanding the Emergence of Regions and the Constitution of Regional Identity," *Fennia* 164: 105–46; Ra'anan, Uri 1991. "Nation and State: Order Out of Chaos," in Ra'anan, Uri, Mesner, Maria, Ames, Keith, and Martin, Kate (eds.) *State and Nation in Multi-Ethnic Societies: The Breakup of Multinational States*. Manchester: Manchester University Press; and Knight, David B. 1992. "Statehood: A Politico-Geographic and Legal Perspective," *Geojournal* 28: 312–13.

[60] See Gottmann, Jean 1975. "The Evolution of the Concept of Territory," *Social Science Information* 14: 34–5.

[61] Friedman, *Legal Theory*, pp. 256–311.

[62] Stoddart, David R. 1966. "Darwin's Impact on Geography," *Annals of the Association of American Geographers* 56: 683–98.

[63] Kristof, Ladis 1960. "The Origins and Evolution of Geopolitics," *Journal of Conflict Resolution* 4: 15–51.

[64] Morgenthau, Hans J. 1963. *Politics Among Nations: The Struggle for Power and Peace*. 3rd ed. New York: Alfred A. Knopf, p. 50.

[65] Israel, *Major Peace Treaties*, p. 645.

[66] See generally, Alexander, Lewis M. 1963. *World Political Patterns*. 2nd ed. Chicago: Rand McNally, pp. 18–28.

[67] Taylor, "The State as Container." The decisions that the Europeans made in dividing up other parts of the world reflected European understandings of sovereignty. Thus, the Treaty of Tordesillas (1494) dividing South America between the Spanish and the Portuguese was premised on the rights of each

country to exercise exclusive control over distinct territorial domains in the Western hemisphere. See Gottmann, *The Significance of Territory*, p. 39.

[68] Pakenham, Thomas 1991. *The Scramble for Africa, 1876–1912*. New York: Random House.

[69] Meinig, Donald W. 1969. "A Macrogeography of Western Imperialism: Some Morphologies of Moving Frontiers of Political Control," in Gale, Fay and Lawton, Graham H. (eds.) *Settlement and Encounter: Geographical Studies Presented to Sir Grefell Price*. London: Oxford University Press, pp. 230–5.

[70] Murphy, Alexander B. 1991. "Territorial Ideology and International Conflict: The Legacy of Prior Political Formations," in Waterman, Stanley and Kliot, Nurit (eds.) *War, Peace and Geography*. London: Belhaven, p. 130.

[71] McNeill, William H. 1986. *Poly-ethnicity and National Unity in World History*. Toronto: University of Toronto Press.

[72] Fox, *Emergence of the Modern European World*, pp. 266–73.

[73] Article 10 of the Covenant of the League of Nations, reprinted in Friedmann, Wolfgang G., Lissitzyn, Oliver J., and Pugh, Richard Crawford 1969. *Cases and Materials on International Law*. St. Paul, Minn.: West Publishing Co., p. 917.

[74] James, Alan 1986. *Sovereign Statehood: The Basis of International Society*. Boston: Allen & Unwin.

[75] Murphy, "Historical Justifications," p. 537.

[76] This point is made forcefully by Mann, Michael 1984. "The Autonomous Power of the State: Its Origins, Mechanisms and Results," *European Journal of Sociology* 25: 210–12.

[77] For the way this process proceeded, see the article by David Strang in this volume.

[78] Krasner, Stephen D. 1988. "Sovereignty: An Institutional Perspective," *Comparative Political Studies* 21: 86.

[79] A similar point was made several decades ago. See Hartshorne, Richard 1954. "Political Geography," in James, Preston E. and Jones, Clarence F. (eds.) *American Geography: Inventory and Prospect*. Syracuse: Syracuse University Press for the Association of American Geographers, p. 169.

[80] In Peter G. Brown's words: "It is sometimes said that the last thing a fish would discover is water. As a basic feature of its environment it is taken for granted. So it appears with twentieth-century men and women and the nation-state. But we not only take the nation-state as a fixed element of our circumstances; we think – or rather assume without reflection – that its existence settles other questions." 1981. "Introduction," in Brown, Peter G. and Shue, Henry (eds.) *Boundaries: National Autonomy and Its Limits*. Totowa, N.J.: Rowman & Littlefield, p. ix.

[81] This point is emphasized in Ashley, Richard K. 1988. "Untying the Sovereign State: A Double Reading of the Anarchy Problematique," *Millennium: Journal of International Studies* 17: 227–62; and in Agnew, "Timeless Space." For critiques of this state of affairs, see Keohane, Robert O. (ed.) 1986. *Neo-Realism and Its Critics*. New York: Columbia University Press; Rosenau,

James N. 1990. *Turbulence in World Politics: A Theory of Change and Continuity.* Princeton: Princeton University Press; Walker, R.B.J. 1984. "The Territorial State and the Theme of Gulliver," *International Journal* 39: 529–52; and Walker, "Security." Prior to the last few years, the only notable figure in American security studies who raised serious questions about the state was John Herz. See his 1957, "Rise and Demise of the Territorial States," *World Politics* 9: 473–93; and 1968, "The Territorial State Revisited – Reflections on the Future of the Nation-State," *Polity* 1: 11–34.

[82] Deutsch, Karl W. 1953. *Nationalism and Social Communication: An Inquiry into the Foundations of Nationality.* Cambridge, Mass.: Technology Press of the Massachusetts Institute of Technology.

[83] See Agnew, John A. 1987. *Place and Politics: The Geographical Mediation of State and Society.* Boston: Allen & Unwin.

[84] Krugman, Paul 1991. *Geography and Trade.* Leuven: Leuven University Press and Cambridge, Mass.: The Massachusetts Institute of Technology Press, p. 2.

[85] R.B.J. Walker has made this point particularly forcefully. See his 1988, *State Sovereignty, Global Civilization, and the Rearticulation of Political Space.* World Order Studies Program Occasional Paper No. 18. Princeton: Princeton University Center of International Studies.

[86] Connor, Walker 1972. "Nation-Building or Nation-Destroying?" *World Politics* 24: 319–55.

[87] Mikesell, Marvin W. 1983. "The Myth of the Nation-State," *Journal of Geography* 82: 257–60.

[88] Symmons-Symonolewicz, Konstantin 1985. "The Concept of Nationhood: Toward a Theoretical Clarification," *Canadian Review of Studies in Nationalism* 12: 221.

[89] Knight, David B. 1985. "People and Territory or Territory and People: Thoughts on Post-Colonial Self-Determination," *International Political Science Review* 6: 248–72.

[90] Chen, Lung-Chu 1989. *An Introduction to Contemporary International Law: A Policy-Oriented Perspective.* New Haven: Yale University Press, pp. 183–92.

[91] Wixman, Ronald 1991. "Ethnic Nationalism in Eastern Europe," in *Eastern Europe: The Impact of Geographic Forces on a Strategic Region.* Washington, D.C.: Central Intelligence Agency.

[92] Murphy, Alexander B. 1994. "A Geographic Perspective on International Governance," in Demko, George J. and Wood, William (eds.) *Reordering the World: Geopolitical Perspectives on the Twenty-First Century.* Boulder, Colo.: Westview Press, pp. 209–24.

[93] Statement by Tutwiler, Margaret 1991. *U.S. Department of State Dispatch/ Bureau of Public Affairs* 2: 395.

[94] 1991. *U.S. Department of State Dispatch/Bureau of Public Affairs* 2: 667.

[95] Polk, William R. 1991. *The Arab World Today.* Cambridge, Mass.: Harvard University Press.

[96] Ibid., p. 3.

[97] See, e.g., Nolte, Richard H. (ed.) 1963. *The Modern Middle East*. New York: Atherton Press.

[98] Williams, Allan M. 1991. *The European Community: The Contradictions of Integration*. Oxford: Blackwell. Although the upheavals following the Danish rejection of the Maastricht treaty have raised some doubts about the community's future, it is unlikely that the framework established over the past several decades will be undone.

[99] See Murphy, Alexander B. 1991. "Regions as Social Constructs: The Gap Between Theory and Practice," *Progress in Human Geography* 15: 22–35.

[100] Foucault, Michel "Questions on Geography," in Gordon (ed.), *Power/ Knowledge*, p. 70.

[101] As Joseph Camilleri argues, "the state's traditional claim to represent a single national will or collective interest is increasingly divorced from reality." Camilleri, Joseph A. 1990. "Rethinking Sovereignty in a Shrinking World," in Walker, R.B.J. and Mendlovitz, Saul H. (eds.) *Contending Sovereignties: Redefining Political Community*. Boulder, Colo.: Lynne Rienner Publishers, p. 37.

[102] Zacher, Mark W. 1992. "The Decaying Pillars of the Westphalian Temple: Implications for International Order and Governance," in Rosenau, James N. and Czempiel, Ernst-Otto (eds.) *Governance Without Government: Order and Change in World Politics*. Cambridge: Cambridge University Press, pp. 58–101; Gill, Stephen 1992. "Economic Globalization and the Internationalization of Authority: Limits and Contradictions," *Geoforum* 23: 269–83. To highlight the discontinuities between the organization of political and economic life is not to suggest that states are irrelevant. For a good statement of why states remain important, see Ruggie, "Territoriality," pp. 4–5.

[103] See Friedmann, John 1986. "The World City Hypothesis," *Development and Change* 17: 69–83.

[104] Biersteker, Thomas J. 1981. "The Limits of State Power in the Contemporary World Economy," in Brown, Peter G. and Shue, Henry (eds.) *Boundaries: National Autonomy and Its Limits*. Totowa, N.J.: Rowman & Littlefield, pp. 147–76.

[105] Mikesell, Marvin W. and Murphy, Alexander B. 1991. "A Framework for Comparative Study of Minority-Group Aspirations," *Annals of the Association of American Geographers* 81: 581–604.

[106] See, e.g., Shue, Henry "Exporting Hazards," in Brown and Shue, *Boundaries*.

[107] See Litfin, Karen 1993. "Ecoregimes: Playing Tug of War with the Nation-State," in Lipschutz, Ronnie D. and Conca, Ken (eds.) *The State and Social Power in Global Environmental Politics*. New York: Columbia University Press, pp. 94–117.

[108] See, e.g., Sikkink, Kathryn 1993. "Human Rights, Principled Issue-Networks, and Sovereignty in Latin America," *International Organization* 47: 411–41.

[109] Most of the world's states signed the declaration, but the Soviet Union, Yugoslavia, and Saudi Arabia abstained. See Chen, *Contemporary International Law*, pp. 207–8.

[110] Ibid., p. 222.

119

[111] See Lyons, Gene M. and Mastanduno, Michael 1992. "Beyond Westphalia? International Intervention, State Sovereignty, and the Future of International Society," pamphlet of The Rockefeller Center at Dartmouth College.

[112] Krasner, "Sovereignty," p. 67.

[113] Luke, Timothy W. 1991. "The Discipline of Security Studies and the Codes of Containment: Learning from Kuwait," *Alternatives* 16: 315–44.

[114] Ibid., p. 323.

[115] On this point see Williams, Colin H. and Smith, Anthony D. 1983. "The National Construction of Social Space," *Progress in Human Geography* 7: 502–18.

[116] For a general discussion of this issue, see Agnew, "The Devaluation of Place."

[117] Luke, "The Discipline of Security Studies," p. 325.

[118] This is because of the possibility for a clear, enforceable, and efficient exercise of power in a territorial system. See Sack, *Human Territoriality*, pp. 32–3.

[119] The resilience and adaptability of the sovereign state system are highlighted in Barnett's chapter in this volume (Chapter 6).

[120] See, e.g., Moynihan, Daniel Patrick 1993. *Pandaemonium: Ethnicity in International Relations*. Oxford: Oxford University Press.

[121] See, e.g., the discussion of the situation in sub-Saharan Africa in Kaplan, Robert D. 1994. "The Coming Anarchy," *The Atlantic* 273: 44–76.

[122] See Lambert, John 1990. "Europe: The Nation-State Dies Hard," *Review of Radical Political Economics* 22: 1–13.

[123] See Murphy, Alexander B. 1993. "Emerging Regional Linkages within the European Community: Challenging the Dominance of the State," *Tijdscrift voor Economische en Sociale Geografie* 84: 103–18.

[124] An example of cross-border cooperation is the effort of the German and French regions along the Upper Rhine to promulgate a joint regional development plan. The geographically dispersed regions of Catalonia, Rhône-Alps, Baden-Württemburg, and Lombardy have signed the "Four Motors Agreement," which calls for interregional cooperation and exchanges to promote scientific research and economic development. See Scott, James Wesley 1989. "Transborder Cooperation, Regional Initiatives, and Sovereignty Conflicts in Western Europe: The Case of the Upper Rhine Valley," *The Journal of Federalism* 19: 139–56.

[125] In July 1990 the European Community established a funded program to support cross-border cooperation schemes. The program, called INTERREG, has a budget of 800 million ecus. Local representatives from border areas may apply for funds to encourage administrative and economic cooperation across the border. The community also recently adopted a program under the name "Exchange of Experience and Regional Network Scheme," which is designed to promote local-level cooperation initiatives across state lines. See Murphy, "Emerging Regional Linkages," pp. 111–14.

[126] Commission of the European Communities 1991. *Europe 2000: Outlook for the Development of the Community's Territory*. Luxembourg: Office for Official Publications of the European Communities.

5 Sovereignty and the nation: constructing the boundaries of national identity

Roxanne Lynn Doty

> The historic idea of a unifying American identity is now in peril in many arenas – in our politics, our voluntary organizations, our churches, our language ....
>
> > (Arthur M. Schlesinger, Jr. 1992)[1]

> Something unique is afoot in Europe, in what is still called Europe even if we no longer know very well what or who goes by this name. Indeed, to what concept, to what real individual, to what singular entity should this name be assigned today? Who will draw up its borders?
>
> > (Jacques Derrida, 1992)[2]

These opening quotes suggest that scholars as diverse as Schlesinger and Derrida sense all is not well with sovereign national identities. They refer specifically to America and Europe, but the issue has much broader resonance. The names Europe and America could be replaced in these passages with Britain, Germany, France, and many other names given to nation-states, and still retain the sense of the two quotes. The instability of national identities recently has attracted attention in both academic and nonacademic circles.[3] Within the mainstream of orthodox international relations, however, there is little interest in this topic. By conceptualizing the state as a given, unitary entity, the dominant realist approach has undermined the distinction between state, nation, and sovereignty. This permits questions of national identity and its relevance to sovereignty to be dismissed because they are presumed not to be problems.[4]

This is an increasingly unsatisfactory point of view. Events in the former Soviet Union and Eastern Europe, as well as longstanding ethnic conflicts in the "Third World," suggest that the issue of national identity is an important force in the contemporary world. The political and social relevance of national identity is not, however, limited to countries experiencing overt and violent conflict, or countries whose boundaries have undergone radical transformations. Issues of national identity remain unsolved in older, well-established and seemingly stable nation-states. These nation-states experience periodic identity crises in which the national identity, the supposedly stable foundation of the nation, is called into question.

This chapter explores questions of political community and national identity and the practices that are implicated in their construction. As an example, I examine Britain during its transformation from an identity based on empire to an identity based on a more refined notion of the nation, and how the inside and outside boundary of the nation-state is constructed. I suggest that this boundary is not simply or solely territorial. Nor is it simply based upon political authority understood as the right to determine the governing rules and policies within a specific geographic territory. Instead, the inside/outside boundary is a function of a state's discursive authority, that is, its ability, in the face of ambiguity and uncertainty, to impose fixed and stable meanings about who belongs and who does not belong to the nation, and thereby to distinguish a specific political community – the inside – from all others – the outside.

This chapter's relevance for sovereignty is twofold. First, it addresses an important component of sovereignty that is generally ignored by international relations, the nation. Second, in drawing on critical, post-structural international relations literature, it suggests a broadened understanding of the concept of sovereignty itself.

In contemporary times, the assertion of sovereignty by a state involves implicit claims to represent an identifiable presence. In other words, it is a political community with some sense of shared national identity. While "the people" have not always served as the foundation for state sovereignty, it is generally recognized that "today no state possesses legitimacy which does not also claim to represent the will of the nation."[5] Such a claim presupposes that the nation's membership can be identified. When it is no longer clear who makes up the nation, a state's internal sovereignty and the existence of the state itself is threatened. When the criteria for differentiating the inside of states from the outside become blurred and ambiguous, the foundational premise of state sovereignty becomes shaky. Without this differentiation, the term "international relations" is indistinguishable from "domestic relations." Orthodox international relations theories have assumed that this inside and outside dichotomy was fixed, and have proceeded to study the world (although not always successfully) as if it were unproblematic. For the real-life practitioners of statecraft, however, the issue of foundations cannot be dismissed so easily. Their task is to constitute as unproblematic a thing that is intrinsically problematic – the nation.[6]

Practitioners of statecraft are ardently and continuously involved in the construction of the nation. This chapter begins with the premise that this task is never completed. National identity is never a finished product; it is always in the process of being constructed and reconstructed. This premise has implications for our understanding of sovereignty. I am not proposing a new and definitive understanding of sovereignty, but I am suggesting that addressing sovereignty's foundations, which are inherently ambiguous, fragile, and always evolving, is to suggest a concept for sovereignty that is an illusion. One cannot point to a nation-state, and simply call it sovereign. To do so would assume that its identity is stable and fixed, a realized ideal. To do so would presume a fixed and unproblematic inside and outside dichotomy. As R.B.J. Walker points out, the attempt to treat sovereignty as a matter of definition and legal principle encourages a certain amnesia about its historical and culturally specific character.[7]

Richard Ashley and Walker offer an alternative understanding of sovereignty that enables the link between national identity and sovereignty to be made. They suggest that any "sovereign presence" (for example, God, nature, citizen, nation, the West), is a contingent political effect. The effect of sovereignty is produced under crisis conditions wherein notions of time, space, and political identity are subject to disruption due to transgressions of the boundaries that attempt to fix time, space, and identity within a social order.[8] Sovereignty itself then is inherently problematic because it is potentially undermined by things such as global economic processes, and also because it emerges in response to a crisis in which the naturalness of foundations has been shaken. One of the research implications that follow from this understanding of sovereignty is the need to interrogate the practices that produce seemingly stable and fixed foundations. This moves analysis away from examining anomalies and deviations from some fixed understanding of sovereignty to focusing on the conditions that lead to attempts to fix meanings and identities, and thereby to produce the foundations presumed by conventional understandings of sovereignty. I use the term "sovereignty effect" to refer to the relatively successful production of such foundations.

Through an examination of New Commonwealth immigration into post-World War II Britain, I examine the production of British national identity. The same characterization Derrida suggests of contemporary Europe applied to Britain. Something unique was afoot in post-World War II Britain, in what was still called Britain. It was unclear what or who went by that name. To what real individuals, to what singular entity the terms "British" and "Britain" would be assigned was a question that prompted debate, political violence, and a series of increasingly restrictive and racist immigration policies. The transformation of Britain from an empire to a nation-state was accompanied by a crisis of national identity that called into question the boundaries of the political community. Who was to be considered on the inside and who was to be considered on the outside? Who was to be considered "truly" British? Who would Britain represent as a political entity? Who would be understood as owing allegiance to and willing to sacrifice for Britain?

These were not small matters. They involved the reinvention of the British "imagined community," and they entailed two very different understandings of political community and British national identity. One understanding, "little England" implied a narrow conception of political community and national identity that focused on the needs of "little England" as opposed to the Commonwealth as a whole. The other understanding, the "Commonwealth ideal," envisioned a multi-racial community cooperating on equal terms in political, economic, and cultural matters. This ideal coincided with the professed ideology of *civis Britannicas sum* – I am a citizen of Britain – that had legitimated Britain's imperial rule. This ideology had not been a totally meaningless facade. The whole empire had been committed to the British war effort, perhaps the ultimate assertion of sovereignty, in 1914 and again in 1939.[9] After World War II, the Commonwealth ideal provided a way of resolving Britain's dilemma of having to choose between either being reduced to the status of a mere European power or accepting some form of American hegemony. It gave Britain a power base that was independent of the United States and Europe, and that enabled Britain to maintain its position as the world's foremost commercial and financial center. It became the foundation of

Churchill's doctrine of "three circles," which consisted of the British Commonwealth, the English-speaking world, and a United Europe, with Britain as the only country that had a part in all three circles. It was thought that this would permit Britain to play a world role commensurate with the superpowers, even though it could not match their capabilities.[10] "If we can preserve a comradeship among all the diverse races who are now in the British Commonwealth and who, during the next few years, will increasingly become independent nations, we shall be able to act as a unified force in the world."[11] However, the Commonwealth ideal required good relations with member countries, especially those countries in Asia and Africa that would increasingly form a majority of the membership.[12] Free movement thus played an important part in sustaining this ideal. Imposition of immigration controls, especially if seen as racist, would jeopardize any sense of unity among the Commonwealth countries. It was just this issue, however, that brought questions of the political community and national identity to the fore and that required the articulation of qualities that, until then, had gone without saying because they were considered natural and in no need of elaboration.

Theoretical framework

Hobsbawm suggests that attempts to establish objective criteria for nationhood have failed because they try to fit historically novel, emerging, changing, and far-from-universal entities into a framework of permanence and universality. Even criteria such as ethnicity, cultural traits, and a common history are "themselves fuzzy, shifting and ambiguous." Subjective definitions are equally questionable. Defining a nation by its members' consciousness of belonging to it is tautological.[13] Others, such as Ole Waever, have noted similar problems with both objective and subjective definitions.[14]

These problems point to a certain conceptual ambivalence regarding the nation and national identity. There seems to be a general acknowledgment of the power that inheres in invocations of the nation and national identity, and the slipperiness in precisely defining these things. Homi K. Bhabha has suggested that we think of the identity of "the people," who constitute the inside of nations and to whom national identities are attached, in a conceptual "double-time." The people are on the one hand the pre-given parts of a body politic and the historical objects that give nationalist discourse its power and authority. On the other hand, the people are the effect of a complex rhetorical strategy of social reference in which the claim to be representative provokes a crisis within the process of signification.[15] Constructing the identity of a people is a continual and never-completed project, but it cannot appear as such. In other words, the people must simultaneously be presumed as given and at the same time be continually reproduced. This understanding fits well with recent arguments by critical international relations scholars regarding the inherently unstable and contingent nature of identity and the boundaries separating the inside from the outside.[16] Boundaries are often blurry, and the unity of the inside is continually subject to disruption from the outside. Unitary claims to a national identity permit the convergence of the state and the people. However, this convergence is never totally fixed.[17]

This suggests that amidst the ambiguities of life, the grounds that states would represent, far from being fixed, are socially, politically, and discursively constructed. The construction of foundational grounds occurs through discursive practices that attempt to fix meanings that enable the differentiation to be made between the inside and the outside. It is not possible to say in advance what these meanings are, especially when it comes to differentiating the inside of the nation from the outside, because they are, as Hobsbawm suggests, often historically novel and changing. The identity of the "we" is a flexible political resource, adaptable to changing circumstances and new crises.

A useful way of conceptualizing the inside in contrast to the outside is as a relational totality that constitutes and organizes social relations around a particular structure of meanings. This conceptualization corresponds to Ernesto Laclau's and Chantal Mouffe's definition of a discourse.[18] A discourse may refer to a specific group of texts, but it also refers to the social practices to which those texts are linked. The linguistic and behavioral aspects of social practices form a complex and inextricably connected whole that is a discourse. The discursive practices that construct a discourse include writing, speaking, and practices often considered to be "behavioral," which are embedded in institutions. Discourses generally work toward closure, creating the effect of an inside that is clearly distinguishable from an outside. But they ultimately fail to escape the irresolvable tension between the interior and the exterior, the inside and the outside.[19] It is here at the margins that the attempts to fix meaning and to institute closure often are most evident. This suggests that rather than conceiving the inside

126

and the outside as dichotomous oppositions, it is more useful to think of them as both mutually constitutive and, at least potentially, mutually undermining of one another. This is particularly evident with the constitution of the inside of nations, especially in times of massive population movements when elements from the "outside" are constantly raising questions as to who should be considered on the "inside," that is, the people.

In this study, I am conceptualizing the political community and the identity that is attached to it as a kind of discourse. This conceptualization is consistent with Hobsbawm's proposal that agnosticism is the best initial posture for students of nationality.[20] To suggest that national identity be thought of as a kind of discourse does not assume an a priori definition of the nation. Instead, the definition is allowed to emerge from specific empirical analyses.

The analytic question that needs to be addressed by such a conceptualization is how discourses are constructed. How is the inside, however provisional and permeable, partially fixed? Theorists of the nation have suggested that it is not possible to reduce national identity to a single dimension.[21] The multitude of social identities – gendered, racial, ethnic, and class – can act as constitutive elements in national identity. They can reinforce or undermine it. If national identity cannot be reduced to a single dimension, then how is it constructed? It stands to reason that there must be certain focal points of meaning around which various dimensions converge to form national identity.

Postmodern theorists have suggested that certain privileged discursive points are essential to the partial fixing of meanings and identities. Laclau and Mouffe refer to these as "nodal points," others, such as Jacques Lacan, call them "privileged signifiers," and Derrida calls them "dominant signifiers." One can examine discursive practices to locate these nodal points that act as privileged signifiers and, at least temporarily and provisionally, work to fix meaning, in this case the meaning of national identity. It might be helpful here to give a brief illustration of a "nodal point." We can, for example, imagine a discourse on democracy in which capitalist market principles serve as nodal points. In such a discourse, the meaning of democracy becomes fixed around these nodal points so that democracy and capitalism are inextricably linked; we cannot imagine democracy where market principles are absent.

This study suggests that it is at the margins of a discourse that we can find the privileged discursive points that constitute national identity. Paradoxically, it is also at the margins that the meaning of national identity is subverted. This creates the continual need for production and reproduction of national identity. The international movement of peoples is one concrete site where the interior and exterior tension is particularly evident. Here, the question of who is inside and who is outside the political community arises, as do the criteria by which this distinction can be made. Human migration highlights the salience as well as the ambiguities of national identity. Terms such as "alien," "immigrant," and "refugee" imply something other than a "normal" national identity and, at the same time, act as constitutive elements in the construction of national identities.

A multitude of practices no doubt go into constructing national identities, and the literature suggests that the state plays a particularly significant role in producing and reproducing national identities.[22] It makes sense to focus on practices generally associated with the concept of the state. A more complete analysis would, of course, show how cultural and symbolic resources are important in their own right in constituting national identities, and how these resources are drawn upon by government officials. My goal in this study is more limited. I am looking at the formal and official hegemonic articulations that create the kind of privileged discursive points discussed earlier.

A useful place to look for these is in the legal realm. The law is both an important instrument of the state and an arena of debate: "the formation of valid legal commands constitutes the highest manifestation of sovereignty."[23] Antonio Gramsci stressed the importance of the law, along with other institutions, as an instrument of the state in creating and maintaining a certain type of society and citizen. Paul Gilroy notes the importance of the law's ability to express and represent the nation-state and national identity, and to articulate the very core of national identity.[24] A fundamental way a state can do this is by exercising its legal prerogative to control entry into its territorial boundaries and to concomitantly regulate those permitted to enter. Without this prerogative, the whole idea of a territorially fixed population that forms the basis of the sovereign nation-state would become highly questionable. I am, of course, not suggesting that Britain's physical or legal ability to control entry into its territory was ever in question. What was important was the fact that, in controlling entry, significant issues concerning the definitions of political community and national identity were raised.[25] Debates on British immigration laws have revolved around these issues.

In focusing on immigration laws and the debates surrounding them, I emphasize Michel Foucault's conceptualization of the dual nature of power: the juridical and the productive. The juridical function of power is manifested in law. Its function is to regulate political life in generally negative terms, for example, through limitation, prohibition, regulation, and control. One might think of this as analogous to the coercive aspect of hegemony in the Gramscian sense. The other function of power, however, is productive. By virtue of being subjected to the juridical function, subjects are themselves constructed, defined as particular kinds of subjects, and given particular identities.

As Foucault notes, the law does not fade into the background when power functions productively. Rather, it operates more and more as a norm. The juridical institution is increasingly incorporated into a continuum of apparatuses whose functions are mostly to regulate and discipline.[26] Law, and the state in whose name it acts, does not exist independently of society. Thus, the power of the law is not solely due to the fact that it is ultimately backed by the sword, that is, the coercive power of the state. It is, therefore, not only the discursive practices manifested in legal statutes that create identities, but also the way that these practices are infused with societal norms and values. In examining the discursive production of national identity, one needs to examine not only laws per se, but the debates, interpretations, and professed needs and interests that surround legal statutes and the social practices to which these are linked.

Below I give a brief background discussion of this case and then examine the discursive practices that constructed British national identity in the post-World War II period. I do this through an analysis of debates on immigration from 1958, when the campaign for immigration control gained considerable momentum in large part due to riots in Nottingham and Notting Hill in August and September of that year, to 1971. The 1958 riots brought the issue of Commonwealth immigration to the attention of the national press, politicians, and the public in general. They also highlighted apparent public hostility to continued Commonwealth immigration. The two immediate reactions to the riots were the condemnation of the violence and the assumption that immigration control was the answer.[27] Britain's immigration control laws have remained basically unchanged since 1971. A citizenship act was passed in 1981, but this did not significantly alter what was already in place.

From empire to nation-state: global transformation and national identity

The period following World War II was one of massive global changes ranging from the reconfiguration of global power to rapid decolonization and the creation of new nation-states in Asia and Africa. These transformations converged upon Great Britain and precipitated an identity crisis that some would suggest has not been resolved to this day. Great Britain *was* the British empire. Decolonization shook that identity to the core. The colonial mission and all that it had entailed could no longer serve as the foundation of British identity. The imperial legacy was not significant only for the British elite and policy-makers. The empire was an important reality at all social levels.[28] It was a matter of great pride to belong to a country that ruled an empire spanning the globe. The impact of the empire was felt through literature, education, film, and other cultural media. Literary figures such as Stevenson and Kipling glorified Britain's imperial adventures and enjoyed tremendous popularity. Many Britons also had direct experience of the empire through government and missionary service.

The collapse of the empire was accompanied by a fall from the circle of leading economic powers exacerbating the crisis of identity.[29] International immigration complicated the relationship between Britain's transformation from an imperial power, its economic decline, and its ensuing crisis of identity. The post-World War II period witnessed massive immigrations from what became known as the Third World into advanced industrialized countries in the First World. Much of this immigration was in response to labor shortages. Like many other European countries, Britain experienced a shortage of labor after World War II.[30] Also like many other countries, the solution lay with immigrant labor. In Britain, this took three forms: the recruitment of Polish workers; European Volunteer Workers; and immigration from the "new" Commonwealth territories of the Caribbean, the Indian subcontinent, the Mediterranean, the Far East, and Africa. This third form was by far the largest, the most significant, and the one that precipitated the debates and controversy, leading to a series of legislative acts that placed increasingly strict controls on immigration. When these "new" Commonwealth immigrants, who were considered British citizens, started coming in sufficient numbers, it led to debates about who should be permitted entry, who was a citizen, and who should enjoy what rights and privileges – in other words, who was "really"

British and who belonged within the nation-state. Post-World War II debates on immigration control can be located within this context of concern with British identity.

Britain and Commonwealth immigration

Immigration is the most important subject facing this country but I cannot get any of my ministers to take any notice.

(Winston Churchill, 1954)[31]

Before 1962, the relationship between citizenship and immigration in Britain was relatively straightforward. British subjects, including anyone born in the empire, were free from immigration control.[32] Underlying this freedom of movement was an ideology consisting of two nineteenth-century ideals: the Commonwealth ideal, whereby every Commonwealth citizen was considered a British subject and thus assured free entry into the mother country; and liberal laissez-faire economic principles that required a free market in labor.[33] With the end of empire, the Commonwealth idea became an important element in British national identity. It helped the British assuage a "sense of personal loss – almost an amputation," which occurred whenever a part of it was granted independence.[34] It also was regarded as a source of moral leadership. The Commonwealth ideology held that all citizens of the British empire were equal subjects of the crown and no distinctions of race or color could be admitted. Free movement posed no problem for the doctrine of solidarity and universal brother-hood as long as this was predominantly from the "old" dominions (Australia, Canada, and New Zealand), also referred to as the "white" dominions. Things began to change with the change in composition of immigration. The "rising tide" of "colored" immigration led to increasing social unease about immigration and political agitation for its control. Thus began a steady move toward an ever more restrictive position on immigration.

Subsequent legislation placed strict limitations on non-white, non-European immigration from the new Commonwealth (former colonies other than Australia, New Zealand, and Canada). The first controls were placed on Commonwealth immigration by The Commonwealth Immigrants Act of 1962 which was passed by a conservative government. This Act broke with the ideals attached to the Commonwealth idea of unity, brotherhood, and equality and served as the precedent for further restrictive legislation. Under the 1962 Act, those with

Commonwealth passports had to apply for a work voucher. Three categories of work voucher were created: category A for employers with a specific job for a Commonwealth citizen; category B for skilled applicants; and category C for all others. In addition, for the first time, Commonwealth citizens could be deported, but only after a court recommendation.[35]

The Labour Party vehemently opposed this Act, citing the obvious, but not explicit, racial content. In debates preceding passage, Labour Party member Gordon Walker referred to the Act as "bare-faced, open race discrimination" that would "do irreparable damage to the Commonwealth."[36] Although the Act was to apply to all Commonwealth immigrants, Gordon pointed out that "the net effect of the Bill is that a negligible number of white people will be kept out and almost all those kept out by the Bill will be coloured people."[37] Despite the lack of official reference to race, the coded language was recognized by the opposition Labour Party. "To use the words we hear so often, 'the social strains and stresses,' in simpler and rather cruder language, that phrase really means colour prejudice."[38]

Despite their strong opposition and their pledge to repeal the Act if they took over government, the Labour Party's position on immigration by 1965 tended to converge with the Conservative Party's position. By 1965, the Labour Party had fully accepted the Conservative Party case for controls on non-white immigration and had implemented even greater controls by eliminating category C work vouchers.[39] The British government now presented a united face in favor of strict immigration control. The Commonwealth Immigrants Act of 1968 placed further restrictions on non-white immigration. The 1962 Act did not affect the United Kingdom and Colonies (UKC). This second category of citizen had been created earlier by the 1948 Nationality Act, provided that their passports had been issued by the United Kingdom and not on behalf of it by a governor. Prompted by the crisis in Kenya revolving around the expulsion of Asians holding British passports and the fear of massive Asian immigration, the 1968 Act stripped such persons in East Africa of the automatic right to enter and settle in Britain unless they had a connection to Britain by birth, naturalization, or descent.[40] The effect of this Act was to create a new class of citizens who were, in effect, stateless.

Further restrictions were introduced in the Immigration Act of 1971 that ended the distinction between the category of "alien," which had been created by earlier immigration acts, and Commonwealth citizens.

The aim of this legislation was to maintain strict control over new Commonwealth immigration, but to permit the entry of those persons living in Commonwealth countries who were of British descent. This legislation introduced the now infamous category of "patrial." A patrial was someone whose parent or grandparent was born in the United Kingdom. Those in this category enjoyed the right of free entry and indefinite stay. Patrials could settle and apply for United Kingdom passports. They were not liable to deportation and were entitled to vote, run for office, work in nationalized industries, and enlist in the armed forces. The category of patrial was important, not just in relation to immigration into the UK, but because patrials constituted a class of citizens entitled to the benefits of European Community (EC) membership as UK nationals under the 1972 Treaty of Accession between the UK and the European Economic Community (EEC). The vast majority who fell within this category were white.[41]

The only major legislation that has altered immigration since 1971 is the British Nationality Act of 1981. Three categories of citizenship were created by this Act: (1) British citizens, people with a close personal connection with the United Kingdom, either because their parents or grandparents were born, adopted, naturalized, or registered as citizens of the UK, or through permanent settlement in the UK; (2) citizens of British Dependent Territories, people who are British citizens because of their own or their parents' or grandparents' birth, naturalization, or registration, or registration in an existing dependency or associated state; and (3) British Overseas Citizenship, a largely formal category with few privileges and no automatic right of entry.

Analysis

> ... the demand for a holistic, representative vision of society could only be represented in a discourse that was at the same time obsessively fixed upon and uncertain of the boundaries of society.
>
> (Homi Bhabha, 1990)[42]

Several important analytic points can be made regarding this case. It has been suggested that the migration and settlement of hundreds of thousands of people from the New Commonwealth was one of the most important social and political developments in postwar Britain.[43] In one sense, this issue can be viewed as "domestic," which involves state and society relations. This had important implications for the legitimacy of the British state and its institutions in terms of its claim to represent and act on behalf of the British people. This case also relates to understanding processes of state expansion. The presence of Commonwealth immigrants led to the creation of new state agencies. Even before the 1971 Act went into effect, a new national police unit concerned with immigration was set up within the Metropolitan Police, the Illegal Immigration Intelligence Unit.[44] This unit worked in close connection with the Central Drugs Intelligence Unit. The 1971 Act also gave police wide powers of arrest without a warrant in cases of suspected illegal entry, breach of conditions of entry, and harboring an illegal entrant. The effect of this was an expansion of the state into areas previously considered part of the "private" realm, for example, the implementation of various race relations acts, and the surveillance and control of the immigrant population as illustrated in "passport raids," and investigation into "marriages of convenience."[45]

This case also had an international dimension, illustrating links across domestic and international levels of analysis. Britain was attempting to carve out for itself a position within an international system undergoing significant changes. Britain's own domestic transformations affected this position. This period of time was marked by new conceptualizations of the world. It was the beginning of not only conceptualizing international relations along an East–West axis, but also along a North–South axis. Changes in international arrangements, norms, and bases of legitimation were linked to domestic conflict and fears of decline and social disorder in Britain.

Such claims are undoubtedly true. Yet, they unwittingly defer an important question. To point to the domestic and international relevance of this issue assumes an unproblematic domestic and international, inside and outside dichotomy and it defers the question of the construction of this dichotomy itself. This replicates what policymakers themselves were doing, which can be best illustrated by examining the specifics of the discourses in this case.

The discussions and debates revolving around immigration control during the period examined above reveal two major discourses: the Commonwealth discourse of inclusion, and a right-wing, anti-immigrant discourse of exclusion. These two discourses were mutually subversive of one another. Each had the potential to destabilize the other. Yet, as suggested earlier, discourses are never fully closed. There exists an irresolvable tension between the interior and exterior of a discourse. It is possible to find points where the interior and exterior of a particular discourse blur and overlap with another discourse. The overlap in these two discourses created a space for the articulation of several themes by which meanings were fixed and which created a new discourse – the immigration discourse. It was within this new discourse that the identity of the British "people" was constructed and reconstructed.

The Commonwealth discourse

The Commonwealth discourse was one of inclusion expressing universalistic aspirations of an "international brotherhood of man" and common citizenship for all peoples of the Commonwealth. One could locate within this discourse the potential construction of a new social and political identity not based on national territorial boundaries. While often associated predominantly with the Labour Party, members of both the Conservative and Labour Parties participated in the Commonwealth discourse.[46] Public opinion on the value of the Commonwealth idea in Britain also agreed with British leaders.[47]

One of the most important and consequential ideals of the Commonwealth was manifested in the fact that there was no distinction between the citizenship status of Britons at home or overseas. They all shared a common allegiance to Britain, which involved obligations and duties such as obedience to established authority and English law, as well as commitments such as service in war. As discussed above, the privilege of free entry for all citizens was codified in the 1948 Act. The Conservative Party had opposed this Act, not because it opposed equal status or free entry for Commonwealth immigrants but because it thought the Act was unnecessary. The party opposed the creation of two categories of citizens, even though these two categories were equal, because it thought this would create the potential for giving primacy to local citizenship and undermining Commonwealth unity.

While ostensibly a discourse of inclusion, equality, and universalism, the Commonwealth discourse nonetheless contained its own inherent limitation. Derrida's notion of exemplarity is useful here in clarifying the relationship between the universal and the particular found within this discourse. Derrida suggests that the value of universality is always "linked to the value of exemplarity that inscribes the universal in the proper body of a singularity, of an idiom or a culture, whether this singularity be individual, social, national, state, federal, confederal."[48] In the Commonwealth discourse, Britain itself was the embodiment of exemplarity. The Commonwealth, while embracing universalistic ideals, was a singularly British idea and achievement. "The Empire and Commonwealth is the supreme achievement of the British People and the most successful experiment in international relations that the world has ever known."[49]

As the "mother country," Britain was the advanced point of exemplarity. A major theme in this discourse was that of national greatness, which coexisted uneasily with the theme of international brotherhood. The Commonwealth ideal was a successor to the ideal of the empire and shared some of its most important features, particularly its moralistic paternalism. This is evident in the words of one of its most ardent supporters:

> *We* are responsible for *them*, and they think of themselves, as anybody who has been there knows, as British people. Oh yes they do. It is rather moving. I found when I was there that *they* look on *us* as the Mother Country in a very real sense.
> (Gaitskell, Member of Labour Party, House of Commons, 1961).[50]

We/they, us/them presumes a difference that at the same time is denied by the Commonwealth ideal. Here we find a tension between universalism and particularism, as well as identity and difference that involves on the one hand the claim that "we" and "they" are the same, a universal brotherhood of man, and on the other hand the claim of difference that is implicit in these terms. This tension could be held at bay, and the question of what this difference was could be deferred as long as most of "them" stayed "there." But when "they" came to the "mother country" in large enough numbers the tension approached its limit.

The relationship between this discourse of inclusion and the presence of Commonwealth immigrants illustrates the kind of relationship between the inside and the outside outlined earlier where each is simultaneously mutually constitutive and mutually undermining of the other. Laclau and Mouffe define this relationship as one of antagonism, that is, a situation in which "the presence of the 'other' prevents me from being totally myself."[51] Antagonism includes the notion of a constitutive outside, which blocks the identity of the inside but is nonetheless the prerequisite for its constitution.[52] Such was the situation in Britain. The universalism of the Commonwealth ideal was itself constituted by the particularism that was evident in the presumptions made about the essence of the British national character, the British people, and the British nation. At the same time, these presumptions prevented universalism, in the form of the Commonwealth ideal, from fully constituting itself because it depended upon a "we/them" opposition. Indeed, these presumptions were shared by the anti-immigrant, right-wing discourse and created the openings by which this latter discourse became hegemonic, and was able to articulate the nodal points, around which the immigration issue was framed.

Right-wing anti-immigrant discourse

This discourse was a particularistic, exclusionary, nationalist one that stressed the indigenous essence of the British people who were threatened by an "invasion" of immigrants from the Commonwealth. This was exemplified by Conservative Party member Cyril Osborne who said, "I do not like to regard the Irish as immigrants. I regard them as British as I am,"[53] and later by the right-wing extremist Enoch Powell. Less extreme views were also party to this discourse. Conservative Home Secretary Butler stated, "The objective here is to excerpt from control – and therefore, to guarantee their continued unrestricted entry into their own country – persons who in *common parlance belong to the UK*."[54]

These remarks can be read as inclusionary instead of exclusionary because they are based on the presumption that there are some who "belong to the UK." and should be regarded as "as British as I am." However, the criteria for belonging remain ambiguous and are made clear only vis-à-vis the racialized "other" who does not belong.

This is evident in the remarks of Labour Party Member Frank Tomney:

> The coloured races will exceed the white races in a few years' time by no less than five to one. This will be a formidable problem for the diminishing numbers of the white races throughout the world. There is a constant dread of the people that the immigrants are seemingly better served than the indigenous population. These are facts which we can ignore only at our own peril.[55]

In general the anti-immigrant discourse focused on three aspects of immigration: the numbers of people, health, and crime. The use of numbers was prevalent throughout as illustrated in the following:

> Because of the sheer weight of these numbers something must be done quickly or there will be such tragedies as will frighten most of us. Difficult and frightening as are the figures of immigrants from West Indies they pale in significance compared with the figures for

the first six months from India and Pakistan. They are really terrifying in their significance.[56]

Explicit in playing this "numbers game" was the idea that fewer Commonwealth immigrants would make better race relations in Britain. The problem could then be defined in terms of the presence of non-white people rather than the responses of the white population. Numbers were used as scare tactics. They served to signify the breakdown of unity and identity rather than to describe any concrete situation. For example, immigrants from Ireland totaled approximately 60,000 to 70,000 annually, while Commonwealth immigrants totaled only 43,000 in 1955 and 21,000 in 1959.[57] Precisely what the "sheer weight of numbers" signified was rather ambiguous. Similarly, phrases such as "keep the flow within reasonable bounds," "uncontrolled immigration," "flood of immigrants," "people pour into this country," "necessity to control the tide" did not point to any concrete reality, but were metaphors that summoned up images of chaos, disorder, and loss of control.

There were also extensive references to the health situation, carrying with them implications of dirt, contamination, and even moral decay. Suggestions were made that Commonwealth immigrants did "not always conform to our ideas of sanitation."[58]

Similarly, the theme of crime was prevalent throughout. Even those opposed to strict immigration control focused on this theme:

> certain types of immigrants possess a propensity to live on the immoral earnings of women and to traffic in dangerous drugs.[59]

> For example, colonial and Commonwealth immigrants are responsible for practically the whole of the drug traffic in this country.[60]

Immigrants also were tied to criminality through the creation and linking of the Illegal Immigration Intelligence Unit and the Central Drugs Unit.[61] These two mutually subversive discourses indicate ostensibly opposed understandings of British national identity; one a universalist, inclusive one, the other an exclusionary, particularistic one. As suggested above, the relationship was not one of pure opposition but rather a mutually constitutive relationship. The invocation of the concept of the British nation and British national character by all parties to the debates created a space for the rearticulation of British national identity. As noted earlier, the anti-immigrant discourse was able to articulate the basic points around which the immigration issue became framed. How this was possible, given the fierce opposition to the 1962 bill and the recognition of it as blatantly (if silently) racist, can be understood in terms of how meanings were fixed around the nodal points of nation and race. Nation and race were the framework for a discourse of order and security. Insecurity and disorder, including national economic decline and decline as a world power, became linked with a dilution of Britishness that was associated with Commonwealth immigration.[62]

While the Commonwealth ideal for all intents died by 1965, it would be too simplistic to suggest that the right-wing, anti-immigrant discourse simply "won." For example, immigrants were not repatriated en masse. Some pro-immigrant legislation came about, for example, a Race Relations Act of 1965 and another one in 1976. The overall result was the turning of boundaries between the inside and the outside into what Bhabha refers to as "in-between spaces through which the meanings of cultural and political authority are negotiated."[63] This is discussed in more detail in the following section.

The immigration discourse

> Surely it is not illiberal for people to be concerned with preserving their own national character and continuity. A question which affects the future of our own race and breed is not one that we should leave merely to chance.[64]

While the right-wing discourse was hegemonic in the sense that it was able to frame the terms in which the immigration issue would be discussed, debated, and acted upon, it was by no means fully closed, fixed, and immune from its exterior. As suggested above, the result was more akin to a constant process of negotiation.

Immigration had raised the issue of who was to count as a British citizen and what this meant. It was presumed by participants to both discourses that there were some discoverable criteria by which one could unproblematically represent what was internal to British identity and what was external to it. It was possible to distinguish the "authentic" British from the "inauthentic." The categorizations explicit in the immigration acts, along with the societal norms and values with which they were linked, were attempts to get at this foundation, this essence of British national identity. The continual reworking of the laws indicated the difficulties inherent in this endeavor, yet people assumed that it was ultimately possible to discover such a foundation.

The immigration discourse illustrates the attempt to construct and reconstruct that foundation. The theme of national greatness at the heart of the Commonwealth discourse overlapped with the right-wing discourse in its presumption of an essential, eternal, and great British nation. It created an opening within which certain themes could be articulated and linked in response to the uncertainty of that identity created by the decline of British empire, economic decline, and the increasing presence of "others" within. Commonwealth immigrants became linked with disorder, loss of authority and control, national decline, dilution of the British national character and living standards, and the decline of Britain as a world power.

What occurred simultaneously with the process of exclusion associated with the increasingly restrictive immigration laws was a process of incorporating Commonwealth immigrants who were already in Britain. Integration of Commonwealth immigrants became a prime concern. This was accompanied by an increasing concern with race relations and discrimination against immigrants. Several statutory agencies – a Race Relations Board, a Community Relations Commission, and local committees – were set up by the Race Relations Act of 1965 and the Acts of 1968 and 1976. The rhetoric revolving around these Acts also was framed in terms of public order and security. Order and security tended to be related inversely to large numbers of non-white people. Dispersal became regarded as necessary for improved race relations.

> social strains tend to develop, as the House knows, where there are large concentrations of coloured people in large towns and cities, and so far as possible coloured immigrants should be enabled to disperse themselves throughout the community instead of congregating together.[65]

> Therefore, I would say that we should be selective in our attitude towards the immigrants whom we take in and to welcome, in particular, those who seek dispersal, that is to say those who do not seek or do not wish to live, for social or cultural or religious reasons, in their own community.[66]

The immigration discourse exemplifies what Bhabha refers to as a process of hybridity, which is the problem of the relationship between the inside and the outside.[67] At the same time that stable foundations, identifying the "authentic" British, were being constructed, elements from the outside were being incorporated into the inside. This suggests that perhaps the power of national identity derives not from the existence of a foundational center, but from the lack of a center that permits a continual process of definition and redefinition, of both exclusion and incorporation. The desire for such a foundation was illustrated in the continual attempt to specify what that foundation was. This attempt, coupled with the ultimate impossibility of arriving at that foundation, created the space that enabled the construction and reconstruction of British national identity. This space consisted of the articulation of meaning around the nodal points of "race" and "nation," which are somewhat ambiguous concepts.

This case illustrates Bhabha's suggestion quoted above, that "the demand for a holistic, representative vision of society could only be represented in a discourse that was at the same time obsessively fixed upon and uncertain of the boundaries of society."[68] British discourse on the new Commonwealth immigration was obsessively fixed upon but uncertain of the boundaries of society. The "immigrant" was deployed as a site for the reconstruction of British identity, for Britain's retrieval of greatness, which was only possible vis-à-vis its "other." "People with a different culture" became the site upon which fears of national decline, loss of empire, and internal disorder could be articulated. This is only too evident in Thatcher's famous "swamping" remark. "People are really rather afraid that this country might be rather swamped by people with a different culture and you know, the British character has done so much for democracy, for law and done so much throughout the world."[69]

Conclusion

In the introduction to this chapter, I suggested that perhaps statecraft is not primarily about relations between different state units, but about the construction and reconstruction of the units themselves. A social constructivist analysis of sovereignty arrives at this important aspect of statecraft by enabling alternative kinds of questions that focus on how practices construct various components such as "the people." In this chapter, I have suggested that the construction of the inside versus the outside of nations is a function of a state's discursive authority and power, that is, its ability to fix meaning and identity in relatively stable ways. It is during times of crisis, when the naturalness of the given order is shaken, that this *sovereignty effect* emerges. Britain's transformation from empire to nation-state occurred during such a period of crisis. What "British" signified was the subject of debate between those who held onto the Commonwealth ideal and those who favored a retreat to "little England." The power to fix meanings and identity was evident in the overlap between the two ostensibly opposed discourses.

Thinking of sovereignty as an effect, a contingent political effect broadens our understanding of sovereignty and the situations that can be considered threats to a state's sovereignty.[70] Sovereignty becomes not so much an ontological problem that questions what sovereignty *is*. Rather, it becomes a question of determining what issues, uncertainties, and transformations elicit responses in discursive practices that attempt to fix meanings and social/political identities. It is also a question of what are the consequences of these practices are. If sovereignty is understood solely as a state's "externally recognized right to exercise final authority over its own affairs," British sovereignty was, of course, never in jeopardy.[71] However, this understanding of sovereignty presumes the very things that *were* in doubt: the internal and external divide and the differentiation of the inside from the outside of the British nation-state. A broadened understanding of sovereignty is necessary to permit the examination of such issues, which are arguably increasingly salient in the post-Cold War era.

The opening quotes to this chapter are meant to suggest that the problematic nature of national identity is not confined to this particular case. Scholars as diverse as Schlesinger and Derrida agree on this point. Other European countries, especially former colonial powers, experienced similar situations in important respects to the one examined in this chapter. This is not to suggest that all cases are identical, either in terms of precipitating factors or in terms of state and nonstate responses. We can learn from this case. It has been argued that the history of the late twentieth and early twenty-first centuries will be written as "the history of a world which can no longer be contained within the limits of 'nations' and 'nation-states,' as these used to be defined either politically, or economically, or culturally."[72] I do not interpret this to imply that these things will simply disappear. Instead, it suggests that there are global forces that may threaten to diminish the importance of these things, and that this can result in a "politics of identity," whereby attempts are made to produce "sovereignty effects," such as practices that seek to reaffirm the foundational elements of belonging to one group as opposed to another, and to exclude those represented as "other." The international migration of peoples is an example of such a force.

If Hobsbawm's prognosis is correct, the times we face are ones in which it will be more difficult to unambiguously signify something

142

like a national identity. It is during such times that practices seeking to do so seem to proliferate. These practices are, of course, not without consequences. For example, xenophobia and a kind of racism inextricably linked with national identity appear to be on the rise today.[73] This inevitably involves the apparatuses of the state. As this study clearly shows, an important issue is determining the inside of nation-states from the outside. Without this distinction, the foundational element of state sovereignty, the nation, is missing. Perhaps it is not so critical to arrive at definitive understandings of important concepts such as national identity, the state, or sovereignty. Perhaps the critical questions revolve around determining the issues and uncertainties that elicit sovereignty-producing practices. Conventional international relations theory is ill-equipped to deal with these issues because the social construction of the various components of sovereignty has not been considered a centrally important aspect of statecraft and hence not a worthwhile scholarly endeavor.

The analysis undertaken in this chapter and the theoretical foundations upon which it rests offer a middle path between those who see state sovereignty as an eternal attribute of global politics and those who stress its imminent demise. Sovereignty as a contingent political effect suggests that the social construction of sovereignty is always in process, and is a never completed project whose successful production never can be counted on totally. This, I believe, is what Bhabha is referring to when he suggests, as noted earlier, that we think of the people in a conceptual double-time, as presumed and always in the process of being produced. The British case nicely illustrates the usefulness of this concept. It is useful to suggest that the practices of statecraft are more general and can be described accurately in this conceptual double-time. These practices are continual and simultaneous, while presuming and constructing the very things that are being presumed, such as spatial boundaries, political authority, and the identity of the people.

Notes

[1] Schlesinger, Arthur M., Jr. 1992. *The Disuniting of America – Reflections on a Multicultural Society.* New York: W.W. Norton, p. 17.

[2] Derrida, Jacques 1992. *The Other Heading: Reflections on Today's Europe.* Bloomington: Indiana University Press, p. 5.

[3] The issue of national identity is at least implicit in the increasing attention devoted to the issue of immigration and the problematic nature of controlling and/or redefining national boundaries. The following are illustrative. In

August of 1992, it was suggested that one of the threats Europeans sensed to their national communities was the growing number of immigrants in their countries. See 1992. *World Press Review* 39: 3. Similarly, it has been suggested that the United States is no longer a nation-state, but rather a multicultural society. See Kurth, James 1992. "The Post-Modern State," *The National Interest* 28: 33. The issue of national identity is, of course, salient in Eastern Europe and the former Soviet republics. See "Baltic Identity: Russians Wonder if They Belong," *New York Times*, 22 November 1992. Scholarly attention to issues of national identity can be found in the literature on nationalism, a topic which mainstream international relations has seriously neglected. On the issue of borders see 1992. "Europe at the Gates," *The Economist* 325:59; *The Atlantic*, May and June 1992, special issues on the US/Mexican border. Mainstream international relations theory has taken national borders as given and unproblematic.

[4] Held, David and McGrew, David 1993. "Globalization and the Liberal Democratic State," *Government and Opposition* 28:261–88. Held and McGrew suggest that the categories of the state, the nation-state, and the nation are used interchangeably, even though they refer to distinct conceptual entities. Mastanduno, Michael, Lake, David A., Ikenberry, G. John December 1989. "Toward a realist Theory of State Action," *International Studies Quarterly* 33:457–74 engage in an internal critique of structural realism in suggesting that the collapsing of the state and the nation-state into one entity by structural-realists has eliminated domestic policy and structures as relevant considerations. Others, such as Ashley, Richard K. and Walker, R.B.J. September 1990. "Reading Dissidence/Writing the Discipline: Crisis and the Question of Sovereignty in International Studies," *International Studies Quarterly* 34:367–416 suggest more profound consequences.

[5] Smith, Anthony D. 1992. "National Identity and the Idea of European Unity," *International Affairs* 68: 55–76, at p. 62.

[6] Conversation with Richard Ashley.

[7] Walker, R.J.B. 1993. *Inside/Outside: International Relations as Political Theory.* Cambridge: Cambridge University Press, p. 166.

[8] See Ashley, Richard K. 1988. "Untying the Sovereign State: A Double Reading of the Anarchy Problematique," *Millennium: Journal of International Studies* 17: 227–62; Ashley and Walker, "Reading Dissidence," pp. 368–77; and Walker, *Inside/Outside,* chap. 8.

[9] See Layton-Henry, Zig 1984. *The Politics of Race in Britain.* London: Allen & Unwin, pp. 33–5.

[10] Blank, Stephen 1978. "Britain: The Politics of Foreign Economic Policy, Economic Policy, the Domestic Economy, and the Problem of Pluralistic Stagnation," in Katzenstein, Peter J. (ed.) *Between Power and Plenty: Foreign Economic Policies of Advanced Industrialized States.* Madison: University of Wisconsin Press; Frankel, Joseph 1975. *British Foreign Policy 1945–1973.* London: Oxford University Press, pp. 96, 157, 222.

[11] Ede, House of Commons, 6 February 1962.

[12] Layton-Henry, *The Politics of Race*, p. 33.

[13] Hobsbawm, Eric J. 1992. *Nations and Nationalism Since 1780*. Cambridge: Cambridge University Press, pp. 5–6, 8.

[14] Waever, Ole, Buzan, Barry, and Kelstrup, Morton 1993. *Identity, Migration, and the New Security Agenda in Europe*. London: Pinter Publishers Ltd.

[15] Bhabha, Homi K. 1990. "DissemiNation: Time, Narrative, and the Margins of the Modern Nation," in H.K. Bhabha (ed.) *Nation and Narration*. London: Routledge, p. 298.

[16] R.B.J. Walker has written extensively about the problematic nature of the inside/outside dichotomy. See especially Walker, *Inside/Outside*, chap. 8.

[17] Ibid., p. 170.

[18] Laclau, Ernesto and Mouffe, Chantal 1985. *Hegemony and Socialist Strategy – Towards a Radical Democratic Politics*. London and New York: Verso, p. 96.

[19] Ibid., especially chap. 3.

[20] Hobsbawm, *Nations and Nationalism Since 1780*, p. 8.

[21] Ibid., pp. 8–11; Smith, "National Identity and the Idea of European Unity," 55–76.

[22] Breuilly, John 1982. *Nationalism and the State*. New York: St. Martin's Press, p. 374 suggests that "the identity of the nation will be related to 'tradition' and to existing cultural practices, but the decisions as to what is relevant and how it should be used in establishing the national identity will rest with the state." Smith, Anthony D. 1991. "The Nation: Invented, Imagined, Reconstructed?" *Millennium: Journal of International Studies* 20: 353–68 suggests that if the narratives and imagery of the nation created by the intelligentsia are to assume concrete shape and be turned into institutions, the organs of the state are required. Smith also suggests that "in many parts of Africa and Asia, it is the state itself, through its economic policies, its political patronage and mass education systems, that seeks, with varying success, to create and narrate the emergent nation." I would not argue with this, but would add that it is not only in Africa and Asia that this takes place.

[23] Poggi, Gianfranco 1990. *The State: Its Nature, Development and Prospects*. Cambridge: Polity Press, p. 30.

[24] Gilroy, Paul 1987. *There Ain't No Black in the Union Jack – The Cultural Politics of Race and Nation*. Chicago: University of Chicago Press, p. 74; Gramsci, Antonio 1985. *Selections from the Prison Notebooks*. Edited and translated by Quinton Hoare and Geoffrey Nowell Smith. New York: International Publishers, p. 246.

[25] This issue of states' ability to control their borders seems to be one of contemporary concern. The cause of concern is not loss of border controls but the issues raised by the exercise of such controls. Heisler, Martin O. and Layton-Henry, Zig 1993. "Migration and the Links Between Social and Societal Security," in Waever, *Identity, Migration, and the New Security Agenda*, suggest that this issue is one of current relevance to Europe and North America. States are not losing the ability to control their borders in a physical sense. The important issues revolve around the social and moral costs of doing so.

Roxanne Lynn Doty

[26] Foucault, Michel 1980. *History of Sexuality*, vol. I. New York: Vintage Books, p. 144.

[27] Layton-Henry, *Politics of Race*, pp. 35–6.

[28] Frankel, *British Foreign Policy*, p. 221–2; Layton-Henry, *Politics of Race*, pp. 7–9.

[29] Freeman, Gary P. 1979. *Immigrant Labor and Racial Conflict in Industrial Societies: The French and British Experiences 1945–1975*. Princeton: Princeton University Press, p. 290.

[30] Gordon, Paul 1985. *Policing Immigration*. London: Pluto Press, p. 14.

[31] Quoted in Layton-Henry, *Politics of Race*, p. 33.

[32] In 1948, Britain reaffirmed the right of all Commonwealth citizens to enter the UK without restriction. The British Nationality Act of 1948 arose from the perceived necessity to clarify and codify the status of persons in the newly independent countries that were creating their own citizenship laws, especially the European settlers there. This Act created two primary categories of British citizenship: (1) citizenship of former colonies that were now independent Commonwealth countries and (2) citizenship of the "United Kingdom and Colonies" (UKC), i.e. the rest of what had been the British empire. Freeman, *Immigrant Labor and Racial Conflict*, pp. 37, 46; Bevan, Vaughan 1986. *The Development of British Immigration Law*. London: Croom Helm, p. 77.

[33] Patterson, Sheila 1969. *Immigration and Race Relations in Britain 1960–1967*. London: Oxford University Press, p. 17.

[34] Frankel, *British Foreign Policy*, p. 225; Strachey, John 1959. *The End of Empire*. New York: Praeger, p. 204.

[35] The Commonwealth Immigrants Act of 1968.

[36] Hansards Parliamentary Debates, House of Commons, 16 November 1961.

[37] House of Commons, 16 November 1961.

[38] Fisher, House of Commons, 16 November 1961.

[39] Gordon, *Policing Immigration*, p. 16; Freeman, *Immigrant Labor and Racial Conflict*, p. 55; Bevan, *Development of British Immigration Law*, p. 79; 1965 White Paper, Command Paper 2739, *Immigration from the Commonwealth*.

[40] Cite 1968 Act, Bevan, *Development of British Immigration Law*, pp. 80–1.

[41] Cite 1971 Act, ibid., p. 83.

[42] Bhabha, "DissemiNation, " p. 296.

[43] Layton-Henry, *Politics of Race*.

[44] Gordon, *Policing Immigration*, pp. 14–24.

[45] Ibid., p. 22.

[46] Foot, Paul 1965. *Immigration and Race in British Politics*. Middlesex: Penguin; Reeves, Frank 1983. *British Racial Discourse*. Cambridge: Cambridge University Press.

[47] Frankel, *British Foreign Policy*, p. 223.

[48] Derrida, *The Other Heading*, p. xxvi.

[49] Quoted in Layton-Henry, *Politics of Race*, p. 14.

[50] House of Commons, 16 November 1961, emphasis added.

[51] Laclau and Mouffe, *Hegemony and Socialist Strategy*, p. 125.

146

[52] Laclau, Ernesto 1990. *New Reflections on the Revolution of Our Time.* London: Verso, p. 17.

[53] Cyril Osborne, House of Commons, 23 March 1965, p. 402.

[54] Hansards Parliamentary Debates, House of Commons, 16 November 1961, p. 695, emphasis added.

[55] Hansards Parliamentary Debates, 5 December 1958, p. 1689.

[56] Hansards Parliamentary Debates, 1 August 1961, pp. 1320–1.

[57] Miles, Robert and Phizacklea, Annie 1984. *White Man's Country – Racism in British Politics.* London: Pluto Press, p. 41.

[58] Hansards Parliamentary Debates, 17 February 1961, p. 1955.

[59] Ibid., pp. 1422–5.

[60] Ibid., p. 46.

[61] Ibid., p. 1967.

[62] Gilroy's book, *There Ain't No Black in the Union Jack,* supports this notion.

[63] Bhabha, "DissemiNation," p. 4.

[64] Quoted from *The Tablet*, a Catholic publication, at the House of Commons in Hansards Parliamentary Debates, 5 December 1958, p. 1563.

[65] Frank Soskice, Home Department Secretary of State, at the House of Commons in Hansards Parliamentary Debates, vol. 711, 3 May 1965, p. 934.

[66] J. Vaughan-Morgan at the House of Commons in Hansards Parliamentary Debates, 23 March 1965, p. 359.

[67] Bhabha, "DissemiNation," 298.

[68] Ibid., p. 296.

[69] Margaret Thatcher. Spoken in a television interview to Gordon Burns on Granada Television's *World in Action*, 30 January 1978. Quoted in House of Common Debates, 31 January 1978, p. 240.

[70] Ashley and Walker, "Reading Dissidence," p. 275.

[71] The resolution of these issues did actually have implications for sovereignty as understood more conventionally. If the Commonwealth ideal had prevailed and all Commonwealth citizens were British citizens in every sense, then the inside of the British nation-state would be much broader and "its own affairs" would be more extensive. For example, an act of aggression against a Commonwealth member might be considered Britain's "own affairs." Related to this, Frankel, *British Foreign Policy*, notes the difference in levels of involvement by Britain in the Indo-Pakistani conflicts in 1965 when the Commonwealth idea was still alive and in 1971 when it was basically dead.

[72] Hobsbawm, *Nations and Nationalism*, p. 191.

[73] See, for example, Balibar, Etienne and Wallerstein, Immanuel 1988. *Race, Nation, Class – Ambiguous Identities.* London: Verso, and Hobsbawm, *Nations and Nationalism*, p. 170. These authors suggest that xenophobia has become the most widespread mass ideology in the world.

6   Sovereignty, nationalism, and regional order in the Arab states system

Michael Barnett

In the first address to the French Parliament by a US president since Woodrow Wilson, President Clinton spoke in June 1994 of the growing challenge posed by nationalism to democracy and international stability. In contrast to Wilson, who went to Paris after the war to champion the idea of national self-determination as the foundation for a more just and stable international order, Clinton arrived after the Cold War to warn that nationalism frequently leads to humanitarian nightmares and international instability. At present, nationalism is identified less with cultural autonomy, freedom, democracy, and sovereignty than it is with chauvinism, expansionism, and assaults on the Westphalian order. If few practitioners or students of security politics fully considered during the Cold War the importance of nationalism, they have been forced into this consideration by the fact that some of the most important sources of regional and international instability are clearly rooted in contending national and ethnic claims and the failure of the state to capture the loyalties of its citizens.[1] Scholars and policymakers are less likely to write of nation-states than they are of nations against states.

The explosive mix of nationalism and state sovereignty is well known to students of Arab politics. Since the beginning of the Arab states system in the 1940s, there has been a vigorous debate over the meaning of Arab nationalism and its implication for inter-Arab practices. Two positions emerged. Perhaps most famous were Arab nationalists who claimed that the Arab state's authority derives not from its citizens, but from the Arab nation that envelops its borders. Far from content with the territorial division of the Arab world and the principle of sovereignty to govern interstate relations, these individuals demanded a political relationship that would be consistent with the interests of the Arabs rather than the West. They also urged Arab states to develop close economic, cultural, and security ties, and contemplated erasing their territorial boundaries to bring them into line with the state and the nation.

Others championed interpretations of Arab nationalism that were consistent with the territorial division of the Arab world and the exclusivity associated with sovereignty. They asserted that the Arab states system should be organized to protect the Arab state's security and to allow each to pursue its own *raison d'état* without necessarily jeopardizing the security of other Arab states. King Hussein of Jordan contrasted his understanding of Arab nationalism and how the Arab world should be organized from that of Egyptian President Nasser in the following way: "My own concept ... is quite different from Nasser's ... He believes that Arab nationalism can only be identified by a particular brand of Arab unity ... I disagree ... Arab nationalism can only survive through complete equality."[2] In general, while all Arab leaders identified themselves as Arab nationalists and advocated Arab unity, they had rival interpretations of the political projects associated with Arab nationalism, which, in turn, had very different implications for organizing inter-Arab politics. National identities and aspirations frequently clashed with Westphalian principles and notions of territorial exclusivity, depositing a legacy of regional conflict.[3]

Yet Hussein's vision has largely carried the day. Before 1967, the principal source of conflict between Arab states concerned whether Arab nationalism was or was not consistent with state sovereignty and the territorial legacy. Since 1967, Arab states have been routinely characterized as having a "real" existence and basis in society, and Arab nationalism as political unification is no longer actively entertained, even at the rhetorical level. The fact that Arab states have seemingly accepted each other's sovereignty and dispensed with pan-Arabism and the goal of political unification is viewed by many students of the region as advancing regional order to the extent that Arab leaders now accept some basic rules of the game. Although inter-Arab rivalries and conflicts still persist, the particularly deadly issue of state versus nation no longer exists, and this change has done much to calm inter-Arab politics.

This chapter argues that the emergence of regional order in the Arab world results from the consolidation of state sovereignty and a changed meaning of Arab nationalism. Specifically, I explore how the Arab states system moved from state versus nation and the acrimonious debate over the region's organizing principles to the simultaneous existence of separate sovereign states, Arab nationalism, and the establishment of relatively stable expectations and shared norms to govern inter-Arab relations. I focus on three related issues to trace this development. First, "neither internal sovereignty, with its conception of citizenship and national identity and loyalty, nor external sovereignty, with its idea of mutual recognition of boundaries and authority over that territory, has a real counterpart in Arab-Islamic history."[4] However, state formation processes, which have increased the masses' identification with the state, and interstate interactions, which have created greater differentiation between Arab states, have contributed to the institutionalization of sovereignty.

Second, many of the same domestic and regional practices that led to the consolidation of sovereignty also promoted an interpretation of Arab nationalism that is consistent with sovereignty. In other words, not only was sovereignty socially constructed, but so, too, was the meaning of Arab nationalism. From the early days of "the Arab Awakening" in the late nineteenth century to the post-Gulf War period, Arab nationalism has displayed considerable conceptual elasticity, and different interpretations of Arab nationalism have had very different consequences for state sovereignty and regional order. Two central issues concerning the relationship between nationalism, sovereignty, and regional order are highlighted here.

Nationalism is frequently treated as an internal phenomenon, that is, its dynamics and consequences for security politics derive from inside the state's territorial boundaries. Therefore, when examining the impact of nationalism on security, many scholars focus either on how the existence of nationless states creates tremendous internal security problems, or how certain forms of nationalism can generate aggressive or peaceful foreign policy behavior.[5] The case of the Arab world, however, directs our attention to how a nationalism that was external to the state's territorial boundaries profoundly shaped inter-Arab behavior. This was particularly dramatic during the pre-1967 period. There was tremendous expectation among many regional actors that an Arab nationalism that demanded a strengthening of the political community would generate a consensual regional order among Arab states, but in fact the simultaneous existence of transnationalism and state sovereignty spawned a legacy of conflict. In short, a nationalism that existed outside the state's territorial boundaries proved to have dramatic consequences for both state sovereignty and regional order.

Moreover, whereas once the prominent theme of inter-Arab politics was nation versus state, over the last few decades it has been increasingly nation(s) and state. In contrast to those who claim that the emergence of state sovereignty has come at the expense, the very death, of Arabism,[6] a striking development is the disappearance of a definition that undermined sovereignty and the emergence of a more "centrist" conception that is compatible with it. In other words, before 1967 state sovereignty and Arab nationalism placed contradictory demands on Arab states, but now Arab nationalism's meaning is more consistent with that of sovereignty. Not only have different conceptions of nationalism had very different consequences for regional stability, but also Arab nationalism seemingly has survived the emergence of the territorial nationalisms of the separate Arab states. This suggests that the territorial nationalism and sovereignty of the various Arab states and Arab nationalism can accommodate each other. It is well-accepted that nationalism is imagined, and this chapter highlights how different imaginings of and meanings associated with the nation have different consequences for regional politics.[7]

Third, the consolidation of sovereignty and the emergence of a "centrist" conception of Arab nationalism enabled Arab states to develop relatively stable expectations and shared norms, that is, to foster regional order.[8] Arab states have a greater incentive and exhibit a greater willingness to recognize each other's sovereignty and honor the principle of noninterference as the basis of their relations. My understanding of the emergence of order in the Arab states system contrasts with realist and neoliberal institutional approaches. Realism claims that regional order is dependent on material configurations, and looks to balances of power, hegemonies, and the like; neoliberal institutionalism examines how state actors with pre-given interests and identities construct institutions to advance cooperation. In contrast, I build on constructivist statements to trace how patterned interactions among Arab states led to the consolidation of sovereignty and a sovereignty-friendly conception of Arab nationalism. This is nothing less than the development of new state identities, roles, and interests, which, in turn, facilitated the emergence of relatively stable expectations and shared norms that are associated with sovereignty.[9] Because the emergence of state sovereignty and convergence on a common set of understandings and mutual expectations fostered regional order,[10] the case of the Arab states system is an important antidote to those who maintain that sovereignty or its absence is inconsequential for understanding interstate dynamics, or that states engage in the same behavior regardless of time, place, and institutional context.[11]

This chapter is organized in the following way.[12] The first section offers an institutional framework for approaching the Arab states system, and focuses on the relationship between institutions, roles, and order. The next section examines how statehood handed Arab states two potentially contradictory roles – that of sovereign state and promoter of the Arab nation – that created regional instability. The final section considers how the self-interested actions of Arab leaders, namely through state formation and interactive processes, promoted a new institutional environment that transformed the meaning of Arab nationalism and institutionalized state sovereignty and its norms. This development, in turn, fostered regional order. I then present a series of indicators to substantiate the claim that Arab states have established relatively stable expectations and shared norms associated with sovereignty to organize their relations.

An institutional preamble to the Arab states system

Whether an institution is understood as a relatively stable set of roles and interests,[13] or as a "persistent and connected set of rules (formal and informal) that prescribe behavioral roles, constrain activity, and shape expectations,"[14] roles appear in most definitions of institutions. Roles can be understood as how the individual (or state) participates in society according to a particular identity and comes to modify his (or its) behavior accordingly.[15] The concept of roles raises three key issues. First, because roles modify and constrain behavior, an important distinction is between position roles and preference roles. The former are generally associated with formal institutions and have well-defined and detailed guides to action, while the latter are more closely linked to informal institutions and are less constraining on behavior.[16] International relations contains both formal and informal institutions, and when investigating their effects on international processes, it is important to recognize that each role type places greater or lesser boundaries on state action. Second, roles shape but do not determine behavior, and this fact highlights the need to examine the state's understanding of and meaning it attaches to its role.[17] The enactment of a role, then, is shaped by how each actor interprets that role, not unlike how different actors will bring different interpretations of the same role to a play.

Finally, state roles have both international and domestic origins.[18] To take seriously both that states are embedded in domestic and international environments and that roles shape but do not determine behavior requires incorporating how international and domestic politics produce and affect actors' conceptions of their roles.

I employ an institutional analysis and focus on the concept of roles to address three central issues in inter-Arab politics: (1) the absence of regional order during the pre-1967 period; (2) the institutionalization of state sovereignty; and (3) the increased regional order after the 1960s. Institutional approaches are most closely associated with theories of change and stability, not theories of instability. Yet the recognition that states are embedded in myriad institutions that distribute different roles and behavioral expectations suggests that the state might occasionally be called upon to enact contradictory roles. It is possible that the state's actions that are consistent with the role requirements of, and stabilizing in, one institution might be inconsistent with, and destabilizing in, another. Therefore, role conflict

> exists when there are contradictory expectations that attach to some position in a social relationship. Such expectations may call for incompatible performances; they may require that one hold two norms or values which logically call for opposing behaviors; or they may demand that one role necessitates the expenditure of time and energy such that it is difficult or impossible to carry out the obligations of another role.[19]

Although "the role selected in response to any situation depends upon the definition and perception of particular events,"[20] often situations structurally overlap in such a way that it becomes difficult to predict which role will predominate. Because of the inability by actors to conform to the requirements of one role, they may be unable to establish the mutual expectations that encourage order.

The possibility that pan-Arabism and state sovereignty allocated potentially contradictory roles informs my portrayal of the pre-1967 period. If Arab leaders were reluctant to treat each other as sovereign entities, frequently challenging each other's authority and territorial basis of existence, it was because of the presence of a rival institution of pan-Arabism that allocated potentially contradictory roles and behavioral expectations. State sovereignty is a social institution; it is not a natural artifact of states but rather a consequence of and dependent upon the discursive and nondiscursive practices of state and nonstate actors. That is, of course, the theme of this volume, increasingly recognized in international relations theory, demonstrated in a variety of historical cases, and present in the case of the Arab states system.[21] Because sovereignty is an informal institution, the behavioral expectations and norms that exist among sovereign states have varied considerably over the ages. That said, an enduring element of sovereignty is that it accords a measure of possessiveness and exclusivity to the state. The state has authority over its domestic space and authority to act as a legitimate member of international society, and such entitlements are embodied in the principle of noninterference.[22] Being recognized as sovereign amounts to a social permission granted by the community of states to act with certain powers, and implies a measure of self-restraint or a "live-and-let-live" attitude by other members of this community.

Arab nationalism also is an institution, but this is less intuitive. It can be viewed as an institution, albeit a weak one, to the extent that it has distributed particular roles to Arab states that have duly constrained and shaped their interests if not their identities, and has contained domestic and regional sanctions for those who were seen as violating its norms.[23] This relates, however, to another important conceptual issue: Arab nationalism has shown considerable conceptual elasticity both historically and spatially; institutions are consequential to the degree that they have some degree of permanence and shape the behavior, if not the identities, of actors. Arab nationalism can be viewed as an institution to the extent that Arab states derive their interests from the Arab nation that envelops their borders, and are expected to work toward political unification and a strengthening of the political community. It is this meaning of Arab nationalism that can be understood best as an institution, and one that conflicts with the norms of sovereignty.[24] However, Arab nationalists have adopted definitions of the nation that borrow, alternatively, from the French and the Germanic traditions. The French tradition demands that a nation is inconceivable without the state, while the Germanic tradition conceives of the nation as an organic entity that is reminiscent of Tonnies's notion of *Gemeinschaft* and is not dependent on a single political authority.[25]

A significant issue in the debate over the meaning of Arab nationalism is whether it entails the political unification of the Arab states or whether the nation can exist and generate political obligations among independent and sovereign Arab states.[26] In order to maintain definitional and conceptual clarity, I refer to pan-Arabism as that version of

Arab nationalism that demands political unification among Arab states because they derive their authority and legitimacy from the Arab nation.[27] In general, an institutional perspective highlights how rival institutions established alternative demands on and expectations for Arab states that impeded the search for regional order.[28]

Institutions both provide the context for strategic interaction and encourage actors to occupy roles, and this informs my understanding of the emergence of regional order in the Arab states system. Specifically, institutions shape historical change as they provide incentives and constraints to action, represent the context of strategic interaction, and guide the direction of historical change. To this extent, an institutional approach is consistent with the view that historical change is path-dependent. "Path-dependent patterns are characterized by self-reinforcing positive feedback. Initial choices, often small and random, determine future historical trajectories. Once a particular path is chosen, it precludes others, even if these alternatives might, in the long run, have proven to be more efficient or adaptive."[29] Initial choices persist because individuals and social groups come to identify with and benefit from past decisions, and because the cost of change becomes more significant over time.[30]

This path-dependent perspective is linked to institutional change in a particular direction: the production of order. By order, I mean the development of relatively stable expectations and shared norms to govern relations among actors; in Arab politics, I am interested in the emergence of a particular order that is associated with sovereignty.[31] International institutions are now widely understood as offering the possibility of order and cooperation among states by encouraging them to adopt a particular role conception and to modify their behavior according to each other's roles, behaviors, and expectations. Once state actors adopt a particular role, they limit their behavior in a continuous and predictable manner that harmonizes mutual expectations and increases system stability.[32] That is, they establish relatively stable expectations and shared norms to govern their relations. This definition distinguishes between factual order and normative order, in other words, between statistical regularity and behavior governed by shared rules and norms,[33] and is consistent with many international relations theories that emphasize how shared rules of the game, including sovereignty, promote international order.

That said, international relations theories can be categorized according to whether they view international order as dependent on

155

material factors (realism); as a consequence of how self-interested states establish norms and institutions to promote cooperation and stability (neoliberal institutionalism); or as a product of the dynamic relationship between agents and their environments (constructivism). Specifically, this latter approach does not view institutions as a product of conscious choice and design but rather as a consequence of patterned interactions, and allows for the possibility that institutions, as a potential source of state interests and identities, can generate order among actors. Below I briefly discuss how the shortcomings of both neorealism and neoliberal institutionalism led me to adopt a constructivist approach to regional order in the Arab world.

Neorealist approaches examine how balances of power, the distribution of power, and hegemonies generate stability among states.[34] In short, they elevate military forces as preeminent in preventing an outbreak of hostilities, deterring the use of force, and maintaining stability. Although some sophisticated versions of neorealism consider how rules might guide interstate life, because such rules are established by the powerful to serve their needs, the rules will change with a change in the power hierarchy. For instance, Robert Gilpin argues that "an international system is stable (i.e. in a stable equilibrium) if no state believes it profitable to change the system," and predicts a change in the rules of the game as a result of a shift in the distribution of power.[35]

As many realists examine the ongoing negotiation of international order, they hint that it cannot be derived from power politics alone; their discussions often refer to how sociological factors also account for interstate stability. This is particularly true of many of the classic realist accounts that acknowledge how state practices and international stability are affected by normative forces.[36] Kissinger began his *A World Restored* by stating that the central issue for the post-Napoleonic order was the construction of a set of socially recognized and collectively legitimated principles, that is, what is permissible and what is prohibited. In short, he situates military power alongside normative power.[37] In the founding neorealist statement, Kenneth Waltz argued that socialization helps to account for how states become like-minded.[38] Although Waltz's conception of socialization is limited to a change in behavior, the collectivist and sociological imagery points to the possibility that international order might be fostered by socializing processes that shape state identity and interests as well (which is more consistent with sociological usage).

This idea highlights an important feature of many realist-inspired narratives of global and regional politics: their insistence on the primacy of power politics is undermined by a more complex portrayal of the workings of the interstate system than either their critics or disciples suggest. They also frequently undermine their plea for individualist purity and the primacy of power politics by resorting to sociological variables when necessary. By resorting to theoretical categories that are residual to their primary claims, many realist scholars reveal some fundamental and unsolved tensions in their work and open the door to substantive theoretical challenges.[39]

These issues surface in many realist accounts of the Arab states system. Specifically, many realist narratives also claim that the post-1967 period is one of greater regional stability. They point to how a change in the regional distribution of power in general, and Egypt's decline as a consequence of the 1967 war in particular, led Nasser to withdraw his support for pan-Arabism and how the rising regional powers, notably the Gulf Arab states, insisted on a region premised on sovereignty.[40] Arab leaders frequently exploited Arab nationalism to serve their ends and the 1967 war had a dramatic impact on regional politics. However, viewing Arab nationalism as parasitic on material factors and looking to shifts in material power to understand these regional changes is unsatisfactory in three ways.

First, changes in the regional distribution of power are not correlated with the decline of pan-Arabism. Shibley Telhami and Stephen Walt, both of whom offer elegant neorealist explanations of regional politics, mark the end of pan-Arabism at radically different historical moments. Specifically, Telhami claims that Egypt's relative power vis-à-vis other Arab states was on the rise, not the decline, following the 1967 war, and that it was not until 1974 that pan-Arabism faltered.[41] Walt stresses how the failed unity talks between Iraq, Syria, and Egypt of the mid-1960s that undermined pan-Arabism resulted "in a new pattern of inter-Arab alignments," and, significantly, has little to say about the effects of the 1967 war on pan-Arabism.[42] In short, two compelling neorealist accounts of inter-Arab politics come to very different conclusions about the timing of pan-Arabism's decline, suggesting that the distribution of power provides at least an inconclusive explanation. In fact, Walt's explanation arguably lends greater support to a process-oriented rather than structural model.

Second, while many of the best-known historical accounts adopt a realist narrative to explain these post-1967 changes, they frequently elevate the importance of normative forces that are independent of power politics to understand regional dynamics and developments. Although best known as a statement concerning the primacy of power politics in a region littered with the language of Arabism, Ajami's *The Arab Predicament* frequently notes how Arab nationalist forces constrained the actions of Arab leaders, and how the decline of pan-Arabism is attributed to a greater collective awareness that unification was both remote and misbegotten (and not solely due to changes in material power). Aspiring to demonstrate the force of structuralism in a region that supposedly takes its ideology seriously, Walt remarks that "a different form of balancing has occurred in inter-Arab relations. In the Arab world, the most important source of power has been the ability to manipulate one's own image and the image of one's rivals in the minds of other Arab elites."[43] In sum, many realist accounts elevate normative and ideational forces alongside the distribution of power to understand the constraints on state action and the dynamics of the region, which suggests that the emergent regional order cannot be derived from material forces alone.

Third, although realists assume that state interests are constant (and identities are irrelevant as an explanatory variable), many nonetheless insinuate that there was an emergence of new interests (and possibly identities) that are tied to the declining salience of Arab nationalism.[44] This implies that the systemic focus overlooks how changes in state–society relations also shape the foreign policies of states. To understand why societal actors no longer responded to the prospect of unification in the same way, or demanded that their governments be associated with the norms of pan-Arabism, requires a greater sensitivity to changes in the domestic context. None of these criticisms implies that material factors are inconsequential for understanding regional changes, but that they alone cannot account for the observed emergence of regional order, and that many realists in fact refer to normative factors when accounting for the dynamics of, and the observed stability in, Arab politics after the 1960s.[45]

Because of these and other unresolved tensions in realist approaches, many scholars have considered how institutions and norms foster international order. It is important to differentiate between rationalist and constructivist approaches to institutions. Rationalist approaches examine how states establish institutions to clarify norms, rules, and principles to guide and define a range of acceptable behavior, and alter (or create greater certainty in) a state's expectations of another state's behavior. Because such dynamics encourage actors to have greater trust in each other and the future, institutions enable states to escape the classic competitive trap fostered by the prisoner's dilemma, and thereby foster cooperation and stability. Moreover, such norms and institutions help to explain the persistence of stability in the face of changes in the distribution of power in the international system.[46]

Constructivist approaches acknowledge that states might establish institutions to encourage cooperation, but they differ from rationalist approaches by raising the possibility that institutions might not be the product of conscious design but rather emerge out of patterned interactions that become routinized and institutionalized; represent an important source of state identity, roles, and interests; and encourage order by creating relatively stable expectations and shared norms among actors that occupy set roles.[47] Roles are always formed in relation to others; it is in the process of interacting and participating within an institutional context that the actor comes to occupy a role.[48] Institutions are important socializing agents, the social context in which norms and values are transferred from one actor to another and new identities and beliefs are formed.[49] As Oran Young observes, while "actors may have an opportunity to choose which practices to join ... [m]ore often ... [they] have little choice about the roles they occupy, because they are socialized into accepting certain roles without question or because they acquire their roles through an interactive learning process that does not involve conscious choice."[50] Institutions encourage actors to occupy particular roles and modify their behavior accordingly. To be sure, actors will obey a particular order for reasons other than feelings of justice or an inherent belief in the norms involved, and this simply recognizes that order is produced in part by norms and in part by coercion.[51] A reasonable assumption, therefore, is that any type of order obtains through a mixture of both coercion and consent, and that this mixture can never be determined a priori, but only through an empirical examination.

This perspective – how institutions shaped the interests and roles of Arab states – provides an alternative explanation for understanding the emergence of regional order. Once caught between pan-Arabism and sovereignty, Arab states have converged on the latter to order their relations. To understand this development requires an explanatory framework that views regional order not as a consequence of balancing mechanisms or hegemony, and not only focusing on how states with pre-given roles and interests establish international institutions to govern their relations. Understanding this development requires a framework that also shows how institutions, by providing the context of strategic action, might shape the interests and roles of state actors in such a manner as to encourage the development of relatively stable expectations and shared norms.

The emergence of sovereignty and the transformation of Arab nationalism

Until the late nineteenth century, inhabitants of the Fertile Crescent existed within a variety of overlapping authority and political struc-tures. The Ottoman empire, Islam, and local tribal and village structures all contested for and held sway over various features of peoples' lives.[52] While the decline of the Ottoman empire, imperi-alism, and new ideas of nationalism combined to challenge local political structures and identities, Great Power intrusions were pri-marily responsible for setting into motion statist and transnational forces that created a disjuncture between where political authority was to reside and the political loyalties of the inhabitants of the region. While the Great Powers established a new geopolitical map, the political loyalties of the inhabitants enveloped these boundaries and challenged the very legitimacy of that map. Because elsewhere I have detailed how the simultaneous presence of pan-Arabism and state sovereignty created role conflict for the Arab state and disorder in the Arab states system,[53] I will discuss these features briefly below.

The disintegration of the Ottoman empire and World War I enabled the Great Powers to reconstruct the Arab world. In the aftermath of World War I and through the mandate system, France ruled Lebanon and Syria, and Britain controlled Jordan, Palestine, and Iraq.[54] The mandate system represented a powerful force behind statism and sovereignty; the fact that the Arab world was divided administra-tively rather than ruled within a single political unit shaped future political activity. In particular, anticolonial movements fought for state independence rather than Arab independence per se. Antonius observes:

> When Great Britain occupied Egypt in 1882, at a time when the national awakening had already begun to translate itself into a politically-minded movement, a new current of ideas emerged whose inspiration was specifically Egyptian and whose aim was, first and foremost, to agitate for the withdrawal of the British army of

occupation. Thus was Egyptian nationalism born and thus did its leaders adopt a course which, as the years went by, made it increasingly distinct from the general Arab movement.[55]

Even if it was not the mandatory powers' intent to calm a pan-Arab movement that was beginning to generate considerable support and enthusiasm,[56] the mandate system spawned new anticolonial movements, and, with them, new categories of political actors. That is, the political actor was becoming shaped and defined – from an Arab political identity to an Egyptian political identity, and so on.[57] Although many independence movements were using the language of Arabism and expressing a greater interest in other Arab lands (and particularly Palestine), the strongest of them directed their activities at immediate independence and only secondarily at Arab unification.[58]

Although most Arab leaders favored the Western-created map, many of the residents of these newly established political units did not share in their satisfaction, and were beginning to express a shared political identity with those in other lands. "A map anticipated reality, not vice versa," observes Benedict Anderson. "A map was a model for, rather than a model of, what it purported to represent."[59] Prior to World War I, pan-Arab movements, responding to new ideas of nationalism, Jewish immigration to Palestine, increased visibility of Western institutions in everyday life, and the Ottoman Empire's attempt to assert control over the area, and capitalizing on new means of communication, transportation, and education, began organizing in Damascus and Beirut and asserting that Arabs shared common identities, enemies, and interests. These social movements, filling a political and intellectual vacuum because of the inability of the political institutions to confront the challenges of the day, began to articulate an alternative vision of Arab political life, to nurture and promote an Arab identity.[60] At this point, however, the idea of Arab political independence and unification had little force in a region where many Arab nationalists also considered themselves Ottomanists.[61]

World War I, the Arab revolt against the Ottoman empire, the death of the Ottoman Empire, and the perception that the region was being assailed by European imperialism through the mandate system and by Jewish immigration to Palestine caused the region's inhabitants to reconsider their political identity and what sorts of political arrangements would be most meaningful and desirable.[62] By the beginning of

World War II, Arab nationalism became a potent political force. Although there was still no singular meaning to Arab nationalism,[63] many who identified themselves as Arab nationalists, particularly those in Iraq, Syria, and Jordan, believed that: (1) "there is or can be created an Arab nation, formed of all who share the Arabic language and cultural heritage"; (2) "this Arab nation ought to form a single independent political unity"; and, (3) "the creation of such a unit presupposes the development among the members of the consciousness ... [and] that their being members is the factor which should determine their political decisions and loyalties."[64]

Once the Arab states gained independence in the mid-1940s a defining issue in inter-Arab politics became how to reconcile the existence of the separate sovereign states and a pan-Arabism that viewed them as artificial and demanded their unification. State elites' vested interest in this territorial division became immediately apparent after independence, when Arab leaders met in Alexandria, Egypt in 1943 to consider the territorial future of the Arab world. When Iraqi leader Nuri al-Said proposed a federation among Jordan, Syria, Lebanon, and Palestine, which would then form a new Arab League with Iraq, the conference rejected this pan-Arab aspiration and essentially embraced sovereignty and independence. "It was as if the founding members [of the Arab League] ... set out deliberately to create an Arab system which did not in any substantial way threaten the vested interests of the respective regimes."[65]

Despite the construction of the League of Arab States with sovereignty at its core, Arab states continued to occupy two social roles that conferred contradictory behavioral expectations: sovereignty demanded that they recognize each other's legitimacy, borders, and the principle of noninterference, while pan-Arabism held that Arab states were to defend the Arab nation, to uphold regional standards of legitimacy, indeed to deny the very distinction between the international and the domestic. Because pan-Arabism provided the opportunity for – indeed, expected – Arab leaders to involve themselves in each other's domestic affairs, it severely complicated the search for stable expectations and shared norms upon which any regional order would be based.[66] If role conflict and regional disorder were to subside, and if stable expectations were to emerge, then either pan-Arabism or state sovereignty would have to bow to the other, or the norms associated with one would have to become more consistent with the norms of the other.

The emergence of regional order

If the first twenty-five years of the Arab states system were marked by tremendous rancor over how Arab states should organize their relations, since then these debates have quieted and the Arab states have apparently settled on sovereignty to govern their relations.[67] If Arab leaders could begin to breathe a little easier on the outside, the inside also offered greater respite. For many scholars the surprise of the post-1967 period was the stability, permanence, and longevity of many Arab regimes.[68] While Arab leaders, like their counterparts elsewhere, continually concerned themselves with their domestic standing, and responded automatically and often repressively to any hint of turmoil, challenges were targeted at the legitimacy of the government and not at the state's borders.

State formation

The simultaneous and related increase in the Arab states' juridical and empirical sovereignty explains why Arab leaders now have begun to consistently adopt the roles and adhere to the norms associated with sovereignty.[69] At independence, the Arab states lacked both external and internal authority because of the colonial legacy in general and pan-Arabism in particular, and they therefore remained dependent on an Arab identity to legitimate their policies and actions. The problem confronting Arab leaders was maintaining the state's sovereignty against the backdrop of an Arab nationalism that acted as both an instrument of political support and as an obstacle to state sovereignty. In this way, Arab leaders replayed the dilemma that confronted European rulers in the seventeenth century:

> The modern European state emerged within the confines of a single civilization united by the normative and religious power of Christendom. During its rise the state sought to free itself from the moral and religious shackles of the medieval world. But while it pursued this aim the state was aware of the dangers of totally undermining earlier notions of an international society ... Quite clearly, the state set out to employ the notion of a wider society of states for the explicit purpose of maintaining international order. Its aim was to enjoy the benefits of preserving an international society without incurring the risk that individual citizens would challenge the state's legitimacy by proclaiming their allegiance to a higher cosmopolitan ethic.[70]

The principal difference, of course, between Arab leaders and their

European compatriots 300 years before was that the Europeans did not have to contend with the idea of nationstates. The paradox, then, was that Arab leaders often needed Arab nationalism to provide a basis for their actions, yet its logical conclusion threatened to undermine their basis of power.

To rid them of that paradox and to better ensure their domestic survival, radical and conservative Arab leaders alike embarked on state formation projects that were designed to encourage the transfer of both subnational and transnational identities to the state, and, therefore, to enhance the state's legitimacy and domestic stability. State formation projects were instrumental in producing new political identities, shrinking the salience of transnational loyalties, and increasing the ability of state actors to act in a manner that is consistent with sovereignty.[71]

State formation can occur through a myriad of activities and processes, but figuring centrally in the comparative politics and the Middle Eastern literatures are material incentives, external threats, and the manipulation of symbols. First, although Arab leaders situated in dependent economies might opt for étatist rather than market-oriented policies for economic reasons (i.e. late industrialization), there are important political benefits to be gained as well. Chief among them is the ability of the state to become the caretaker, to act as the primary financial guardian and material source of support. Economic development came to be associated with a *state*-led effort (for good or for bad).[72] Consequently, citizens link their material interests to the state and not to local or international actors. To be sure, this was a major reason why the capitalist class in the newly independent Arab states was most loyal to the state's independence and most resistant to pan-Arabism, and why the lower classes were generally more sympathetic to pan-Arabism and a new regional order. Accordingly, the promotion of a welfare state would link the citizens' material interests and political loyalties and identities to the state. In this model, material forces propel changes in political identities. The danger is that using material benefits to win support, which does not guarantee that it will alter an individual's political identity, is a costly strategy for most resource-poor states.

External threats have played an important role historically in the growth of state power. Not only do wars and external threats generally act as an important impetus behind the state's penetration and control over society, but such challenges also can build a sense of camaraderie and develop a national identity.[73] Whereas conflicts between Arab and non-Arab states increased an Arab identity and unity witness the increase in pan-Arabism following the 1956 war, the chronic infighting and rivalry between Arab states has only highlighted their perceived differences. For instance, some Arab officials suggested that one of the paradoxes of the Gulf War was that Saddam Hussein's attempt to cast himself as leader of the pan-Arab movement only "sharpened a sense that pan-Arabist slogans had outlived their relevance," and consequently increased the sense of difference between neighboring Arab states.[74] There is little doubt that Iraq's invasion of Kuwait bolstered the idea of a Kuwaiti national identity.[75] Moreover, separate statenational identities were also reinforced by the Arab–Israeli conflict, wars that were ostensibly waged in the name of the Arab nation (though not for Arab unification). Conscripts were trained in state armies, wore state uniforms, were buried in state graves, and honored with state holidays. In general, external conflict accelerated the sense of separateness and the growth of state-national identities.[76]

Finally, Arab leaders have wielded and manipulated a variety of symbols to create a state-national identity. Manufacturing consent through the reconstruction of political identity can prove to be a cost-effective method of creating support, and there is abundant evidence that nearly all Arab leaders attempted to infuse the state with a sense of permanence. For instance, even Libyan leader Mauammar Qaddafi, who aspired to become the champion of pan-Arabism after Nasser's death in 1970, attempted to create a "Libyan Arab" national identity through historical texts, holidays, and monuments.[77] And in Iraq, the Ba'athist party, which stresses pan-Arabism and the singularity of the Arab people, established an ongoing project to demonstrate that there existed an Iraqi identity with roots in Mesopotamia.[78]

Additionally, many Arab leaders also attempted to appropriate and be associated with the symbols of Arab nationalism, but in a way that was consistent with the state's interests. Because many Arab leaders feared that their counterparts would seek to appropriate pan-Arabism to enhance their regional power and to destabilize their neighbors, they attempted to minimize their susceptibility to transnational issues by giving their own spin on Arabism's demands – one that was consistent with the state's interests.[79] "Little by little the vocabulary of Arabism was altered to accommodate ideas and concepts designed to highlight regional differences and local particularity."[80] This attempt to define "Arab" issues in ways that were consistent with the state's interests led to a decreased sensitivity to "Arab" causes. For example, because of Palestine's centrality in Arab politics, Arab leaders strove to ensure that their definition of and solution to the problem was not outstripped by another Arab leader's appraisal; the attempt by the Egyptian government to insulate its citizenry from pan-Arabism led to "an increasing passiveness toward ... Arab causes, especially that of Palestine."[81]

In sum, as Arab leaders worked for integration at one level, they promoted fragmentation at another.[82] There is solid empirical evidence at the regional and state levels that a state-national identity is better able to compete with an Arab identity because of a deliberate strategy to pursue what Baram terms "territorial nationalism,"[83] and that these states are now "legitimate in the eyes of society, or at least of a significant part of it."[84] What is central is that there is a greater allegiance to the state; that state-based identities are better able to compete with Arab nationalism for the citizens' political loyalties; that Arab societies are less likely to demand that their leaders follow pan-Arabism's cues; and that Arab leaders have less incentive to resort to pan-Arabism's demands to enhance their legitimacy.

Interstate interactions

My concern here is how inter-Arab interactions contributed to a decline in pan-Arabism and greater differentiation between Arab states. Wendt's discussion of how reciprocal interactions can create new and separate roles and interests provides a useful organizing device for considering how the interaction between Arab states produced a decline in transnational identities and obligations.[85] While prior to the initial interaction, both actors might have cautiously optimistic or wary feelings toward each other; this first contact generates expectations for future encounters. Such knowledge not only informs future behavior, but this patterned behavior also encourages the formation of the roles and interests of these actors. In short, while this initial interaction can be positive or negative, as much as it and subsequent behavior appears threatening, "the self is forced to 'mirror' such behavior in its conception of the self's relationship to the other."[86] Ominous behavior produces a more wary and cautious outlook, a sense of conflicting interests, and the potential for distinct identities. Path-dependent behavior becomes institutionalized and establishes separate roles that are rather impervious to change.[87] Therefore, anarchy alone cannot account for the emergence of these roles; rather, these roles are created by states and through their actions; it is structure through action.[88] This process-oriented model nicely captures how initial pan-Arab sentiments and a sense of shared identity and interests were steadily replaced by greater fragmentation among Arab states, as well as an acceptance of the roles and behavioral expectations associated with sovereignty.

Consider the following historical sketch: At independence, Arab leaders were considerably ambivalent toward each other. There was widespread recognition that Arab states had shared interests, but this cooperative spirit was coated with tremendous apprehension and suspicion that pan-Arabism was a Trojan horse for Arab leaders. This approach–avoidance behavior emerges as a major theme of many excellent historical narratives of the period.[89]

Future interactions only reinforced these suspicions and fears. Perhaps most damaging to the spirit of pan-Arabism were the outcomes of pan-Arab projects. Most significant were the twin failures of the 1960s: the death of the United Arab Republic in 1961 and the 1967 Arab–Israeli War. If the UAR began with much public fanfare, privately both Nasser and Syrian leaders were only too fearful of the costs associated with this unification agreement.[90] These fears were prophetic. In 1961, Syria withdrew from the UAR amidst charges that it was little more than a vehicle for Nasser to expand his power at Syria's economic and political expense.[91] If the 1963 Iraqi–Syrian–Egyptian unification talks provide evidence that unification remained a formidable force, the talks ended with a flurry of accusations, only dampening the desire for Arab unity.[92]

The other major defeat of pan-Arabism resulted from Israel's military victory in June 1967. Because Arab leaders paved their road to war with Israel with the language of pan-Arabism, Israel's victory represented a defeat not only for the Arab states but also for pan-Arabism.[93] The fact that the 1967 war was such a fatal blow to pan-Arabism, however, is a testimony to its already frail condition. It was in this context, with the fading popularity of pan-Arabism and the possible Arab response to Israel, that Arab leaders gathered in Khartoum in fall, 1967. If the pretext was to discuss the collective Arab response to Israel's military victory, the prominent subtext was the meaning of Arab nationalism. During the immediate months after the June 1967 war, Arab leaders exchanged indictments. The underlying theme was how much pan-Arabism, which represented the principal split in the Arab world, could be blamed for the defeat. Saudi Arabia and Jordan were particularly vocal in claiming that any successful confrontation of Israel depended upon greater inter-Arab cooperation, that is, jettisoning the radical pan-Arab agenda. Amman's *ad-Dustar* reflected the emerging mood: "Co-existence is a need which we must recognize at the present stage. An attempt to force others to adopt a certain system would ... eventually divide the Arab ranks."[94]

To close these divisions and increase inter-Arab cooperation would mean concluding the five-year confrontation in Yemen between Saudi Arabia and Egypt. When Egyptian troops intervened in Yemen in 1962, it represented a flashpoint between radical and conservative Arab states and a symbol of Nasser's attempt to export his revolution. The continuing Egyptian presence five years later, therefore, was an obstacle to inter-Arab cooperation. Accordingly, the continuing conflict in Yemen was an important agenda item at Khartoum, and the subsequent agreement by Egypt and Saudi Arabia to end the war was considered one of the summit's crowning achievements. Nasser agreed to resign as the sponsor of pan-Arabism and to target his activities and energies against Israel, not his Arab brethren, and Saudi Arabia agreed to help him financially to do so. The result of these developments was a broadening consensus on the basic norms that should govern Arab relations, aptly symbolized by Nasser's shift in rhetoric from "unity of ranks" to "unity of purpose" and the "new pragmatism," which suggested that cooperation need not imply unification.[95] The Jordanian newspaper *ad-Dustar* summarized the prevailing view:

> We [the Arab world] have not yet reached the state where we can overcome problems created by the existence of separate entities, which would, thus, pave the way for the complete elimination of separateness. This in turn imposes on us the duty to tolerate more than one viewpoint ... Because, if we do not tolerate the interaction of Arab experiments, we will never progress toward Arab coexistence and will never approach our basic aim – Arab unity."[96]

In short, through an ongoing interactive process, Arab states converged on both sovereignty and relatively stable expectations about how to organize their relations.

Inter-Arab relations since Khartoum have only reinforced this path of fragmentation, a belief that Arab states might have distinct interests, and that they should organize their relations around sovereignty's norms. The decision by Nasser and others (but not Syria) to abstain from intervening in Jordan during its military campaign against the Palestinian Liberation Organization in fall, 1970 was viewed by many as recognition of the arrival of sovereignty and the new conservatism in the Arab world – even the PLO, the representative of the Palestinian people and the conscience of the Arab world, should not challenge the sovereignty of the existing Arab states. Although the 1973 war and the subsequent oil embargo suggested the possibility of a greater collective spirit in the Arab world, Egypt's decision to take a separate road to peace with Israel signaled that state interests and Arab interests did not always coincide, even on defining issues. The emergence of subregional organizations such as the Gulf Cooperation Council and the Arab Maghrebi Union rather than pan-Arab associations was the dominant trend in inter-Arab cooperation in the 1980s.[97] The Iraqi invasion of Kuwait ushered in a new era in inter-Arab relations, as Arab leaders became less apologetic about defending their policies as furthering the state's – as opposed to the Arab nation's – interests.[98] In sum, the historical legacy of inter-Arab interactions is not greater cooperation and a deepening of the political community but rather greater differentiation and particularism among Arab states.[99]

Although such developments spell the demise of pan-Arabism, they do not necessarily mark the end of Arab nationalism. If Arab states are more fully treating each other as having a "real existence," Arab leaders and masses alike have apparently converged on a more centrist definition of Arab nationalism that implies interstate cooperation and consultation, but little else.[100] Arab nationalism and sovereignty, therefore, are no longer contradictory concepts. Arab nationalism's meaning and expected behaviors are increasingly comparable to those of inter-national society.[101]

The ascendance of this centrist conception of Arab nationalism is a product of some of the same state-formation and interactive processes that are responsible for the institutionalization of sovereignty. Political concepts cannot be divorced from political practice, their historical context, the meaning that actors attach to those concepts, and how they address new difficulties in new surroundings.[102] Briefly, three broad periods in inter-Arab politics, defined by three different international and domestic contexts, affected the debate over and the meaning of Arab nationalism. The first was from the late nineteenth century through the early twentieth century, defined by the breakdown of the old order as a consequence of the demise of the Ottoman empire, the emergence of nationalism, and the spread of the world economy. As their political, economic, and cultural institutions crumbled, individuals in the Fertile Crescent were forced to reconsider their political

identity, how they wanted to live with one another, and who constituted the political community.[103] Modernity and imperialism provided
an impetus for Arabs to discover their common identity and destiny,
and to suggest that a meaningful response to these economic, cultural,
and political dislocations required collective action on an expansive
scale. The emergence of a pan-Arabism that attempted to link up with
the modern-day project of nationalism and the creation of a nationstate
is directly related to how individuals responded and attempted to
make sense of these fundamental transformations.

The period from political independence through 1967 that was
defined by the coexistence of state sovereignty and pan-Arabism
occurred as Arab leaders wanted to build strong and modern states in
relationship to an international system that left them vulnerable to
other artificial states with which they shared a history, language, and
destiny, and to their own societies that treated them as illegitimate and
artificial. Therefore, the debate over Arab nationalism is related to the
attempt by Arab leaders to reconcile the desire to protect and promote
the interests of both the Arab nation and the Arab state due to
transnational and territorial logics, respectively. Accordingly, the
debate over Arab nationalism was a debate not only over how much
Arab states had uniform interests, but also over the necessity of
political unification to give meaning, permanence, and purpose to the
Arab nation.

The growing differentiation among Arab states, which were increasingly taken for granted and endowed with a "real basis" due to state-
formation projects and interactive processes, produced a corre-
sponding change in the meaning of Arab nationalism. Specifically, the
language of Arab nationalism still can be heard as Arabs continue to
confront the fundamental changes in international and domestic politics within a new context, that of Arab sovereign states responding to
perceived common challenges. While there is little support for unification, the continued existence of an Arab identity that serves as a bridge
between Arab states and the awareness by Arab states of the permeability of borders to cultural and economic forces preserves an interest
in close relations.[104] Arab nationalism still provides a powerful pull on
Arab states and provides a symbolic incentive for cooperation. This is
particularly true when states are viewed as under assault by outside –
notably Western – forces.

In sum, Arab leaders have a greater incentive to act consistently with
the role allocated by and norms associated with sovereignty because of

domestic and international changes. State-formation processes have increased the masses' willingness to identify more closely with the state. Accordingly, Arab leaders no longer have the same incentive to be seen as working toward Arab unification nor the need to legitimate their actions in the name of pan-Arabism because that language no longer has the same salience for their citizenry. Interstate interactions, moreover, have undermined pan-Arabism, if not the very desire for close cooperation, and encouraged greater differentiation between Arab states. Domestic and international processes institutionalized sovereignty, promoted a more sovereignty-friendly definition of Arab nationalism, and enabled Arab leaders to adopt more consistently the roles associated with sovereignty and to develop relatively stable expectations concerning how to organize their relations.

Indicators of change

The institutionalization of sovereignty and the changed meaning of Arab nationalism encouraged Arab leaders to act more consistently with the behavior associated with sovereignty, which in turn increased regional order. Yet on what basis can we claim that sovereignty has been institutionalized? Although many scholars of Arab politics also have observed a fundamental shift in behavioral patterns in the Arab states system, they frequently base their claims on selected historical episodes; for example, Sadat's trip to Jerusalem, the Iraqi invasion of Kuwait, and the Declaration of Principles between Israel and the PLO raise several methodological and conceptual issues. First, actors might share common interests, goals, and definition of the situation, yet disagree over the appropriate measures and actions required to achieve their objectives. Second, actors might have numerous interests, and interests sometimes can conflict. The fact that one set of interests emerges over another at one moment does not represent conclusive evidence that other interests are not also present. Overlooking these two issues "would run the risk of misinterpreting a contingent choice reflecting immediate constraints for one representing the more basic and stable interests of the agent."[105]

Third, many historical episodes can be interpreted as a vindication of Arab nationalism or sovereignty, that is, as the result of either Arab norms or the norms of international society. Consider Iraq's invasion of Kuwait, which many scholars offer as conclusive evidence that Arab nationalism is dead because an Arab state invaded another, supposedly violating a cardinal tenet of Arab nationalism.[106] There have been numerous instances of inter-Arab military conflicts since 1945, but the fact that a norm is broken does not preclude its absence. The immediate and shocked reaction of the Arab states to the Iraqi invasion of Kuwait can be viewed as evidence that the normative prohibition against Arab states invading each other was broken; that is, evidence of the norm can be detected in the reaction of those observing its violation. Finally, both sovereignty and pan-Arabism permit a range of behaviors that often overlap. For instance, because sovereignty allows for political unification, it is theoretically consistent with pan-Arabism's goal of unification; neither the active nor abandoned search by Arab states for regional integration represents conclusive evidence of the institutionalization of sovereignty. In general, the same event used by some to indicate Arab nationalism's decline can be appropriated by others to indicate the very opposite.

To make the case that sovereignty has been institutionalized, pan-Arabism has declined, and Arab states have established relatively stable expectations and shared norms to govern their relations requires greater attention to those practices that are fundamentally inconsistent with sovereignty. In particular, Arab states have ceased challenging each other's authority and debating the rules of the game, which is evidence of the institutionalization of sovereignty. There are three indicators to support the claim that Arab states have converged on sovereignty and its norms to organize their relations: (1) the decline of unity talks and agreements; (2) the agenda at Arab summit meetings; and, (3) Arab leaders no longer actively promote themselves as the champion of pan-Arabism and political unification.

Perhaps the clearest sign of the rise of sovereignty is the near extinction of unification talks and treaties. Whereas there were seven unity agreements between Arab states of the Fertile Crescent between 1949 and 1964, the lone post-1967 instance came in October 1978 between Syria and Iraq.[107] The dramatic downturn in the number of unification efforts suggests the institutionalization of sovereignty. And, in contrast to current European integration efforts that are advocated by state elites primarily on economic and political grounds, Arab unification efforts are derived from a belief in the Arab state's "artificiality" and lack of legitimacy, and the desire to bring the state and nation into correspondence. What matters, then, is not the attempt of integration per se but rather the meaning and motivation attributed to such actions. Therefore, a decline in unification talks suggests a decreased belief in the artificiality of the Arab state among Arab state and nonstate actors. A prominent interpretation of these unification efforts shows an attempt by Arab leaders to maintain their domestic legitimacy. Consequently, a decline in these efforts provides an indirect indicator of an increase in the Arab states' legitimacy and empirical sovereignty, and/or that pan-Arab claims are no longer effectual because they are unattractive.[108]

The agenda of Arab summit meetings represents another avenue for tracing the rise of sovereignty, the decline of pan-Arabism, and the development of shared norms and relatively stable expectations to organize their relations.[109] Although the formal agenda of pre-1967 meetings concerned Arab–Israeli issues, the informal agenda and many pre-summit preparatory meetings had as a central issue the debate over pan-Arabism and political unification.[110] Simply put, the participants debated the basic norms that should govern inter-Arab relations. The post-1967 agenda is no longer colored by issues of political unification or debates over how to organize their relations. Although these summits are still fraught with conflict, such tensions revolve around differences over how to solve and how to coordinate their responses to issues of mutual concern rather than whether Arab states should accept the norms of sovereignty to guide their relations.

Another method for demarcating the emergence of sovereignty derives from the definition of the threat to regional stability. Threats may originate from considerations other than military power alone; they might derive from those state and nonstate actors that challenge the principle of sovereignty and the authority of the state. In this respect, revolutionary actors are those that present and promote an alternative principle for organizing international relations. Prior to the 1960s, the threat frequently posed by Arab states was not military but presentational, having to do with their willingness and ability to forward a particular understanding of the Arab state's rôle and relationship to other Arab states. By suggesting that the purpose of the Arab state was to work toward political unification, those Arab leaders who aligned themselves with pan-Arabism undermined the state's external and internal sovereignty. Accordingly, an Arab state that successfully wielded the pan-Arab card threatened to subvert the state's internal and external security. In this respect, even relatively weak states represented a potential threat to stronger states.

It is noteworthy that while the post-1967 period still contains attempts by Arab leaders to claim leadership in the Arab world, such bids revolve around leadership on issues of mutual interest rather than overturning or defending the region's organizing principles. For example, Walt catalogues numerous alliances in the Middle East since the 1950s. It is notable that their number significantly decreases after 1967 and the identified source of these threats is no longer associated with Arabist challenges, that is, a threat to the region's organizing principles.[111] In short, the changed definition of the threat in general, and that Arab leaders are no longer actively promoting themselves as the champion of political unification suggest the institutionalization of sovereignty.[112]

Changes in these three indicators – unity attempts, the agenda at Arab summits, and a changed presentation of purpose for the Arab state and the definition of the threat – underscore a significant development in inter-Arab politics: the institutionalization of sovereignty, the acceptance of a meaning of Arab nationalism that is consistent with sovereignty, and the development of relatively stable expectations and shared norms for organizing regional life.

Conclusion

The debate over Arab nationalism represented a debate over how regional life should be organized in general and how the Arab states should manage the legacy of Westphalia in particular. Since the beginning of the Arab states system, there has been an active and occasionally violent dialogue among state and nonstate actors over how the region should reconcile the sometimes contradictory demands and expectations associated with sovereignty and Arab nationalism. If Arab leaders seemingly embraced Dumbarton Oaks with the establishment of the Arab League in 1945, their actions over the next several decades testified that such arrangements were not entirely satisfactory to many in the region. Arab nationalists demanded a rethinking of how Arab states should organize their relations and suggested that the state did not exhaust the political loyalties or identities of the inhabitants of the Arab world.

The Arab states have engaged in a lengthy dispute over how to organize their relations, and this highlights how Westphalia and the norms of international society conflicted with and shaped the existing and emerging regional society.[113] There were overlapping international societies at the regional and at the global levels, and the debate over Arab nationalism was, in effect, a debate over the degree of commitment to global or regional norms, and even what should constitute these regional norms. "An international society is not simply a yes or no issue. Within a yes, a spectrum of both levels of development and degrees of participation are possible."[114] While many Arab leaders were on the frontlines defending their sovereignty and territoriality, other state and nonstate actors both saw state sovereignty as little more than a conservative, Western-sponsored construct that divided the Arab nation, and, accordingly, demanded in its place a regional system that reflected the identities and desires of its inhabitants. In this respect, Arab states were not only sovereign states but also, at a basic level, *Arab* states, deriving their legitimacy from the Arab nation and its representatives; these different social identities contained different behavioral expectations. Far from reading their interests or roles from anarchy's logic alone, Arab states were embedded in overlapping international and regional societies that undermined their sovereignty, offered rival behavioral expectations and standards of legitimacy, and weighed heavily on their foreign policy.

The debate among the region's inhabitants over how to adjust and respond to these global norms unleashed tremendous regional instability. In the absence of an agreement on the relationship between sovereignty and Arab nationalism, Arab leaders failed to coordinate the social roles they were expected to play vis-à-vis their societies and each other, depositing a legacy of unfulfilled expectations and conflict. Interstate conflict, in other words, was not solely a product of insecurity driven by anarchy; rather, it was insecurity driven by transnational forces. The transfer of sovereignty to the Arab world represented an institutional revolution for organizing regional political life; and similar to most revolutions, this transfer was neither uncomplicated nor free of conflict.

State sovereignty emerged once the state understood itself as occupying certain roles; and there was a revolution in loyalties such that subnational loyalties were transferred to the state and transnational loyalties receded in importance.[115] The combined effects of unsuccessful pan-Arab activities and relatively successful state-formation projects increased the state's internal and external sovereignty, encouraged the differentiation between domestic and international space. The boundaries of the Arab states system and the desired and realized normative structure were a result of material and ideational forces. Material forces, embodied in external and internal threats, the collapse of empires, and economic forces, decidedly altered the incentives and interests of state and nonstate actors. But ideational forces also contributed to the development of the Arab states system. These forces were reflected by contending and shifting national identities, as well as by the ways interstate interaction produced new intersubjective understandings of the role and purpose of the Arab state.

Institutions such as sovereignty generate their stabilizing properties once actors consistently adopt a particular role conception, and modify their behavior according to each other's roles, behaviors, and expectations. The institution of sovereignty now holds center stage, and the concept of Arab nationalism is now frequently interpreted in a way that is consistent with sovereignty. This means that Arab states are more apt to adhere to the roles allocated by sovereignty, and to limit their behavior accordingly. During the first decades of the Arab states system sovereignty and nationalism often contained competing standards of behavior and expectations for Arab states, but progressively since the 1970s Arab nationalism no longer contains the same meaning or has the same implications for state sovereignty. My approach to regional order, therefore, highlights not balancing mechanisms, hegemony, or other often-used indicators of the state's strength in the international system; instead it emphasizes how institutions encourage and socialize state actors to adhere to a stable set of roles and behavioral expectations, and the willingness of Arab states to recognize each other's existence.

Yet sovereignty is not permanently anchored and Arab nationalism is not exactly dead. Arab leaders must continually work to reproduce the state's sovereignty, its domestic and international authority, the distinction between domestic and international space. While pan-Arabism has receded as a threat to the state's authority and Arab states are not generally

> threatened by a higher level of integration, ... statist ideologies are still unable to convince the Arabs that the present states are resilient against all kinds of challenges, or that there is no possible loyalty beyond state borders. In fact, both nationalism and isolationism (*qawmiyya* and *qutriyya*) seem to be in a historical impasse.[116]

The failure of statist ideologies has resurrected primordial, ethnic, and, most famously, religious identities, which, in turn, represent a potential threat to state sovereignty.[117] The existence of social forces that continually challenge the state's sovereignty remind us that state leaders are endlessly engaged in differentiating between domestic and international space. Far from a completed task, the reproduction of state sovereignty is an ongoing, all-consuming project for nearly all Arab leaders.

Many of the social processes and patterns that furthered the consolidation of sovereignty also altered the meaning of and the political projects associated with Arab nationalism. This observation runs counter to much scholarship on Arab nationalism, which frequently has an either/or quality: the Arab nation either takes precedence over all other identities, or it is meaningless; either Arab nationalism necessitates political unification or it is without force. Arab nationalism has always had a conceptual elasticity, had different meanings both historically and spatially, depending on who was being asked and when that person was being asked. Indeed, nationalism has "rapidly 'invaded' the Arab mind but not converged on a clear definition of the nation itself."[118] This suggests that many who identify themselves as Arab nationalists do not have political unification in mind. Although a standard definition of nationalism is the drive for and maintenance of a modern national state, Arab nationalism has meant both this and other expressions of a strengthened political community. If a hallmark of Arab nationalism is the desire to deepen and strengthen the political community, such a desire does not require immediate political unification.[119] The danger of adhering to a restrictive definition of nationalism is that it prematurely dismisses both the presence of national sentiments, and the possibility of mass political mobilization for political projects short of political unification.

Once the prominent theme of inter-Arab politics was nation versus state, but over the last few decades it has been increasingly nation(s) and state. Not only have these different conceptions of nationalism had very different consequences for regional stability, but Arab nationalism also has seemingly survived the emergence of the territorial nationalisms of the separate Arab states. Therefore, in contrast to "pigeon-hole views of nationalism" that discount the possibility that there might be simultaneously "nation-state nationalisms" and more inclusive nationalisms,[120] Arab politics suggests how territorial nationalism can coexist alongside other national identities. While it is tempting to assume that national identities are mutually exclusive and have clearly differentiated boundaries – that is, that "us" and "them" are clearly demarcated – the case of the Arab world suggests how national identities are more fluid than is frequently acknowledged. Territorial nationalism of the Arab world does not contain the same degree of exclusivity associated with the territorial boundaries of the state and the ideal type of the nationstate, and this can be attributed to the presence of an Arab identity. It is quite possible, for instance, for an Egyptian to identify with the Egyptian and the Arab nation; in Jordan, Palestinian, Jordanian, and Arab national identities mingle, and only occasionally come into conflict. Although it is tempting to conclude that nations are distinct and segregated entities, one of the intriguing features of Arab politics is the existence of contending national identities and political allegiances that occasionally accommodate each other – sometimes blurring into one another and not always portending regional instability.

Notes

I thank the following individuals for their helpful suggestions and critiques: Emanuel Adler, Gehad Auda, Raymond Duvall, Peter Katzenstein, F. Gregory Gause, Ellis Goldberg, Moshe Maoz, Robert McCalla, Joel Migdal, Craig Murphy, Bruce Maddy-Weitzman, Malik Mufti, John Odell, Avraham Sela, Janice Thomson, Cindy Weber, Jutta Weldes, Alexander Wendt, Crawford Young, many others at the SSRC-sponsored workshop at Brown University, 26–8 February 1993, and several anonymous referees at *International Organization*. I also thank the research assistance of Ashshraf Rady in Cairo, Avi Muallen in Tel-Aviv, and Michael Malley in Madison, Wisconsin. This research was supported by the MacArthur Program in International Peace and Security and the Global Studies Research Program at the University of Wisconsin.

[1] See, for instance, Van Evera, Stephen 1994. "Hypotheses on Nationalism and War," *International Security* 18: 5–39; Posen, Barry 1993. "The Security Dilemma and Ethnic Conflict," in Brown, M. (ed.) *Ethnic Conflict and International Security*. Princeton: Princeton University Press, pp. 103–24; Barkins, J.S. and Cronin, B. 1994. "The State and the Nation," *International Organization* 48: 107–30; Gottleib, Gidon 1993. *Nation Against State*. New York: Council on Foreign Relations Press; and Moynihan, Daniel Patrick 1993. *Pandaemonium*. New York: Oxford University Press.

[2] Cited from Walt, Stephen 1987. *The Origins of Alliances*. Ithaca: Cornell University Press, p. 213.

[3] See Ben-Dor, Gabriel 1983. *State and Conflict in the Middle East*. New York: Praeger Press; Hudson, Michael 1977. *Arab Politics: The Search for Legitimacy*. New Haven, Conn.: Yale University Press, p. 54; and Noble, Paul 1984. "The Arab State System: Opportunities, Constraints, and Pressures," in Korany, B. and Dessouki, A. (eds.) *The Foreign Policies of the Arab States*. Boulder: Westview Press, pp. 48–50.

[4] Tibi, Bassam 1991. "The Simultaneity of the Unsimultaneous: Old Tribes and Imposed Nation-States in the Modern Middle East," in Khoury, P. and Kostiner, J. (eds.) *Tribes and State Formation in the Middle East*. London: I.B. Taurus, p. 127.

[5] The relationship between nationless states and internal security is, of course, most thoroughly explored in the case of Third World security dynamics. See, for instance, Gottleib, *Nation Against State*. For the relationship between nationalism and aggressive behavior, see Van Evera, "Hypotheses on Nationalism and War," and Comaroff, John and Stern, Paul 1994. "New Perspectives on Nationalism and War," *Theory and Society* 23: 35–45. For the possible relationship between nationalism and pacific behavior, see Haas, Ernst 1993. "Nationalism: An Instrumental Social Construction," *Millennium* 22: 505–45.

[6] The classic statement is Ajami, Fouad 1978/79. "The End of Pan-Arabism," *Foreign Affairs* 57: 355–73.

[7] Anderson, Benedict 1991. *Imagined Communities* 2nd ed. New York: Verso Press. Also see Haas, "Nationalism."

[8] For sociological statements that inform this conception of order, see Wrong, Dennis 1994. *The Problem of Order*. New York: Free Press; Goffman, Erving 1983. "The Interaction Order," *American Sociological Review* 48: 1–17; Berger, Peter and Luckmann, Thomas 1967. *The Social Construction of Reality*. New York: Anchor Press; and Alexander, Jeffrey 1987. *Twenty Lectures.* New York: Columbia University Press, chap. 1.

[9] See, for instance, Wendt, Alexander 1992. "Anarchy is What States Make of It," *International Organization* 46: 391–426; Koslowski, Rey and Kratochwil, Friedrich 1994. "Understanding Change in International Politics," *International Organization* 48: 215–48; Adler, Emanuel and Haas, Peter 1992. "Conclusion: Epistemic Communities, World Order, and the Creation of a Reflective Research Program," *International Organization* 46: 367–90; Caporaso, James 1989. "Microeconomics and International Political Economy: The Neoclassical Approach to Institutions," in Czempiel, Ernst-Otto and Rosenau, James (eds.) *Global Changes and Theoretical Challenges*. Lexington, Mass.: Lexington Press, 137–8.

[10] Rather than presupposing the inherent desirability of one type of order over another, i.e. that of separate, sovereign, states over alternative organizing principles and actors, I am attempting to explain how the consolidation of sovereignty produced a particular response to the problem of regional order.

[11] Fischer, Marcus 1992. "Feudal Europe: Discourse and Practices," *International Organization* 46: 427–66.

[12] I examine the original members of the League of Arab States, namely Yemen, Egypt, Jordan, Lebanon, Iraq, Syria, and Saudi Arabia. Although the League's membership has expanded considerably since 1945, it was this original group that is the focus of most discussions of inter-Arab politics and highlights the changing relationship between state and nation.

[13] Wendt, "Anarchy is What States Make of It," 399.

[14] Keohane, R. 1989. *International Institutions and State Power*. Boulder: Westview Press, p. 3. Also see Young, Oran 1989. *International Cooperation*. Ithaca: Cornell University Press, p. 5.

[15] See Berger and Luckmann, *The Social Construction of Reality*, pp. 72–4; Stryker, Sheldon 1980. *Symbolic Interactionism: A Social Structural Perspective.*

Reading, Mass.: The Benjamin/Cummings Publishing Company, p. 57; Rosenau, James 1990. *Turbulence in World Politics.* Princeton: Princeton University Press, p. 212; and Jackson, J.A. (ed.) 1972. *Roles.* London: Cambridge University Press.

[16] See Searing, Donald 1991. "Roles, Rules, and Rationality in the New Institutionalism," *American Political Science Review* 85: 1249. Also see Rosenau, *Turbulence in World Politics,* p. 212.

[17] See Hollis, Martin 1994. *Philosophy of the Social Science.* New York: Cambridge University Press, pp. 163–82; Giddens, Anthony 1987. "Erving Goffman as a Systematic Social Theorist," in his *Social Theory and Modern Sociology.* Stanford: Stanford University Press, pp. 109–39. As Keohane acknowledges, "Institutions may also affect the understandings that leaders of states have of the roles they should play and their assumptions about others' motivations and perceived self-interest." "Neoliberal Institutionalism: A Perspective on World Politics," in Keohane, *International Institutions and State Power,* p. 6, emphasis added. Also see Holsti, K.J. 1970. "National Role Conceptions in the Study of Foreign Policy," *International Studies Quarterly* 14: 245–6.

[18] Sovereignty, however, led the early advocates of role "theory" to minimize systemic in favor of domestic forces. Holsti, "National Role Conceptions," p. 243.

[19] Stryker, *Symbolic Interactionism,* p. 73.

[20] Young, Crawford 1976. *The Politics of Cultural Pluralism.* Madison: University of Wisconsin Press, p. 38.

[21] See Wendt, "Anarchy is What States Make of It"; Bull, Hedley 1977. *Anarchical Society.* New York: Oxford University Press; Ruggie, John 1986. "Continuity and Transformation in the World Polity," in Keohane, Robert (ed.) *Neorealism and Its Critics.* New York: Columbia University Press, pp. 131–57; On Europe, see Spruyt, Hendrick 1994. *The Sovereign State and Its Competitors: An Analysis of Systems Change.* Princeton: Princeton University Press. On Africa, see Young, Crawford 1991. "Self-Determination, Territorial Integrity, and the African State System," in Deng, F. and Zartman, I.W. (eds.) *Conflict Resolution in Africa.* Washington, D.C.: Brookings Press, p. 384; Davidson, Basil 1992. *The White Man's Burden.* New York: Times Books, p. 106; and Jackson, Robert and Rosberg, Carl 1982. "Why Africa's Weak States Persist: The Empirical and Juridical in Statehood," *World Politics* 35: 1–24.

[22] For instance, John Ruggie argues that the development of the institution of sovereignty differentiated "among units in terms of possession of self and exclusion of others," and created an international order that enabled states to become the principal units of international life. Ruggie, "Continuity and Transformation in the World Polity," p. 145.

[23] See Barnett, Michael 1993. "Institutions, Roles, and Disorder: The Case of the Arab States System," *International Studies Quarterly* 37: 271–96, for a defense of pan-Arabism as an institution.

[24] It is also this meaning of Arab nationalism that most closely conforms to most definitions of nationalism. Specifically, nations are understood as having

a shared identity, past, and future, and nationalism is a political movement that demands that there be a correspondence between the nation and political authority. In short, modern-day nationalism is associated with the demand for a modern state. See Hobsbawn, E.J. 1990. *Nations and Nationalism Since 1780.* New York: Cambridge University Press; Gellner, Ernst 1983. *Nations and Nationalism.* Ithaca: Cornell University Press; Kedourie, Ellie 1994. *Nationalism* 4th ed. Cambridge: Basil Blackwell; and Haas, "Nationalism."

25 Tonnies, Ferdinand 1955. *Community and Association.* London: Routledge & Kegan Paul.

[26] Tibi, Bassam 1990. *Arab Nationalism,* 2nd edn. New York: St. Martin's Press, pp. 22–3.

[27] This is consistent with Tibi, ibid., p. 14.

[28] There are interesting parallels between the emerging European state system and the Arab states system. Two issues are particularly striking. First, European leaders learned a different conception of the state's interests; that is, they did not immediately understand or promote the distinction between their individual interests and the needs of the whole. See Hinsley, F.H. 1963. *Power and the Pursuit of Peace.* New York: Cambridge University Press, chap. 8. Moreover, both the early European state system and the Arab state system were characterized by the existence of overlapping authority claims that derived from substate, state, transnational, and religious institutions.

[29] Krasner, Stephen 1988. "Sovereignty: An Institutional Perspective," *Comparative Political Studies* 21: 83. Also see Gould, Stephen Jay 1989. *Wonderful Life: the Burgess Shale and the Nature of History.* New York: W.W. Norton; and Putnam, Robert 1993. *Making Democracy Work.* Princeton: Princeton University Press, p. 6.

[30] Young, *International Cooperation,* p. 65; North, Douglass 1990. *Institutions, Institutional Change, and Economic Performance.* New York: Cambridge University Press, pp. 86–7.

[31] Wrong, *The Problem of Order,* see, especially, chaps. 1 and 3. Oran Young similarly defines an international order as "broad, framework arrangements governing the activities of all (or almost all) the members of international society over a wide range of specific issues. We speak of an international political order, for example, as a system of territorially based and sovereign states that interact with one another in the absence of any central government." *International Cooperation,* p. 13.

[32] Magid, A. 1980. " 'Role Theory', Political Science, and African Studies," *World Politics* 32: 328; Buzan, Barry 1993. "From International System to International Society: Structural Realism and Regime Theory Meet the English School," *International Organization* 47: 345.

[33] See Wrong, *The Problem of Order,* chap. 3; Alexander, *Twenty Lectures,* chap. 1; and, Rosenau, James "Governance, Order, and Change in World Politics," in Rosenau, J. and Cziempel, E. (eds.) 1992. *Governance without Government: Order and Change in World Politics.* New York: Cambridge University Press, pp. 9–11.

[34] See Lebow, Richard Ned 1994. "The Long Peace, the End of the Cold War, and the Failures of Realism," *International Organization* 48: 252–9, for a good overview and criticism of the neorealist focus on the role of force for understanding international stability and change. On the polarity debate, see Waltz, Kenneth 1964. "The Stability of the Bipolar World," *Daedelus* 93: 881–909; and Niou, Emerson and Ordershook, Peter 1990. "Stability in Anarchic International Systems," *American Political Science Review* 84: 1207–34. On hegemonies, see Gilpin, Robert 1981. *War and Change in World Politics.* New York: Cambridge University Press. On balances of power, see Waltz, Kenneth 1979. *Theory of International Politics.* Reading, Mass.: Addison-Wesley, chap. 6.

[35] Gilpin, *War and Change in World Politics*, p. 50.

[36] For instance, E.H. Carr writes, "The homo politicus who pursues nothing but power is as unreal a myth as the homo economicus who pursues nothing but gain." 1964. *The Twenty Years' Crisis.* New York: Harper & Row, p. 97.

[37] Moreover, Kissinger's narrative intimates that these legitimation principles were not shaped by the distribution of military power alone. 1964. *A World Restored.* Boston: Houghton Mifflin.

[38] Waltz, *Theory of International Politics*, p. 74–7. In 1993. *The Logic of Anarchy.* New York: Columbia University Press, pp. 39–40, Barry Buzan, Charles Jones, and Richard Little also focus on the relationship between socialization and international order.

[39] As Jeffrey Alexander writes: "For the sake of interpretation it is often more useful to move backwards, from one's discovery of the residual categories back to the basic tensions which they have been developed to obscure." *Twenty Lectures*, pp. 124–5. "It follows from this," writes Talcott Parsons, "that the surest symptom of impending change in a theoretical system is increasingly general interest in such residual categories." 1968. *The Structure of Social Action*, vol. I. New York: Free Press, p. 18.

[40] For realist-inspired explanations, see Vatikiotis, P.J. 1971. *Conflict in the Middle East.* London: Allen & Unwin; Vatikiotis, P.J. 1984. *Arab and Regional Politics in the Middle East.* New York: St. Martin's Press; Walt, *Origins of Alliances*; Telhami, Shibley 1990. *Power and Leadership in International Bargaining.* New York: Columbia University Press; and Owen, Roger 1992. *State, Power, and Politics in the Making of the Modern Middle East.* New York: Routledge Press, pp. 90–2.

[41] *Power and Leadership*, pp. 94–104. Moreover, the rise of the Gulf Arab states postdates the widely observed decline of pan-Arabism.

[42] Walt, *Origins of Alliances*, p. 87.

[43] Ibid., p. 149.

[44] See, for instance, Vatikiotis, *Arab and Regional Politics*; and Dessouki and Korany (eds.) *The Foreign Policies of the Arab States.*

[45] Another view holds the superpowers responsible for the decline of pan-Arabism and the rise of statism. See Barakat, Halim 1993. *The Arab World.* Berkeley: University of California Press, for this position. Although the superpowers have affected the region, and the Middle East can be understood as a

"subordinate system" since it is penetrated and affected by Great Power rivalries, I ally myself with those who portray the superpowers as accommodating themselves to, accentuating, or mitigating present inter-Arab dynamics. See Ajami, Fouad 1981. *The Arab Predicament*. New York: Cambridge University Press; Ben-Dor, *State and Conflict in the Middle East*; Brown, L. Carl 1984. *International Politics and the Middle East*. Princeton: Princeton University Press; Noble, "The Arab System"; Korany, Baghat and Dessouki, Ali 1984. "The Global System and Arab Foreign Policies," in Korany, B. and Dessouki, A. (eds.) *The Foreign Policies of Arab States*. Boulder: Westview Press, pp. 19–39; and Walt, *Origins of Alliances*, p. 158.

[46] See Keohane, Robert 1984. *After Hegemony*. Princeton: Princeton University Press; Krasner, Stephen (ed.) 1992. *International Regimes*. Ithaca: Cornell University Press. This rationalist approach is consistent with the British school. For instance, Hedley Bull argues that states construct international institutions such as sovereignty to organize their relations and to increase the prospect of order. In this respect, a primary goal of the society of states is the survival of the sovereign state, which is dependent on there being "a sense of *common interests* in the elementary goals of social life." *The Anarchical Society*, p. 53 (emphasis in original). This also parallels Bull's definition of international order: a "pattern of activity that sustains the elementary or primary goals of the society of states, or international society," p. 8. The issue in the Arab states system, however, was an inability to establish some rules of interaction because of a debate over whether, in fact, the Arab world should be organized around sovereignty, and whether, in fact, Arab states should survive. Closer to the mark, in this respect, is R.J. Vincent's summation of Bull's view on disorder: "The precariousness of order in international society can be understood as a direct reflection of the degree to which these sovereign states have not agreed to fundamental rules, particularly those who view themselves as victims of this system." Vincent, R.J. 1991. "Order in International Politics," in Miller, J.B.D. and Vincent, R.J. (eds.) *Order and Violence*. New York: Oxford University Press, p. 54.

[47] See Wendt, "Anarchy is What States Make of It"; Adler and Haas, "Conclusion," p. 368; Caporaso, "Microeconomics and International Political Economy," pp. 137–8; and Dimaggio, Paul and Powell, Walter 1991. "Introduction," in Dimaggio, P. and Powell, W. (eds.) *The New Institutionalism in Organizational Analysis*. Chicago: University of Chicago Press, pp. 1–40.

[48] See Berger, Peter 1966. "Identity as a Problem in the Sociology of Knowledge," *European Journal of Sociology* 7: 105–15; Young, *International Cooperation*, p. 197; Mead, G.H. 1962. *Mind, Self, and Society*. Chicago: University of Chicago, pp. 136–43. Institutions also signal who are the central agents. See Stryker, *Symbolic Interactionism*, p. 57. In this reading, sovereignty is more than simply a constraint on state action, for it also denotes that states are the central actors in international politics, and this gives them particular identities.

[49] See Ikenberry, G. John and Kupchan, Charles 1990. "Socialization and Hegemonic Power," *International Organization* 44: 289; and Wendt, "Anarchy is What States Make of It," p. 399.

[50] Young, *International Cooperation*, p. 212.

[51] Goffman, "The Interaction Order," pp. 5–7.

[52] See Karpat, Kemal 1988. "The Ottoman Ethnic and Confessional Legacy in the Middle East," in Esman, M. and Rabinovich, I. (eds.) *Ethnicity, Pluralism, and the State in the Middle East.* Ithaca: Cornell University Press, pp. 35–53; Hourani, Albert 1991. *A History of the Arab Peoples.* Cambridge, Mass.: Harvard University Press; and Mansfield, Peter 1973. *The Ottoman Empire and Its Successors.* New York: St. Martin's Press, for an overview of the international relations of the Middle East during this period.

[53] See Barnett, "Institutions, Roles, and Disorder."

[54] See Fromkin, David 1989. *A Peace to End All Peace: The Fall of the Ottoman Empire and the Rise of the Modern Middle East.* New York: Henry Holt, for a detailed study of this period. One reason for the mandate system was to instruct these potential states in the norms of international society in general and sovereignty in particular, thereby adhering to the Great Powers' interests. See Louis, Wm. Roger 1984. "The Era of the Mandates System and the Non-European World," in Bull, H. and Watson, A. (eds.) *The Expansion of International Society.* New York: Oxford University Press, pp. 201–13.

[55] Antonius, George 1965. *The Arab Awakening.* New York: Capricorn Books, p. 100. See Gershoni, Israel and Jankowski, James 1987. *The Search for Egyptian Nationhood.* New York: Oxford University Press, for an excellent study of Egyptian nationalism.

[56] This charge is raised by Antonius, *The Arab Awakening*, pp. 248–9, and Khadduri, Majjid 1946. "Towards an Arab Union: The League of Arab States," *American Political Science Review* 40: 90.

[57] See Taylor, Alan 1982. *The Arab Balance of Power System.* Syracuse: Syracuse University Press, p. 15; Breuilly, John 1982. *Nationalism and the State.* New York: St. Martin's Press, p. 124; Antonius, *The Arab Awakening*, pp. 325–6; Sharma, J.P. 1990. *The Arab Mind: A Study of Egypt, Arab Unity, and the World.* Dehli: H.K. Publishers and Distributors. One possibility is that had the Arab world remained politically whole, and not divided into separate administrative units, Arab independence movements might have become more pan-Arab in character. See Jackson and Rosberg, "Why Africa's Weak States Persist," for a similar observation concerning the West African states.

[58] Many statist-oriented movements were associated with particular class interests. See Khoury, Philip 1987. *Syria and the French Mandate.* Princeton: Princeton University Press; Hourani, Albert 1946. *Syria and Lebanon: A Political Essay.* New York: Oxford University Press, p. 118; and Batatu, Hanna 1978. *The Old Social Classes and the Revolutionary Movements in Iraq.* Princeton: Princeton University Press.

[59] Anderson, *Imagined Communities*, p. 73.

[60] Khalidi, Rashid 1991. "Arab Nationalism: Historical Problems in the Literature," *American Historical Review* 96: 1363–73; Khalidi, Rashid, Anderson, Lisa, Muslih, Muhammad, and Simon, Reeva (eds.) 1991. *Arab Nationalism.* New York: Columbia University Press.

[61] Tibi, *Arab Nationalism*, p. 16.

[62] Hourani, *A History of the Arab Peoples*, p. 316.

[63] See Antonius, *The Arab Awakening*; Hourani, *A History of the Arab Peoples*, p. 343.

[64] Hourani, *Syria and Lebanon*, p. 101. See Duri, A.A. 1987. *The Historical Formation of the Arab Nation*. New York: Croom Helm; Tibi, *Arab Nationalism*; Khalidi, "Arab Nationalism"; and Khalidi, et al. *Arab Nationalism*, for good overviews of Arab nationalism.

[65] Taylor, *The Arab Balance of Power*, p. 23. Also see MacDonald, Robert 1965. *The League of Arab States: A Study in the Dynamics of Regional Organization*. Princeton: Princeton University Press, pp. 33–8.

[66] See Owen, Roger 1983. "Arab Nationalism, Arab Unity, and Arab Solidarity," in Asad, T. and Owen, R. (eds.) *Sociology of the "Developing Societies": The Middle East*. New York: Monthly Review Press, p. 20, and Salame, Ghassan 1988. "Inter-Arab Politics: The Return to Geography," in Quandt, W. (ed.) *The Middle East: Ten Years After Camp David*. Washington: Brookings Press, pp. 345–6, for how pan-Arabism led to state policies that violated the principle of noninterference.

[67] For a related argument emphasizing sovereignty, see Gause, F. Gregory, III, 1992. "Sovereignty, Statecraft, and Stability in the Middle East," *Journal of International Affairs* 45: 441–67. Brynen, Rex 1991. "Palestine and the Arab State System: Permeability, State Consolidation, and the Intifada," *Canadian Journal of Political Science* 24: 594–621.

[68] See the essays in Luciani, Giacomo (ed.) 1990. *The Arab State*. Berkeley: University of California Press.

[69] The distinction between juridical and empirical sovereignty is consistent with that offered by Jackson, Robert 1990. *Quasi-States: Sovereignty, International Relations, and the Third World*. New York: Cambridge University Press.

[70] Linklater, Andrew 1990. "The Problem of Community in International Relations," *Alternatives* 15: 136.

[71] See Brynen, "Palestine and the Arab State System," p. 606, and Gause, "Sovereignty, Statecraft, and Stability," for additional claims that state-building has hardened the Arab territorial state and led to a decline in pan-Arabism.

[72] Bloom, William 1990. *Personal Identity, National Identity, and International Relations*. New York: Cambridge University Press, pp. 100–3; Mayall, James 1990. *Nationalism and International Society*. New York: Cambridge University Press, p. 121.

[73] Barnett, Michael 1992. *Confronting the Costs of War: Military Power, State, and Society in Egypt and Israel*. Princeton: Princeton University Press.

[74] *New York Times*, 8 July 1991, A2.

[75] Viorst, Milton 1991. "A Reporter at Large (Kuwait)," *New Yorker* 30: 38–9.

[76] See Davis, Eric 1992. "State Building in Iraq in the Iran–Iraq War and the Gulf Crisis," in Mildarsky, Manus (ed.) *The Internationalization of Communal*

Strife. London: Routledge & Kegan Paul, for the relationship between war and Iraqi nation-building.

77 Anderson, Lisa 1991. "Legitimacy, Identity, and the Writing of History in Libya," in Davis E. and Gavrielides, N. (eds.) *Statecraft in the Middle East*. Miami: Florida International University Press, p. 72. Also see the various contributions in Davis and Gavrielides (eds.) *Statecraft in the Middle East*. See Silberman, Neil Asher 1989. *Between Past and Present: Archeology, Ideology, and Nationalism in the Modern Middle East*. New York: Henry Holt, for a discussion of how archeology is used by Middle Eastern states to forge a national identity.

78 Baram, Amatzia 1990. "Territorial Nationalism in the Middle East," *Middle Eastern Studies* 26: 426–7; al-Khalil, Samir 1991. *The Monument: Art, Vulgarity, and Responsibility in Iraq*. Berkeley: University of California Press.

79 Brynen, "Palestine and the Arab State System," p. 611; Owen, "Arab Nationalism," p. 21.

80 Owen, "Arab Nationalism," p. 21.

81 Brynen, "Palestine and the Arab State System," p. 613.

82 Luciani, Giacomo and Salame, Ghassan 1990. "The Politics of Arab Integration," in Luciani (ed.), *The Arab State*, p. 398.

83 Baram, "Territorial Nationalism." Also see Hourani, *A History of the Arab Peoples*, p. 451. Gause, "Sovereignty, Statecraft, and Stability," p. 460, shows how an increasing percentage of the gross national product of these states is utilized by the government, demonstrating that the citizens' needs are more closely linked to the state.

84 Hourani, *A History of the Arab Peoples*, p. 448.

85 Wendt, "Anarchy is What States Make of It," pp. 405–7.

86 Ibid., pp. 406–7.

87 On interaction, social identities and roles, and order, also see Berger and Luckmann, *Social Construction of Reality*; Abercrombie, Nicholas 1986. "Knowledge, Order, and Human Autonomy," in Hunter, J. and Ainlay, S. (eds.) *Making Sense of Modern Times: Peter Berger and the Vision of Interpretive Sociology*. New York: Routledge & Kegan Paul, pp. 18–19; and Turner, Jonathan 1988. *The Theory of Social Interaction*. Palo Alto: Stanford University Press.

88 Boden, Deirdre 1990. "The World as it Happens: Ethnomethodology and Conversational Analysis," in Ritzer, George (ed.) *Frontiers of Social Theory*. New York: Columbia University Press, p. 189. This view, of course, is consistent with Wendt's phrase, "anarchy is what states make of it."

89 Porath, Yehoshua 1986. *In Search of Arab Unity*. London: Frank Cass; Seale, Patrick 1986. *The Struggle for Syria*. New Haven: Yale University Press; and Maddy-Weitzmann, Bruce 1993. *The Crystallization of the Arab State System*. Syracuse: Syracuse University Press.

90 Seale, *The Struggle for Syria*.

91 Kerr, Malcom *The Arab Cold War*; Taylor, *The Arab Balance of Power*, p. 37; Vatikiotis, *Arab and Regional Politics*, p. 84; and Owen, *State, Power, and Politics*, p. 88.

92 For these talks see Kerr, *Arab Cold War*.

[93] Ajami, *The Arab Predicament.*

[94] *BBC World Broadcasts,* ME/2519/A/8, 18 July 1967.

[95] Ansari, Hameid 1986. *Egypt: The Stalled Society.* Albany: State University of New York Press, p. 150.

[96] *BBC World Broadcasts,* ME/2561/A/6, 6 September 1967. Also see the editorials in the Baghdadi *al-Fajr al-Jadid* and the Egyptian *al-Akhbar al-Yawm,* reprinted in *BBC World Broadcasts,* ME/2558/A/3, 2 September 1967, and ME/2559/A/4, 4 September 1967, respectively. See Ajami, *The Arab Predicament,* for a fuller treatment of the symbolic significance of Khartoum.

[97] The decline of pan-Arabism also encouraged more regional affiliations and loyalties: "A North African (*maghribi*) or a Gulf Arab (*khaliji*) identity, which had once been an anathema, was no longer so, and the 'Egypt-first' slogan that had once been held in check gradually became acceptable." Salame, "Inter-Arab Politics," p. 322.

[98] For instance, Shaykh al-Nuhayyan of the United Arab Emirates observed that: "The Arab nation's split and fragmentation existed before the Gulf War, but this war has aggravated and deepened this split." "President on Prospects for Arab Unity," *FBIS-NES,* 20 March 1994, p. 25. Also see Lewis, "Rethinking the Middle East," pp. 103–4, and Karawan, Ibrahim 1994. "Arab Dilemmas in the 1990s: Breaking Taboos and Searching for Signposts," *Middle East Journal* 48: pp. 433–54.

[99] The rise of statist interests had immediate implications for regional security arrangements. The real importance, and the only surviving principle, of the Damascus Declaration of 1991, which was ostensibly designed to create a security alliance between the Gulf States and Syria and Egypt, was its insistence on sovereignty as the basis of inter-Arab politics. Coming on the heels of Iraq's denial of Kuwaiti sovereignty and claim that Gulf oil belonged to the Arabs, the Gulf Cooperation Council states held sovereignty and security as indistinguishable. *FBIS-NES-92–241,* 15 December 1992, pp. 10–11. As acknowledged by then Egyptian Minister of State for Foreign Affairs Boutros Boutros-Ghali, "The painful realities resulting from Iraq's invasion of Kuwait and its usurpation of the territory of a fraternal Arab state include the collapse of the traditional concept of pan-Arab security." (Interview and date not given.) Cited in *FBIS-NES-91–059,* 27 March 1991, pp. 9–10. Moreover, because there is less reason to differentiate between Arab and non-Arab states, it is possible to consider the inclusion of all regional actors in strategic alliances and balancing formulations. See "Arafat Suggests Formation of Mideast 'Regional Order'," *FBIS-NES,* 4 February 1994. Finally, at the recent Arab League conference, Arab states agreed for the first time that each could identify its own security threats. Granot, Oded "Outcome of Arab League Conference Analyzed," *Ma'ariv,* in *FBIS-NES,* 31 March 1994, p. 3.

[100] As Bernard Lewis notes, "The decline of pan-Arabism as a force shaping the policies of Arab governments can be measured in the level and intensity of their support for other Arab governments and peoples." "Rethinking the Middle East," p. 100. Prior to the 1970s Arab unity efforts generated much

public enthusiasm. Notable here is the 1958 announcement of the United Arab Republic between Syria and Egypt; it sent shock waves throughout the Arab world, and, relatedly, gave birth to the Arab Federation (*ittihad*) between Jordan and Iraq. Dann, Uriel 1989. *King Hussein and the Challenge of Arab Radicalism: Jordan, 1955–1967*. New York: Oxford University Press, chap. 6.

[101] See Hourani, *A History of the Arab Peoples*, p. 451.

[102] Farr, James "Understanding Conceptual Change Politically," in Ball, T., Farr, J., and Hanson, R. (eds.) 1989. *Political Innovation and Conceptual Change*. New York: Cambridge University Press, p. 33. See Tibi, *Arab Nationalism*, introduction to the 2nd ed., for a related discussion.

[103] See Tilly, Charles 1994. "States and Nationalism in Europe, 1492–1992," *Theory and Society* 23: 131–46, for a discussion linking the demise of empires and the rise of nationalism.

[104] Salame, "Inter-Arab Politics," pp. 321, 340, 351.

[105] Connolly, William 1983. *The Terms for Political Discourse* 2nd ed. Princeton: Princeton University Press, p. 70.

[106] Lewis, Bernard 1992. "Rethinking the Middle East," *Foreign Affairs* 71: 100–1.

[107] Mufti, Malik 1996. "Sovereign Creations: Pan-Arabism and State Formation" in *Syria and Iraq, 1920–1992*. Ithaca: Cornell University Press. Indeed, the 1978 Syrian–Iraqi agreement, which produced little excitement and was given little significance outside a narrow political spectrum or the state's borders, was a surprise and was viewed as a blatant attempt by Iraq to replace Egypt as leader of the Arab World and Assad to consolidate his domestic position. Owen, *State, Power, and Politics*, p. 91.

[108] There is also evidence that the language of legitimation has changed: while Arab leaders still claim that their actions further the interests of the Arab nation (though after the Gulf War Arab states are less reserved in defending their policies in the name of state interests), they no longer suggest that such actions are designed to accomplish the ultimate goal of political unification.

[109] See Mansbach, Richard and Vasquez, John 1981. *In Search of Theory*. New York: Columbia University Press, chap. 4, for a full treatment of the methodological and theoretical issues involved in using agendas to trace shifts in international politics. Sela, Avraham "Middle East Politics and the Arab–Israeli Conflict," unpublished manuscript, argues that the very decision to convene an Arab summit in 1964 signaled that Nasser was beginning to abandon pan-Arabism. Although Arab summit meetings are a recent historical phenomenon, Arab leaders have had various top-level meetings since the 1940s, and are equally worthy of such an analysis. Indeed, my survey of these pre-1964 meetings of Arab heads of state suggests that pan-Arab concerns and the prospect of unification were defining items of the agenda.

[110] That no summit occurred in 1966 was testimony to the re-emergence of Arab radicalism. Vatikiotis, *Arab and Regional Politics*, p. 87.

[111] Walt, *The Origins of Alliances*, pp. 287–8.

[112] Also see Salame, "Inter-Arab Politics"; Brynen, "Palestine and the Arab

State System," p. 603; and Lewis, "Rethinking the Middle East," p. 117, for other arguments and indicators concerning the willingness of Arab leaders to recognize the principle of noninterference.

[113] See Bull, Hedley and Watson, Adam 1988. *The Expansion of International Society*. New York: Oxford University Press, for the general theme of the interaction between the expanding norms of international society and regional systems.

[114] Buzan, "From International System to International Society," p. 345.

[115] Linklater, "The Problem of Community," p. 149.

[116] Salame, Ghassam "Integration in the Arab World: The Institutional Framework," in Luciani, G. 1988. (ed.) *The Politics of Arab Integration*. New York: Croom Helm, pp. 278–9.

[117] While Islamic movements may or may not be compatible with juridical sovereignty, they challenge the internal sovereignty of many Arab states. See Piscatori, James 1986. *Islam in a World of Nation-States*. New York: Cambridge University Press, for an argument concerning the compatibility between Islam and juridical sovereignty; see Tibi, Bassam 1992. "Religious Fundamentalism and Ethnicity in the Crisis of the Nation-State in the Middle East," Working Paper 5.4 University of California, Berkeley: Center for German and European Studies, for the opposing claim. See Tibi, *Arab Nationalism*, pp. 17–20, for a discussion of the relationship between Islam and Arabism. For subnational identities see Khoury, Philip and Kostiner, Joseph 1990. "Introduction: Tribes and the Complexities of State Formation in the Middle East," in Khoury, P. and Kostiner, J. (eds.) *Tribes and State Formation in the Middle East*. Berkeley: University of California Press, pp. 1–22.

[118] Luciani, Giacomo 1990. "Introduction," in Luciani, Giacomo (ed.) *The Arab State*. Berkeley: University of California Press, p. xxx.

[119] See Smith, Anthony 1991. *National Identity*. Reno: University of Nevada Press, chap. 1; and Hall, John 1993. "Nationalisms: Classified and Explained," *Daedalus* 122: 1–28, for statements that do not equate nationalism with the creation and maintenance of a territorial state.

[120] Layne, Linda 1994. *Home and Homeland: The Dialogics of Tribal and National Identities in Jordan*. Princeton: Princeton University Press, p. 20.

7 Binding sovereigns: authorities, structures, and geopolitics in Philadelphian systems

Daniel Deudney

The Westphalian and the Philadelphian systems

The relationship between forms of legitimate political authority and the capacities of coercive power has been at the center of the Western study of politics since the ancient Greeks began systematically investigating politics. At least since the Middle Ages, these debates have been about "sovereignty."[1]

Because the modern European system has expanded globally over the last half millennium, students of international politics have focused on the Westphalian system of sovereign states as a paradigm so much that it seems inevitable and universal.

The essentials of the Westphalian system, codified as the core of realist international relations theory, are widely accepted. Westphalian realists presume a dyadic conception of political order: hierarchy inside and anarchy outside. Thus sovereign authority has two faces, an inside and an outside. Inside the territorial units, the sovereign state monopolizes the violent power that creates a hierarchy of higher and lower authorities. To avoid ambiguity, a hierarchically structured unit should be called a "hier-state."[2]

Outside and between states, authoritative governance is absent or fleeting. But interstate order exists, primarily because of two institutions and practices: mutual recognition of sovereignty and the balance of power. State sovereigns extend to one another the system of mutual recognition that creates a society of states, reflecting and embodying state supremacy, while moderating state power and anarchy. As Martin Wight, Hedley Bull, and others have noted, this European society of states existed in addition to the anarchical and balance-of-power system of states.[3] The external face of sovereignty in the

Westphalian system was a recognized claim to have exclusive authority over a particular territorial space and mutual nonintervention in the internal affairs of other sovereigns.[4]

The primary security practice of the units in the Westphalian system was balancing. Multifaceted and ill-defined, the balance of power refers both to a distribution of power among the units capable of maintaining the units, and, secondly, defending at least the largest unit, from conquest by a state seeking to overthrow the plural state system and to create a system-wide hierarchy, either loosely as a hegemony or tightly as an empire. The phrase "balance of power" also encompasses a constitutive practice of balancing or what the early modern Europeans spoke of as "counterpoise." Many realists see balancing activity as automatic, pervasive, and natural, while others see it as a social practice.[5]

Although the Westphalian system of authority and power has been hegemonic in modern world politics, it has not been universal. At the periphery and in the gaps of the Westphalian system, there have existed different political orders. Most notable of these are the Hanseatic League, the Swiss Confederation, the Holy Roman Empire, the Iroquois Confederation, the Concert of Europe, and the early United States.[6] These systems are alike because they are constituted without exclusive sovereignty within the units and are amalgamated with other similar units in ways that go beyond instrumental alliance or confederation. Realist theorists have had an extremely difficult time making sense of these political orders in terms of the central concepts of the Westphalian system. Beginning with the debate between Jean Bodin and Samuel Pufendorf over the constitution of Switzerland and the German empire, realist theorists have insisted that they are either federal states or interstate confederations, but never anything in between.[7]

Of the polities not fitting the Westphalian model, the Philadelphian system in the United States of America between the establishment of the Union (1781–89) and the Civil War (1861–65)[8] is of particular interest. The American political order and behavior is widely recognized as being "exceptionalistic."[9] Its size and internal diversity often lead to its being thought of as "what a United States of Europe would be," an alternative to the European Westphalian system rather than an oddly constituted state within it.[10] It had elaborate institutions that went beyond confederation, but stopped short of being an internally sovereign state. The American Union also interests international relations analysts because its designers had a clear grasp of the dynamics of the European anarchical state system. However, they sought to design and build institutions in North America that would not fall prey to these patterns of violent competition and conflict. The institutions in the United States were designed to avoid the Europeanization of North American politics. It is the only large-scale historical prototype of a political order explicitly designed as a self-conscious alternative to the Westphalian system of hier-states in anarchy.

The key to understanding the Philadelphian system is republicanism. Unfortunately, the fullest and strongest republican alternative to the realism centered upon Westphalian models has been overlooked by recent international theorists.[11] Like realism becoming neorealism, early republicanism's becoming liberalism and then neoliberalism has been greatly narrowed as well as refined. Of course, a full recovery of the ur-liberalism of republicanism is beyond the scope of this chapter, but much of the value of such a recovery can be found through the related early republican concepts of popular sovereignty,[12] social practices of binding, and social structures that are in between anarchy and hierarchy, not a hybrid of them.

Practices, social structures, and deep structures

Before exploring the Philadelphian alternative to the Westphalian system, a few general observations about social practices and structures are needed. The Westphalian starting and ending point for discussions of sovereignty in international relations has been challenged recently by various sociologically oriented theorists known as postmodern, reflectivist, and constructivist. These theorists have insisted that the Westphalian system is one of perhaps an unlimited number of possible configurations for political authority in large and extensive political orders. They argue that patterns of authority, legitimacy, and identity are more constitutive of interstate systems than are power capacities and relations, reversing the realist presumption that structure and power matter more than socially recognized norms. They also emphasize that social practices generate, sustain, and reproduce political orders.

One promise of constructivism is its opening to variation in the forms of authority, sovereign or otherwise, and social practices that constitute political order. Realizing this promise requires a conceptualization of different forms of authority and sovereignty relations, and of different social practices, both domestic and international, that generate and sustain security structures. In other words, the general constructivist attack upon premature closure will remain an ontological anxiety instead of a new set of insights into political order unless it can generate a set of variations in sovereignty and security practices.

In its strongest forms, constructivism challenges the very notion of social structure, but in milder forms, it also opens avenues for structural theory. The constructivist opening to variance and social practice should not be seen as an alternative to structural theory. Once social structures are recognized as constructed, international theory can explore how different social practices and social structures interact with one another. As such, constructivism is a way of enriching rather than overthrowing realist and structural theory.[13]

At the same time, the engagement between social construction and social structure should not be confined to the relatively narrow form of international structural theory that is associated with Kenneth Waltz's neorealism. A fuller structural theory must consider more variation in system structures than Waltz admits, and must consider the interaction between system and unit-level structures. In formulating such a broadened structural theory, the legacies of republicanism are particularly valuable because they provide conceptualizations of both unit and system-level structures that go beyond the neorealist dyad of hierarchy and anarchy.

Analysis of the interaction of authority, practices, and social structure, although broader than either social structuralism or constructivism, is incomplete without attention to deep material structures that are not generated by social practices. In correcting for the reification of social structures, constructivism risks its own blindness in failing to distinguish between social structures constituted by social practice, and material or deep structural realities that are not socially constructed. Natural and material realities structure human action, and such structures are subject to various socially constructed interpretations, but they are not generated by social practices.

In sum, an international theory enriched by constructivist insights about authority and practice – operating with a full set of unit and system structural variation, but still anchored in deep material structures – enables us to theorize about the relations between different forms of authority, social practices, social structures, and deep or material structures, as summarized in Figure 7.1.

Operating with these concepts and assumptions about the relevant

Factor	Range of variation
Inter-unit system structure	Anarchy, hierarchy, negarchy
Foreign policy practices	Hiding, balancing, binding extended popular
Unit-level authority	Extended popular sovereignty vs. state or national
Unit-level structure	Hier-state vs. federal republic
Deep (material) structure	Degree of geopolitical separation

Figure 7.1: Elements of system theory

components of a system of political order, this chapter advances a simple set of related claims that will be clearer after the terms have been more fully defined. I argue that sovereignty situated in an extended people produces governmental authorities structured neither as a hierarchy nor as an anarchy, but as what I call a "negarchy." Securing such a popular sovereignty requires distinctive social practices, both internally and externally. Such sovereigns prefer the foreign policy practices of hiding and binding over balancing. Successful binding replaces system-level anarchy with unions structured as negarchy rather than as hierarchy. But the choice between hiding and binding and the likely success of these practices depend upon particular deep material structural conditions.

The Philadelphian system: sovereignty, security structures, and social practices

The architects of the American political order proudly referred to it as a *novus ordo saeclorum*, a "new order of the ages," distinctive from the earlier republican city-states, and from the overall political order of Europe. Throughout the late eighteenth and early nineteenth centuries, many American and European observers echoed these bold claims, emphasizing that the American political order was unlike the European because of the central role of popular sovereignty in constituting the order, and the absence of a state in it. In contrast to the state or monarchical sovereignty of Europe, sovereignty in the American system rested with the people. As Alexis de Tocqueville observed, "The people reign over the American political world as God rules over the universe. It is the cause and end of all things; everything rises out of it and is absorbed back into it."[14] Also distinguishing it from the European pattern, the United States lacked a state, as Hegel and others noted.[15] It is easy enough to determine what this system was not, but to grasp what it was we must look more closely at popular sovereignty and governmental structures and the social practices that constituted them.

The location and salience of sovereignty

The first step in unraveling the Philadelphian system is to examine its distinctive patterns of authority. The Westphalian system had a particular pattern of sovereign authority, but to grasp alternatives to it one must return to the broader and earlier conceptions and distinguish sovereignty from governmental authority, unit autonomy and mutually recognized autonomy. Sovereignty is often thought of as a fundamentally contested concept, but simple semantic discrepancies obscure the actual disagreements and make the conceptual problems much worse than they are. In its original and basic meaning, sovereignty is the ultimate source of all legitimate authority in a polity.[16] As William Blackstone, the most authoritative eighteenth-century English constitutional commentator, said, "there is in all [types of government]

195

a supreme, irresistible, absolute, uncontrolled authority, in which the *jura summi imperii*, or the rights of sovereignty, reside."[17] This meaning of sovereignty is often conflated with the related question of authority, which refers to the actual exercise of legitimate power; autonomy, which refers to the independence of a polity vis-à-vis other polities; and recognized autonomy, which involves the rights, roles, and responsibilities of membership in a society of states.

These distinctions help clear up several confusions. Scholars who insist that freedom can survive only in political orders in which sovereignty is divided are not making a claim about divided sovereignty, but are conflating sovereignty and political authority. Republican talk of divided sovereignty is an imprecise expression of the claim that authorities should be exercised by several distinct bodies, and should retain some autonomy in relation to one another. Conversely, statists do not distinguish sufficiently between authority and sovereignty, and tend to leap from the definitional impossibility of divided sovereignty to the mistake of thinking a system of multiple authorities that are not hierarchically arranged is impossible or inconsistent with sovereignty.

Sovereignty can be situated in principle and practice in any of several places in a political order, and different locations result in very different authority structures. Most commonly, sovereignty rests either in the hands of the people as a whole or in the state apparatus or the leader of the state.[18] The relationship between the sovereign and the exercise of authority is generally one of salience: to what extent does the sovereign body actually wield authority? The sovereign body may be either engaged or recessed in exercising authority. The sovereign is engaged when it actually wields governmental authority. Although they disagreed often, Hobbes and Rousseau insisted that the sovereign be engaged. The sovereign of a polity is recessed when the exercise of authority has been delegated to some other body or bodies.

Location and salience can be combined to generate four fundamentally different political orders. (See Figure 7.2.)

A popular and engaged sovereign produces direct democracy. Such political orders must be small, for otherwise it would be impossible for the sovereign people to exercise political power directly. Alternatively, sovereignty can be located in the state leader or apparatus and, when engaged, produces the real-state. The third possibility is that of sovereignty situated in a single individual who does not directly exercise political power, which is known as a limited monarchy or a

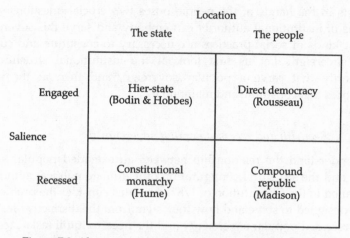

Figure 7.2: Alternative sovereignty configurations

constitutional monarchy. This possibility entails the delegation of authority from the sovereign monarch to various ministers.

Publius: *an extended popular sovereign*

The fourth possibility, sovereignty located in the people but recessed, is the basis of the American Union as described by the *Publius* trio of John Jay, Alexander Hamilton, and James Madison in *The Federalist Papers*. They argue that the new generative principle of the American Union is a popular sovereignty[19] that is spatially and numerically extended. The preamble of the Constitution begins "We the People." As Madison wrote, "the ultimate authority, wherever the derivative may be found, resides in the people alone."[20]

Because the sovereign people are so numerous and dispersed, the actual governance of a recessed sovereign public must be carried out by authorities with power delegated by the people rather than directly by the people. A large, extensive sovereign necessarily will be recessed in its exercise of political power. The structures of the American Union aim to exploit the opportunities and cope with problems that arise in delegating power. The delegated authorities of a recessed sovereign must be structured to serve its interests while preventing its sovereignty from being usurped.

To proclaim that the ultimate legitimate authority – the sovereignty

– rests in the hands of the people poses two crucial questions: what forms of institutional authority can embody and serve this sovereign? What kinds of social practices are necessary to constitute and sustain this sovereign? Let us first look at the institutional structures of authority that serve a popular sovereign, and then at the social practices that constitute and maintain it.

Security and recessed popular sovereignty

To understand the relationship between an extended popular sovereign and the structural configuration of legitimate political authorities specified in the Constitution of 1787, one must consider the problems it was designed to solve and how they stem from the distinctive features of a recessed popular sovereignty and the need to fulfill tasks faced by all political orders.

The provision of security by the control of violence was a primary concern of the framers of the American Constitution.[21] The Declaration of Independence of 1776 lists "life" before "liberty and the pursuit of happiness" as the natural animating goals of human beings. The *Federalist Papers* mention security 116 times. Montesquieu, the most cited authority of the era, defined political liberty as "a tranquillity of mind arising from the opinion each person has of his own safety."[22]

To be effective instruments of security, the governmental authorities in the service of an extended and recessed popular sovereign must simultaneously cope with two prime and interrelated threats, anarchy and despotism, which represent too little and too much order. Anarchy and despotism, which are absolute opposites, are mutually generating. Both anarchy and despotism are threats within and between the states; therefore security threats come in four forms: domestic revolution and tyranny and external war and empire.

Anarchy within states was associated with unconstrained democracy and factional strife. It was ameliorated in America by a union that guaranteed republican government within the units and possessed a union government with the authority and capability to maintain order or repel revolution in the units. Interstate anarchy is a hydra-headed source of insecurity, directly through war and invasion, and indirectly as a stimulus to the growth of governmental power and despotism within the units. To combat the threat of interstate anarchy, the framers of the Constitution formed a union between the American states that circumscribed the military autonomy of the states, and a union governmental apparatus focused upon counterbalancing threats from other states still in an anarchic relation to the union. The framers of the Constitution also saw despotism – the accumulation of unchecked and oppressive power in the state apparatus – as a threat to security. To combat this threat they constituted the union government with an elaborate system of power constraint devices such as popular election of office holders, limited terms of office, and separations, vetoes, and balances of power. But fearing that such measures might ultimately fail, they relied upon the armed citizen militia to reduce the need for a large standing army in the hands of the union government and to serve as an ultimate external check to its potential for oppression.

Republican versus state security

In the Westphalian model, the institutional outcome of the hier-state apparatus invested with full political authority follows simply and directly from where the sovereignty is situated. To generate institutional structures from *Publius*'s recessed and extended sovereignty involves a second, not so simple, translation.[23] As with the Westphalian model, the American system rested upon the presumption that the governmental structure should be configured first and most essentially to serve the security interest of the sovereignty in whose name and on whose behalf it rules. But the American Union solution to the security problem cannot simply depend upon the centralized state apparatus. For an extended popular sovereign, the state is as much a potential source of security threat to the sovereign as it is an indispensable instrument in providing security from outside threats. Another security threat that can arise in a polity based upon popular sovereignty is the tyranny of the democratic majority against the interests of other parts of the polity.

The first step toward security is the suspension of anarchy by the creation of a government, but the government created to provide security can itself be a threat to the security of the body politic. Government may be the protector of the citizenry in principle, but is often a predator of the populace in practice.[24] Or as James Madison classically noted, "You must first enable the government to control the governed; and next place oblige it to control itself."[25] Good government optimizes security rather than maximizing order. In designing institutions to control violence, the Founding Fathers sought to strike a balance between two simultaneously necessary but inconsistent goals. Like Hobbes, they sought to maintain internal order between the parts and security from outside threats. They also sought to guard the guardians, and to guarantee that the institutional solutions to the problems of internal order and external security did not themselves become security threats to the inhabitants of the country.

The basic insight here is that security from violence is intimately connected to civic and political freedoms. To be a subject or slave is to be inherently insecure against the predations of the master or absolute ruler. For the individual, despotic state power can be more threatening than the anarchic state of nature because it is more systematic and relentless. In etching his extreme vision of the state of nature where life was "nasty, brutish and short," Hobbes emphasized that even the strongest man is vulnerable in the state of nature, because even he must sleep.[26] But in an unfree polity, the strongest man is vulnerable to the exercise of arbitrary state power even if he is awake and actively resisting. As John Locke observed, anyone is "in much worse condition, who is exposed to the arbitrary power of a man, who has the command of 100,000, than he that is exposed to the arbitrary power of 100,000 single men."[27]

Concentrations of unconstrained power threaten security because they are apt to be abused. This republican opposition to hierarchy is based upon assumptions of human frailty, commonly associated with realism rather than liberalism: humans are generally self-interested and rational in relating means to ends, but particular individuals are prone to lapses in judgment and instrumental rationality, and the opportunities of extreme power can produce corruptions. As Montesquieu observed, "every man invested with power is apt to abuse it."[28] Advocates of authoritarian and hierarchical orders often emphasize the depravity and weakness of humans as a reason why strong government is necessary, but in doing so they raise the stakes for statecraft. Either state structures constrain the leaders, or else the leaders must somehow rise above the maladies of human frailty.

Structure I: anarchy, despotism, and union

To achieve security against the full panoply of threats recognized by republican political theory required a complex architecture of political structures, whose main features we must examine to grasp the institutional implications of an extended popular sovereign.

The drafters of the Philadelphia Union feared anarchy, violent disorder, and revolution within the states.[29] They were committed to popular sovereignty, but saw democracy as a source of instability and insecurity. History showed that the small city-state government in ancient Greece and early modern Italy were "the wretched nurseries of unceasing discord," in a "perpetual vibration between the extremes of tyranny and anarchy."[30] Direct democracy slid into mob rule and then succumbed to coups and despotism. A union of such polities with a federal government, authorized and equipped to intervene and prevent revolution or coup, would preserve democracy in the states by curing its excesses. Hence, the Constitution (in Article 4) guaranteed the members of the Union a "republican form of government." Extension is crucial because turmoil in all the states at once is unlikely, and enables the chief federal magistrate to suppress revolutions in one republican state with forces drawn from the others, which is what the Washington administration did to suppress the Whiskey Rebellion.[31]

Another possible source of insecurity was violent conflict between the several states in anarchy. Capturing the essence of what today is known as Waltzian neorealism, Hamilton observed, "To look for a continuation of harmony between a number of independent unconnected sovereignties situated in the same neighborhood would be to disregard the uniform course of human events."[32] The most probable scenario was that the governors of the larger states would use their militias to settle conflicts with their neighbors.[33]

Interstate anarchy is also an indirect security threat because it strengthens internal central power, risking internal despotism. To respond to outside threats, more concentrated power is needed. An internal imbalance of power must be created to address the imbalance created by the external source of power. This creates a tragic trade-off for free government. As Hamilton observed "To be more safe become willing to run the risk of being less free."[34] Inter-unit anarchy and the state of war stimulate preparations for war, which in turn form concentrated government power threatening to public security.

The solution to both the direct and indirect threats of anarchy is union. This solution is consistent with the sovereignty of an extended public. For polities in which sovereignty is situated in an extended recessed public, union extends the constitutive principle of the units to the inter-unit system level, and reinforces sovereign prerogatives. The creation of a union security government entails the further division of authorities and the relocation of some of them in a new tier of government erected above the existing ones. Popular sovereigns can throw new governments over existing ones, as well as overthrow governments that have been usurped or corrupted. Union replicates the constitutive logic of recessed popular governance upon a larger scale. Recessed popular sovereigns use union to avoid the threat posed by the expansion of their own governmental authorities. In polities with a recessed popular sovereign, union preserves sovereignty. At the same time, the strenuous defense of their polities' full autonomy through government expansion into a state risks compromising it.

The union to solve the problem of anarchy fell far short of a complete merger. The Constitution did not eliminate the independent military power of the several states, but constrained the ends to which the states could employ its militias: the governors of the states could call up the militias to maintain order within the borders of their own states but not for activities beyond them.[35] Unrestrained by the union, state militias were perceived to be an instrument of potential interstate conflict. Within the American Union, however, they could play a vital role of counterbalancing power centralized in the union government, a role that would be lost should they be eliminated, or if their control was vested solely in the hands of the central government. The constraint of the states was reinforced by the application of federal law upon individuals rather than upon states. If they sought to exercise violent power outside the parameters set in the Constitution, individual office holders in the states were liable to criminal prosecution in the federal courts.

Structure II: external threats and concentrated power

The union between states eliminated anarchy between them, but was not so universal as to completely eliminate the threat of foreign powers exercised in the anarchic state of war. The newly independent American states feared that European states would attempt to reassert imperial control over them.[36] To combat this threat, the central government was endowed with two key authorities: raising a standing army and navy and the revenues needed to support them, and calling the state militias into action. The framers of the Constitution also created an office of chief magistrate, the president, whose most important power was commander-in-chief of the armed forces. Executive command of the armed forces could be an instrument of domestic oppression, but a concentration of power was a necessary accommodation to political and military realities.

The American union also sought to secure itself from foreign predation by gaining recognition from the European powers of its independence and rights under international law. Given the greater relative power of the European states in the late eighteenth century, Americans were forced to interact with the Europeans on terms largely established by the Europeans. By playing the sovereign recognition game as it had been established by the Europeans, the Americans could reduce European intervention into their affairs. The members of the Continental Congress clearly sought to achieve recognition as sovereign by the European powers, and a union government was needed to create a repository for this externally recognized sovereignty.

Structure III: limited and divided centralized powers

The centralized power of the union government in turn required careful constraints. In an extended union, there is more power potential; consequently relative power against any outside threat increases greatly. Yet the extent of the union makes it formidable enough to deter aggression without a strong state. The importance of the negative as a principle for structuring governmental agencies rises as the people are more extended. The union security government entailed the delegation of authorities at even greater distance from the sovereign, and, all else being equal, this increases the chances of usurpation unless accompanied by an increase in how much the negative dominates. The further power is removed from the people, the more it must be constrained.

The political theorists most widely read by Americans and their own recent experience taught the citizens of the newly independent American states that standing armies were the critical tool by which central political authorities could oppress and dispossess them.[37] The colonists believed that the English Constitutional constraints on the monarchical power had been circumvented or corrupted by the crown's ability to raise a standing army. The Declaration of Independence attacked George III's effort "to render the Military independent of and superior to the Civil Power." Questions concerning the establishment of a standing army were the most hotly contested in the debates over ratification, as the antifederalists painted it a grave threat to the citizenry.[38]

To combat this security threat, the founders went to great lengths to prevent the central government from initiating war on its own accord. The election of the office holders within the central government was an important but incomplete restraint. Since elections were infrequent, war-making authority was divided between the legislature and the executive. Although they felt compelled to centralize command of the armed forces, they vested the authority to declare war, raise taxes, set military policy, and ratify treaties in the Congress.[39] By carefully separating the war-making authority between the executive and the legislature, the founders sought to insure that the decision to make war would involve a process with checks and balances, and that the authority to initiate and sustain a war were removed from the hands of the commander-in-chief and vested in the branch of the central government closest to the people.[40]

Binding union and structural negarchy

More than a confederation of states in anarchy, and less than a state with extensive devolution, the complex structure of the Philadelphian system seems to defy simple classification, in contrast to the simplicity and elegance of anarchy and hierarchy as structural principles.

Was the Philadelphian system a hierarchy? To begin with, it is important not to confuse order with hierarchy, as many realists have been doing at least since the times of Hobbes. The Philadelphian system was not a hierarchy in the sense of a structure of authorities in which one rules over another because the center did not rule over the parts. The federal or union government had significant authority in many functional areas but did not have the authority to command the states. One cannot say that the Constitution ruled because it is inappropriate to say that an agreement or charter, rather than a human, ruled. The Constitution set out the fundamental rules of the system, but did not itself rule, and the Supreme Court was more a referee than a ruler. The relationship between the states, the federal government, and various groupings of the people was neither anarchic nor hierarchical.

Could it not be said that there was a hierarchy because there was an ultimate authority, a sovereign, that is, the extended people as a whole? There was hierarchy in the Philadelphian system to the extent that there was one sovereign in the system. However, because this sovereign encompassed all the people and acted as sovereign only to create the Constitution, and to amend it through the principle of concurrent majority, there was not a hierarchy of actors in which some ruled over others because all actors were subsumed as constitutive members of the sovereign.

The institutional architecture of a government in the service of an extended and recessed popular sovereign must be more complex than a Westphalian hier-state. In its overall structure, it is a cross-cutting arrangement of negatives and constraints. It is a rounded system of constraining the power of the states, democratic majorities, sectional tendencies, the central government, and foreign governments. Its essence is what John C. Calhoun called the Constitution of the negative: "the power of preventing or arresting the action of the government, be it called by what term it may, veto, interposition, nullification, check, or balance of power."[41] Instituting a government to regulate relations between members of the polity is the first and most necessary of political tasks, but it remains incomplete – or too complete – without negatives.

Because the overall system architecture negates, it is appropriate to call the structural principle of this order negarchical and the overall order a negarchy. The tasks that define security negarchies are not arbitrary, and are intimately connected to the logics of both hierarchy and anarchy. *Negarchy is the arrangement of institutions needed to prevent simultaneously the emergence of hierarchy and anarchy.* In a workable negarchy, the particular configurations of negatives vary with the relative strengths of multiple threats, but the antithesis to hierarchy and anarchy remains constant. Understood in this way, negarchy is a third – and liberal – structural principle of political order, along with hierarchy and anarchy.

Social practices I: popular freedom and virtue

To take the next step in analyzing the Philadelphian system, we must relate its distinctive patterns of sovereignty and security structure to its specific social practices. This chapter does not provide a full analysis[42] of the constitutive social practices of this system, but a brief review of three related clusters of social practices will help demonstrate the mutual dependence of particular social structures and social practices upon one another.

The Philadelphian system rested upon the people, therefore the social practices of the people in constituting themselves as a people played an important role. To constitute themselves as a sovereign, the people of the United States had to assume and sustain a particular political community and identity. Americans often referred to themselves as making up a "nation," but the late eighteenth- and early nineteenth-century meanings of this term were relatively empty, and had few of the connotations of ethnic homogeneity that are today associated with this protean term.[43] As many historians have observed, American nationality was distinctive from its European counterparts because of the central position of regime principle over ethnic or state dimensions.[44]

Directly related to its distinctive authority patterns and governmental structures was the American republican civic identity. Americans primarily thought of themselves as free and virtuous. Unlike subsequent liberal and neoclassical economic approaches, which take free and self-directed individuals to be an unquestioned starting point, the republicanism of the founders held that free men depended upon powerful social institutions that were demanding to create and maintain. At a time when individual freedom, political democracy, and social egalitarianism were rare and widely perceived to be precarious, this fundamental liberalism of the American people was both a powerful and distinguishing basis of political identity.[45]

Republican civic identity was reinforced and reproduced through mass public education, ceremonies and rituals, and public architecture and iconography.[46] Its most important basis, however, was the political economy of "possessive individualism."[47] Private property, adequate in scope and productivity and widely distributed, gave practical viability to the juridical and social constructions of the autonomous individual. The centerpiece of early social republicanism[48] was the "freehold" or "yeoman" farmer. Hymns to the independent agricultural proprietor were omnipresent in the political discourse of the era. Perhaps the most elaborate statement of this agricultural social republicanism was Harrington's *Oceana*, which firmly linked the widespread distribution of landed property to the constitution of a free people. The animus against both manufacturing and purely commercial activities expressed by Thomas Jefferson, John Taylor, and others that seems so archaic in highly developed market capitalism, was motivated by the fear that economic dependence was incompatible with political freedom.[49] A crucial reason why the American pursuit of social republicanism centered on "free soil, free men" was so successful was the existence of large quantities of land that could be readily developed with the technology of the time.

Unlike subsequent liberal and democratic emphasis upon rights and interests over responsibilities, the early American republican civic identity gave equal status to civic self-restraint, or *virtue*. The record of earlier self-governing regimes, carefully studied and constantly referenced by Americans of the time, suggested that popular liberty was precarious and readily lost without citizen virtue. The vocabularies of virtue and its antithesis, corruption, were as protean as they were ubiquitous in American public discourse.[50] But primarily, to be virtuous in republican America meant to practice self-restraint. Decentralized political structure and absence of a coercive hierarchy were understood to be possible only if the people disciplined themselves. Without popular self-discipline, conflicts would be too sharp and passions too extreme to be mediated by the negarchically configured governmental structures. Republican virtue also meant putting the interests of the public over private ones.[51] George Washington, the exemplar of the republican virtue of self-restraint, was memorialized as Cincinnatus rather than Caesar.[52] At the macro-level, the virtue of self-restraint meant the practice of compromise between states and sections, without which the union could not have held together.[53] Finally, American republican virtue also meant that citizens had a skilled knowledge of procedures and mechanisms, both of which were objects of extensive educational effort.

The long record of illiberal and hierarchical political orders demonstrates the ease with which humans may be socialized or disciplined into obedience. Yet where can free individuals gain the psychological practices (or, in the language of moral philosophy, "character") of self-discipline without also assuming deference to traditional or hierarchical authorities? In ways not fully appreciated by the Turner School, the frontier was partly the source of self-discipline. The frontier life of the pioneer, while anarchic in many ways, was also very rugged. Converting the untamed wilderness into cultivated land and then cultivating it required enormous effort that exerted a great disciplining effect on early Americans. The encounter with the never fully subduable "other" of nature provided the *paidaia* (education) of the "rugged individual" by providing discipline without a social disciplinarian.[54]

Social practices II: legal proceduralism and constitutionalism

The second cluster of social practices constituting the Philadelphian system were legal proceduralism and constitutionalism. The governmental structure of the American Union was complex, and depended upon actors able to operate it.

The American emphasis upon laws and procedures to resolve conflicts and allocate social goods was deeply rooted in the American social and economic structure. Feudal vestiges were few and steadily shrinking, particularly after the flight of many royalists. The dominant social class in America consisted of property owners who purchased rather than inherited land, and this interstate network of business elites was a bastion of union support. The land tenure and criminal justice systems were served by a large number of lawyers, and, as Tocqueville observed, the "American aristocracy" was the "bench and the bar."[55] Lawyers were the Gramscian organic intellectuals of capitalist society, and their social practice of resolving conflict by independent courts and applying tort law gave a distinctively pacific cast to American politics.

The power of the American practice of legal proceduralism to moderate the dynamics of anarchy was demonstrated in the interstate territorial conflict between Connecticut and Pennsylvania over the Wyoming Valley (in what is now northeastern Pennsylvania) that stemmed from overlapping charter grants. Several violent skirmishes indicated that this conflict would be resolved by armed struggle, but both states accepted legal arbitration of the dispute by a special court in Trenton established by the Confederation Congress.[56] For Americans, the crucial element in land ownership was juridical recognition and not hereditary right. This societal orientation made recourse to interstate violence less appealing than contracts and arbitration.[57]

The importance of the norm of compromise and the practice of legal proceduralism also can be seen in the great intersectional compromises that kept the Union intact during the rapid expansion of the early nineteenth century. Admission of new states in the West had important ramifications for the balance of power between slave-holding and free states in the Senate and Electoral College. In 1820, 1833, and 1850, sectional Great Compromises saved the Union. These wide-ranging and multi-sided agreements were similar to interstate alliances and regimes.[58] Had compromise not been reached, the new state aspirants to admission, although located on American land, would have gradually meant the emergence of an interstate system. In part, the Great Compromises depended upon the ability to roughly pair new entries to the Union, but also depended upon the strength of proceduralist practices and compromise norms.[59]

The apex of the American practice of complex proceduralism was, of course, the Constitution itself. Throughout the early nineteenth century the Constitution occupied a position of particular reverence in American politics and popular culture. The widespread notion that the Constitution was a "machine that would go by itself" constituted the great myth of Constitutionalism, reflecting the belief that its processes were just, and legitimating the practices of proceduralism without which it would have just been another piece of paper.[60]

Social practices III: popular arms control

The third social practice intimately connected with the viability of the American security structures was popular arms control. The founders were not content to rely upon elections and the separation of powers within the federal government; they sought to guarantee that a robust and permanent counterbalance to the central government continued to exist in the hands of the several states and the citizenry. Echoing Hobbes's admonition that covenants without the sword are unreliable, the founders were unwilling to rely solely upon parchment barriers, but instead sought to guarantee that the sword would remain firmly in the hands of the sovereign, the people. William Blackstone had insisted that all citizen rights ultimately depended upon the possession of arms by the citizen body.[61] The history of state-building in early modern Europe also seemed to demonstrate that an armed people and militia were a vital bulwark against monarchical absolutism.[62] The maintenance of a robust military capacity in the hands of the citizenry served as the ultimate counterweight against a despotic concentration of power in the federal government. Should the limitations on the government fail, the people retained the capacity to balance against it, which was enshrined in the Second Amendment's guarantee: "A well-regulated Militia, being necessary to the security of a free State, the right of the people to keep and bear Arms, shall not be infringed."[63] The Constitution did not legalize rebellion, but it did legalize the instruments necessary to do so. Maintaining a significant proportion of the polity's armed force in the militia also constrained the ability of the central government to wage unpopular foreign wars because it required the active mobilization of civil society to wage war.

Publius *versus Webster and Calhoun*

The final step in our exploration of the role of sovereignty concerns the American Civil War of 1861 to 1865. The basic causes of this conflict were slavery, particularly problematic in a polity based upon individual liberty, and the effects of rapid expansion upon the balance of power between the sections. Competing conceptions of sovereignty also were at issue, and a brief glance at the alternative constructions of popular sovereignty will help sharpen our understanding of *Publius's* extended popular sovereign.

At the core of the first United States Constitution as interpreted by *Publius* is popular sovereignty. But *which people* were sovereign in the American polity became fundamentally contested. In the period between the founding and the Civil War, there were two challenges to the *Publius* sovereign. Both also claimed to be forms of popular sovereignty, but they were radically subversive of the *Publius* institutional design. These struggles over the nature and possessor of sovereignty in the American Union culminated in the American Civil War of 1861 to 1865, in which eleven Southern states sought to secede to form their own separate confederate union, but were militarily conquered and occupied by the Union government controlled by the Northern states.

One challenger, stated most powerfully by Senator John C. Calhoun of South Carolina, was the proposition that sovereignty resided in the peoples of the states and that the Union Constitution was in effect a confederative one that could be ended if the peoples of the several states decided to do so. Calhoun sought to demonstrate that the right of secession was implicit in the Constitution of 1787, but more important, that it was an inherent attribute of sovereignty situated in the hands of the peoples of the several states.[64]

The other challenger did not have the philosophical sophistication of Calhoun but ultimately was the victor in the bloodbath of the 1860s. This interpretation, stated most powerfully by Senators Daniel Webster of New Hampshire and Robert Livingston of Louisiana, argued that sovereignty was situated in the people of the American nation as a whole, and was exercised by democratic majorities operating through the structures of the central government created by the Constitution of 1787.[65]

The views of Webster and Calhoun had radically different implications for the political viability of the American Union, but are quite similar at their core. The powers that Webster attributes to the people of the United States, Calhoun also attributes to the people of the states. Both concepts of sovereignty are readily encompassed as variants of the essential Westphalian scheme: Webster, a national liberal democratic state; Calhoun, a confederation of national but not necessarily liberal democratic states. The view of *Publius* sits alone outside this realist typology of orders because it alone constitutes sovereignty in the people as a whole, denying both the statist and democratic popular claims to sovereign authority.

These competing views of sovereignty in the American system were intimately connected with the central political struggles in the American Union. *Publius*'s view was an artful synthesis of the competing nationalist and federalist views in the Convention of 1787 and in the subsequent debate between the advocates of the Constitution and its antifederalist opponents. As the Union entered its great crisis in the middle of the nineteenth century, few people still held the *Publius* understanding of sovereignty in the American Union. The views of sovereignty became polarized, with Southerners adhering to Calhoun's view, and Northerners tending toward Webster's.[66] The fate of this clash over the nature of sovereignty in the American system was resolved in favor of Webster's position during the extraordinary presidency of Abraham Lincoln, who subscribed to Webster's view and was able to exercise the extra-constitutional powers that helped preserve and change the Constitution.

Popular sovereignty and the beginnings of the civil war

The Kansas–Nebraska Act of 1854 and the bloody conflicts it unleashed marked a crucial step toward the breakup of the American Union and the Civil War.[67] The open civil war that raged between settlers from the North and South on the frontier in "bleeding Kansas" rehearsed the great conflict that was to engulf the core regions of the Union.[68] This episode is particularly interesting because of the role popular sovereignty played in it. The question of the composition of new states in the Union had been of utmost importance in the constitutional architecture of the Union since the founding. The Northwest Ordinance of 1787, negotiated separately from the Constitution of 1787, established a system for entry to the Union for states lying north of the Ohio River. It provided that slavery would not be allowed in the region. At the same time, the Western cessions of the southern slave states that later became Kentucky, Tennessee, Alabama, Mississippi, and much of Louisiana were being settled by people from the slave states. With the Missouri Compromise of 1820, the Compromise of 1833, and finally with the Great Compromise of 1850, the question of slavery in the new states – and of the balance of power between the sections in the Senate and the Electoral College – was decided by an elaborate and carefully negotiated agreement between the sectional factions in Congress. In each of these agreements, the question of slavery within the units was subject to decision by a general compromise between the major sectional interests.

The Kansas–Nebraska Act of 1854 marked a new, and ultimately catastrophic, procedure to determine the free–slave state balance: it was up to the settlers in the territories to decide. In this Act, the principle of popular sovereignty within the units was empowered to resolve a question that touched upon the core balance of power and interests of the entire Union. This "squatter's sovereignty" was democratic, and consistent with the general rhetorical commitment to democracy and popular sovereignty in the American polity. But it was fundamentally different from the popular sovereignty that *Publius* conceived of as being invested in the extended people instead of in any part or in a majority of them.

In resolving the question of general Union importance with popular sovereignty at the state level, the first blows of the Civil War were struck. Partisans from both North and South poured into the state and sought to set up rival state governments. Violence broke out as extremists from both sides sought to intimidate and kill their opponents. The radical abolitionist John Brown and his followers murdered pro-slavery settlers, and, evading capture, returned to the East, where they sought to seize the federal arsenal at Harper's Ferry in Virginia and ignite a general rebellion of slaves in the South. For the first time since the Revolution, American citizens were killing each other over political questions. The norms of political compromise that had been so central to the virtue of the Constitution of 1787 were undermined.

Between two systems: Westphalian and Philadelphian relations

Our analysis has focused thus far almost entirely on the internal side of the Philadelphian system. But securing popular sovereignty required measures to deal also with the world outside the Union. A major aim of the Union was to create enough centralized power to balance against foreign threats; the various military and foreign policy authorities delegated to the central government were seen as necessary evils to deal with outside security threats. The limited power that these central institutions possessed was only possible because the United States was geopolitically separated from Europe. Establishing centralized authority and then being able to keep this authority limited in power are readily predicted by Westphalian realists. If this were all to the story of the United States and the world, its value as an alternative to the Westphalian system would be limited.

Yet popular sovereignty's consequences do not end at the water's edge, and they are not variances explained only by the water's width. The conceptual apparatus and the explanatory power of international theory can be advanced by considering the relations between internal sovereignty configurations, foreign policy practices, and system structures. The argument begins with two sets of theoretical claims about the relationships between foreign policy practices and sovereignty and about the relationships between system structure and foreign policy practices. The argument then proceeds through a rapid overview of American and European relations between the American founding and the present to make a first rough assessment of how much the actual historical phenomena vindicate the theoretical arguments.

Hiding, balancing, and binding

The first step in capturing the relationships between different forms of sovereign authority for foreign policy practices and system structure is to expand our conceptual menu of practices beyond the distinction between balancing and bandwagoning extensively explored by neo-realists.[69] I propose a fuller spectrum of foreign policy practices that stretch from hiding through balancing to binding. With this expanded spectrum, we can then theorize about how these practices strengthen or weaken particular sovereignty configurations through the interaction of external and internal balances and the need for state autonomy.

To identify security practices other than balancing, one need not look outside Europe, but look more closely within Europe. One must look beyond neorealism, but not beyond the actual practice of the European political order. In several path-breaking analyses of European diplomatic practices during the eighteenth and nineteenth centuries, the diplomatic historian Paul Schroeder has identified two additional foreign policy practices, hiding[70] (his term) and binding (my term). Many examples of hiding and binding are well known, but not recognized as distinctive in the categories of neorealism. Hiding refers to the practices of avoiding interaction with potential adversaries and potential conflicts. Nonentanglement, isolationism, and neutrality are examples of the practice of hiding. Alternatively, binding is a foreign policy practice of establishing institutional links between the units that reduce their autonomy vis-à-vis one another. In the European context, Schroeder identifies many *pacta de contrahendo* (pacts of constraint) that were "devices that specifically unite rivals."[71] Such binding pacts aimed not to aggregate capability to balance against adversaries, but to tie a potential adversary into a relationship of friendship to reduce possible conflict and predatory behavior. These are, however, mild forms of binding, and for reasons that will soon be clear, European hier-states generally eschewed stronger forms of binding. The best example of a stronger binding practice was in the establishment of the American Union. Here, as we have seen, the thirteen independent American states sought to bind each other through union to suppress the dynamics of anarchy.

These two additional practices, when added to the well-known balancing, provide a spectrum of foreign policy practices needed to make good on the constructivist opening to variation. Combining these three possible practices with the variation in sovereignty – hier-state versus compound republic – enables us to generate propositions regarding the ways sovereignty and foreign policy practices relate to one another.

The three foreign policy practices are not equally congenial with all configurations of sovereignty. *Balancing is congenial with and reinforces a salient state sovereignty, while hiding and binding are uncongenial and subversive to it. Conversely, balancing is uncongenial to and subversive of an extended popular sovereign, while hiding and binding are naturally congenial to it and strengthen it.* (See Figure 7.3.)

The reasons that hiding, balancing, and binding have such different implications for different configurations of sovereignty is that they entail very different roles for central state authorities. Hiding strengthens the sovereignty of an extended and therefore recessed popular sovereignty because hiding reduces the need to centralize power to balance against outside threats. Conversely, hiding undermines the hier-state sovereignty configuration by reducing power and enhancing the autonomy of the state apparatus. By the same logic, the foreign policy practice of balancing strengthens the hier-state by altering the internal balance of power in favor of the center at the expense of the rest of the polity. This same practice of balancing

214

	Hiding	Binding	Balancing
Hier-state (sovereignty in state apparatus)	Weakens	Strengthens	Weakens
Compound republic (sovereignty in extended people)	Strengthens	Weakens	Strengthens

Figure 7.3: Impacts of foreign policy practices upon sovereignty

threatens to weaken the sovereignty of an extended popular sovereign because the internal balance of power is tilted in favor of the center at the expense of other authorities in the polity.

A foreign policy of binding undermines the sovereignty of a hier-state. Binding, however, strengthens the sovereignty of an extended popular sovereign. When a polity binds with another polity to suppress the dynamics of anarchy, the need to concentrate power and grant autonomy to the central government is reduced in both. Furthermore, the negarchical structures of government generated by such sovereigns are well-suited to being bound by interstate arrangements. Disaggregation allows sector-by-sector binding, and the insulation of components of governmental capability from hierarchical direction makes it possible for small states to bind with larger ones with much less fear of being hegemonically dominated.

Even when the binding must be strong enough to yield a union government that must hold considerable authority, the sovereignty of an extended people is enhanced. The creation of a union through binding replicates at a larger scale the internally constitutive move of such a sovereign. Just as a popular sovereign can overthrow governmental authorities that have strayed from their subservient role, such a sovereign also can throw over governmental authorities by placing some authorities in a corporate body generated by the union with another polity. To deny that a sovereign can so delegate authorities is to deny its sovereignty. Reshuffling the architecture of delegated

215

powers strengthens the sovereignty of a public because it reduces the need to centralize power and grant autonomy to its own governmental apparatus that risks usurpation. Of course, the crucial assumption is that the government created by the binding union is also carefully circumscribed. Moreover, sufficient authorities and capabilities must remain closer to the direct control of the extended popular sovereign to balance against, or, if necessary, overthrow or withdraw from a union government's embrace.

An initially paradoxical implication of this hypothesis is that the preferred foreign policies of a unit structured as a compound republic will be the completely opposite practices of hiding and binding, of avoidance and embrace, and of isolationism and internationalism. Compound republics will want either nothing or everything to do with other polities, and they will find the routine balancing behavior of Westphalian hier-states to be inhospitable and uncongenial. From the standpoint of a theory of international relations in which the Westphalian system is paradigmatic, the foreign policy practices of compound republics seem prone to excesses and illusions, and recalcitrant to socialization. Conversely, from the perspective of an international theory with a broader capacity to conceptualize foreign policy practices and a fuller understanding of the security problem, hier-states appear hobbled and prone to incapacities in pursuing security.

Geopolitical separation, foreign policy practices, and system structure

So far we have hypothesized relations between different forms of sovereignty and different foreign policy practices. As realists correctly emphasize, foreign policy practices are not simply expressions of the internal personality of the units of an international system, but adaptations to external realities that units cannot dictate and that often are harsh in their implications for achieving security. Internal factors shape how competently a unit acts, but which actions are needed for competence are not determined internally. Therefore, as the realists point out, as long as external realities demand balancing, then the hier-state will predominate, and other forms of polity will languish.[72]

Indeed, realists have traditionally emphasized that the anomalous structures of the early United States were possible because of America's anomalous geopolitical relationship to the Great Powers of the

European state system.[73] Given the technology of the time, the United States was geopolitically separated from Europe. Distance diluted the power of the European states, and made it possible for the United States to achieve security from their predations without building up strong central state institutions. The implications of this geopolitical separation were keenly grasped by the Founding Fathers.[74]

Geopolitical separation is, however, far more important in the realist response to the apparent anomaly of the United States than it is to neorealist theory of structure, which emphasizes anarchy and the material distribution of powers between the units. However, in eighteenth- and nineteenth-century international theories of republicanism and geopolitics, material separation was accorded a much more central and explicit role. Montesquieu and others who theorized about Europe's then anomalous plural political order in naturalist and republican terminology thought that material separation was at least as constitutive of the system as the balance of power – that is, the rough equality of power potential of the major state – and more constitutive than any practice, whether balancing or other.[75] Material separation, particularly the fragmentation of Europe by topography (grouping arable land into relatively discrete clusters, mountain and marine barriers to military mobility), was constitutive because it accounted for the existence of separate states rather than a universal empire.[76]

It is generally recognized that material separation was very important in the case of the early United States, but material separation is absent from recent neorealist understandings of structure. But the basic insight is contained in concepts of strategic interdependence, vulnerability, and in Barry Buzan's interaction capacity.[77] As with sovereignty, it is useless to theorize about material separation without defining some variance within it. Material separation can be measured along a simple spectrum, from *isolation*, (a high degree of separation), though *proximity*, a medium degree of separation, to *closeness*. The early United States was in an isolation relationship with Europe, but given their small size and the incongruence between their juridical borders and the topographical barriers, the thirteen original states were in a close relationship with one another. Conversely, the states of Europe were in a relationship of proximity with one another during the operation of the classical balance-of-power system.

What relationship exists between the different forms of geopolitical separation and social practices and institutional structures at the unit and system levels? (See Figure 7.4.)

Material (deep) structure: geopolitical separation	Security practice	Unit-level structure	System structure
Isolated	Highly variable	Highly variable	Nullarchy (interaction too low to support system government)
Proximate	Balancing dominant	Hierarchical (hier-state)	Anarchy (governance absent, but possible)
Close	Binding dominant	Negarchical (compound republic)	Negarchy (binding union to recover separation)

Figure 7.4: Congruent deep, unit, and system structures

The Westphalian realists emphasize that in a situation of proximity, balancing is needed and hiding is difficult to achieve. Although, as Schroeder demonstrates, binding was also an important tool for managing conflict, it was ultimately secondary to balancing. But what of isolation or closeness? In these situations, the practice of balancing will be either unnecessary or insufficient. When polities are isolated, a great deal of variation is viable in both unit structure and practice. Hiding fits well with isolation: a policy of isolationism is likely to fare well in a situation of isolation, but states could pursue imperialism and choose to be more involved with their distant neighbors than they need to be. In a situation of isolation, binding is not appealing and is difficult or impossible to achieve, because there is little reason to pursue binding and there are insufficient interactions to make a binding union necessary or viable. In geopolitical isolation, binding (and all the structural architectures it generates) is utopian.[78]

In a situation of little geopolitical separation – of closeness – binding is the most appropriate and viable foreign policy practice, and its exercise can result in a nonanarchical system structure. Because of the absence of material separation, hiding will be nearly impossible and balancing will not achieve security. In a situation of closeness, a practice of binding will be very attractive as a means of regulating the many inevitable interactions. To respond to the structural imperatives of closeness, the practice of binding will have to be strong enough to go beyond ad hoc alliances to a union. In a situation of closeness, one possibility emphasized by realists is that binding will not be reciprocal but hierarchical. If there is a significant asymmetry of power between the units, and if the units are hier-states, it is more likely that an imperial or tight hegemonic union will replace anarchy. Alternatively, the security threats of geopolitical closeness can be managed by binding that leads to a negarchical union. Here the distinctive unit-level structures and binding practices of compound republican polities are most adaptive to the material structural context. To the extent that units are socialized by the imperatives of their security environment, hier-states are likely to fade and compound republics are likely to spread.

To grasp the full value of these theoretical distinctions and propositions requires an examination of the actual patterns of history. Does the historical record vindicate our model's hypothesis that the viability of hiding, balancing, and binding is correlated with the degree of geopolitical separation? In answering this question and making a first rough test of our hypothesis, the pattern of American history offers a revealing set of cases because the position of the United States vis-à-vis the core of the Westphalian system in Europe has, in succession, been one of isolation, proximity, and closeness.

Escape from Westphalia

The ambition to escape from interaction with the European balance of power operating in the Westphalian system animated much of the early Union's thinking about foreign affairs. The United States pursued a foreign policy of hiding in three ways: strategic nonentanglement, support for and participation in the neutrality regime, and by attempting to convert the Americas into an autonomous subsystem of the international order. The main thrust of American thinking was that participation in the Westphalian system was a corrupting influence, and therefore should be minimized. In his farewell address, George Washington classically expressed these aspirations to escape "entangling alliances" and to "remain aloof from the quarrels of Europe."[79] The Americans thought their distinctive political order would be forced to evolve in ways hostile to its animating goals if they were forced to interact extensively with the European states through the balance-of-power system. Extensive socialization into European political processes would spell the death of their experiment.[80]

The regime of maritime neutrality offered the early United States one means of remaining aloof from European conflicts.[81] Although this regime predated the formation of the United States, early American diplomacy placed great emphasis upon the assertion and protection of neutral rights.[82]

The United States' strategy of escape and isolation found its greatest expression in the Monroe Doctrine of 1823, in which the United States asserted that the New World was off-limits to the predations of the European powers. This doctrine was a direct challenge to the norms of the Westphalian system. The Europeans recognized the doctrine in fact, but never granted it legal status.[83] Subsequent historiography has emphasized that the Monroe Doctrine was an early declaration of American hegemony and imperial ambition, but it also can be interpreted as an effort to establish a buffer zone between the Westphalian system and the Philadelphian Union. Like the constitutive states of the American Union, other countries in the Americas under the Monroe Doctrine possessed semiautonomy, or semisovereignty in Westphalian terms. As expected, the United States initially sought to hide when it was isolated and isolationism worked in this situation.

American exceptionalism and the Westphalian balance

America was never fully isolated and, as time passed, it became less so. America's semiautonomous subsystem was never fully disconnected from the Westphalian system at whose periphery it sat. How did America's exceptionalistic foreign policy practices affect the Westphalian system and the operation of its core power-balancing dynamic? What happens to a balancing system when a polity pursues a foreign policy practice of hiding and binding, but eschews balancing?

The operation of balancing in a plural state system is most important in responding to a hegemonic challenge to its very existence. During the late eighteenth and early nineteenth centuries, the threat to the plural order from revolutionary and Napoleonic France and the counterhegemonic alliance led by Great Britain followed the classic

Westphalian pattern. From the standpoint of the overall system balance, the United States' policy was quite eccentric. During this period, the United States waged a de facto war against France at sea in the Quasi-War of 1797–1801[84] and against Great Britain in the War of 1812. In both cases, the reason the United States went to war against powerful European states was not to help maintain the balance of power in Europe, but to sustain its strong interpretation of neutral rights in the face of the refusal of the European states to respect them.

The grave consequences of consistent hiding in a period of hegemonic challenges to the plural order can be seen in the War of 1812. The main cause of this conflict was Britain's violation of American neutral rights.[85] Consistent with the universality and reciprocity of the neutrality regime, Jefferson and Madison emphasized that their policy did not aim to discriminate between Britain and France. But because France had been largely swept from the seas after Trafalgar, America's exercising of neutral rights worked almost entirely to Britain's disadvantage.[86] Waging war against Great Britain, the leader of the anti-hegemonic coalition, made the United States the de facto ally of Napoleonic France at the zenith of its hegemonic challenge. Federalist critics of Jefferson and Madison's anti-British policy anxiously noted that a French victory would mean that "the iron scepter of the ocean will pass into his hands who wears the iron crown of the land."[87] As Ludwig Dehio has emphasized, the successful resistance to imperial consolidation at the core of the European system was dependent increasingly upon drawing resources from the flanks.[88] Because Britain, the typical balancer state, drew much of its strength from its expanding holdings outside of Europe, the American attempt to maintain subsystem autonomy threatened to choke off balancing at the core. Despite the drain on the resources of Great Britain when its resources were most extended, Napoleon was defeated; but had his challenge to the plural system been successful, historians would no doubt assign some of the blame to the hiding policy of the United States. Hiding through support for a neutrality regime can moderate the anarchic dynamics of a plural state-system. But if hiding occurs at the periphery of the system rather than dominating its core, it can retard the operation of balancing. In situations of hegemonic challenge, this retarding could be a decisive factor in the system collapse from plurality to hierarchy.

During the long peace that ensued after the defeat of Napoleonic France, the continued withdrawal of the United States from the

European balance-of-power system probably helped reinforce the peace of Europe by helping to remove colonial rivalry as a cause of war between the Great Powers. The peace administered by the concert was based in part on the absence of conflict in the periphery. During the eighteenth century, the rivalry between France and Britain in North America, as well as in India, was a major cause of the Seven Years' War.[89] In the late eighteenth and early nineteenth centuries, however, North America and then all the New World were effectively removed from the balance of European power because of the American War of Independence, subsequent American expansion into the interior of North America, and the Monroe Doctrine. The only European effort to expand at the American periphery, the French adventure in Mexico during the 1860s, occurred when the American Civil War had reduced the United States' ability to enforce the Monroe Doctrine. On the other flank of the system in eastern and southern Europe, the Crimean War, which was caused by the competing expansionist aims of Russia and Austria in the vacuum left by the recession of Ottoman power, constituted an important blow against the concert's system of conflict regulation.

In the late nineteenth and early twentieth centuries, the relationship between the American practice of hiding and the European balance-of-power system was changed by the great decrease of geopolitical isolation and the great increase in American power. Because of the new technologies of the industrial revolution, the material relationship between the United States and Europe was transformed from one of isolation to one of proximity. In this changed situation, a state socialized fully into the norms and practices of the Westphalian system would have abandoned the practice of hiding and begun to balance. Ultimately this happened, with a significant time lag caused by the United States' stubborn adherence to the practice of hiding. Isolation had ended, but American isolationism had not; the United States was trying to hide when it was inevitably part of the larger system and dependent upon its balance for survival.

The first consequence of the United States for the Westphalian system was to cast the plural system in Europe into an altogether different light and to provide both a model and impetus for its overthrow. Not only were Europe and America becoming proximate, but also the great size of the United States meant that within the expanded sphere of the system, the US was a major player, capable of altering outcomes at the core.[90] The failure of Confederate secession

222

and the success of the Union reconstruction of the defeated South meant that a balance-of-power system was absent in North America. As the intensifying industrial revolution shrank distance further, the United States became the paramount power in the still politically fragmented regions in Europe and East Asia.

By the later years of the nineteenth century, anxious Europeans examined the American colossus for indications of the future of the West.[91] Looking through the lens of their political history and practices, many Europeans saw the United States as a model of a new scale of political organization that could – and many believed would – inevitably be emulated elsewhere. It seemed that Europe would be dominated by either America or Russia, unless the plural balance-of-power system was overthrown or otherwise replaced by a unified Europe.[92]

The European imperialism of the late nineteenth and early twentieth centuries outside and inside Europe was driven partly by the desire to balance against the United States. The lag in the United States' abandonment of hiding had even more direct, profound, and unsettling effects upon the European balance of power. At the beginning of both German challenges to the plural system on the continent, the United States remained aloof. In both cases, a significant reason why the United States was drawn into the war was over its assertion of neutral rights, and the unwillingness of the Germans to respect those rights.[93] Had Germany been more adept in managing its maritime relations with the United States, it is likely that the United States would not have been drawn into the wars in time to stop or reverse German domination of the continent.

The consequences of American exceptionalistic preference for hiding and binding over balancing for European political order were strikingly evident in the settlement of World War I and the twenty years leading up to the outbreak of World War II. After hesitating to balance until late in World War I, the United States did not seek to restore order through a balancing system, but to push for an ambitious binding union. At the Versailles Peace Conference, President Woodrow Wilson proposed an ambitious scheme to alter interstate anarchy with an elaborate international institution, the League of Nations, conceived at least in part as an effort to replicate the strategy and architecture of the American Constitutional Union on a larger scale.[94] As Wilson emphasized, this plan aimed to end balancing as the main security practice in Europe and replace it with a fairly strong binding union.[95]

Like the earlier Philadelphian system, it was dependent upon the willingness of the decentralized parts of the system to exercise self-restraint and to help punish violators. For a variety of reasons – its architecture, the European political scene, and Wilson's mismanagement or miscalculation in the US Senate debate over the ratification of the League Treaty[96] – the binding union was never established. The League institutions that emerged were so weak and incoherent that their collapse led many realists to conclude that binding unions are inevitably utopian enterprises.

In the wake of this binding failure, the United States immediately reverted all the way back to hiding, eschewing the more limited commitments to the European balance entailed in security alliances with Britain or France.[97] The result of the reversion of the United States to its traditional practice of hiding was what E.H. Carr famously called the "twenty years' crisis."[98] The United States was in a proximate relationship with Europe and the most powerful country in the system, but it refused to balance. American hiding helped create the power vacuum in central and eastern Europe that Nazi Germany and Soviet Russia sought to fill. A crucial puzzle for all actors in Europe was whether the United States would balance again against German expansion.[99] German prospects for success depended upon continued American hiding and British hopes of the counterhegemonic coalition hinged upon American balancing. As war approached in Europe, there was a great gap between the capability and commitment of the United States.[100] In contrast to the well-known problem of commitments exceeding capability, the United States' capabilities exceeded its commitments. Because of this lagging commitment to balancing, states that might have been deterred by American capability were not.

The return of the Philadelphian system?

To the extent that circumstance dictated involvement, Americans always have harbored ambitions to transform the norms of the Westphalian international system into ones more compatible with their own principles of legitimacy and association. After World War II, the United States was in a position for the first time to realize this goal. The further development of technology, particularly long-range aerial bombardment and the development of nuclear weapons, had pushed the geopolitical relationship of North America from proximity to closeness. Also, the devastation of the war and the discrediting of the

224

strong national statism of Nazi Germany and Imperial Japan created a power vacuum within which American goals could be realized at lower costs than ever before. In the nineteenth century, the Westphalian system expanded and the Philadelphian system declined, but in the twentieth century, events have followed a reverse pattern at the core of the Western states system. America's other preferred practice of binding has been successfully pursued, producing a system-level structure in the world of liberal democracies quite unlike a Westphalian anarchy.[101]

The paths by which America became so intimately involved in European affairs were twisted and defy simple description or explanation. Realists explain the extended American system with two powerful arguments: bipolarity and hegemony. For neorealists, the bipolar distribution of power between the United States and the Soviet Union provided the United States with ample incentive to ally with the West Europeans and the Japanese, and even more incentive for the Europeans and the Japanese to ally with the United States. Within the Western group of states threatened by Soviet expansion, the United States had a sufficiently preponderant share of the organizational, ideological, and material capabilities to organize the Western states along hegemonic lines.

These realist arguments may be necessary, but they are not a sufficient explanation of the relationship between the United States and the rest of the West. Understanding this system beyond realist bipolarity and hegemony is difficult because of the underdevelopment and atrophy of macro-liberal international theory, which exists mainly as scattered fragments. Part of this tradition are the early twentieth-century British progressives and internationalists who viewed the United States as the prototype of a fundamentally new form of political life and thought that Europeans would have to reconfigure their institutions along similar lines. Perhaps the boldest of such thinking was H.G. Wells's prediction in 1900 that a "great synthesis" encompassing the North Atlantic and "headquartered" in the northeastern corner of North America would replace the Great Power interstate system.[102] Another part of this tradition is the effort to conceive a "Union of the Democracies" or later an "Atlantic Union" or "western community."[103] Karl Deutsch's concept of a "pluralistic security community" is weaker on advocacy but stronger on description and explanation.[104]

There is not enough space to allow either a full reconstruction and extension of the scattered theory of macro-liberalism, or a full engagement with the powerful realist arguments. However, features such as popular sovereignty, binding practices and negarchical structures, semiautonomous states (in Westphalian terms semisovereign) in the extended political order of the United States and Western Europe follow the expectations of our hypotheses, but are not explained by Soviet–American bipolarity and American hegemony. Taken together, these features suggest the emergence of a political order in Europe and, to a lesser degree, in East Asia that bears more resemblance to the Philadelphian system than the classic Westphalian system.

In the NATO alliance system, binding practices have supplanted anarchy with negarchy. The proverbial goals of the alliance are "to keep the Russians out, the Germans down, and the Americans in." In keeping the Russians out, NATO is a standard balancing alliance. Its other two goals have been met through binding and the other European states are secured by a Germany bound to broader European institutions.[105] American power is kept attached to Europe through an "empire by invitation" that makes the relation unlike coercive hegemonies.[106] The relationships within the extended American system are not bilateral, as Westphalian realists might expect; they are multilateral, as John Ruggie and others have pointed out.[107] So great is the reliance upon proceduralism in the extended Western system that Anne-Marie Slaughter has postulated the existence of a "liberal community of law" in which conflicts are routinely resolved through legal institutions.[108]

The resulting structure of European and North American politics resembles the early Philadelphian system more than anarchy of the nation-states that fought in World Wars I and II. Like the Philadelphian system, violence capability in the Western alliance has two tiers: a sovereign state lower level and a pooled region-wide one. Binding has compromised state autonomy, producing semisovereignty. The two most important states,[109] West Germany and Japan, have elaborate constitutional prohibitions against the use of force beyond their borders. So extensive are these constraints that Peter Katzenstein believes West Germany is semisovereign.[110] A similar pattern characterizes post-World War II Japan.

External binding and the resulting nonanarchical and nonhierarchical system structure depend partly upon restructuring the internal constitutions of Germany and Japan along American lines. The negarchical unit structures and popular sovereignty contribute incentives and capacities to make binding unions with other European states.

Binding practices are also widely evident in the formation of the institutions of the European Union. Perhaps forgetting the earlier *pacta de contrahendo*, Hans Morgenthau observed that the European Coal and Steel Community was revolutionary because instead of balancing by a system of alliances, France was trying to draw "Germany into its arms in order to disarm it and to make the superior strength of Germany innocuous."[111] Also, the United States has been a major supporter of European integration. This policy in effect supports the emergence of a large, powerful, close, and potentially competitive state, and is irrational to Westphalian realists.

Three difficult tests: binding über alles

Over the last decade, three crucial junctures – German reunification, the Maastricht Treaty, and the relations between the Western alliance and the Soviet Union and Russia at the end of the Cold War – offer additional evidence for the strength of binding practices and the decline of balancing. In each of these cases, fundamental security interests were at stake. Balancing alternatives were seriously contemplated but binding practices won out, posing major anomalies for Westphalian realist theories. In all three cases, Germany, traditionally an aspiring hegemon and object of intensive balancing alliances, practiced binding and sought to be bound by its traditional adversaries. "Keeping Germany down and keeping the Russians out" increasingly has been replaced by practices and structures to keep the Germans and the Russians – as well as the Americans – in.

Having been subject to German aggression twice in the twentieth century, Britain, France, and the Soviet Union believed that German reunification posed a major potential threat. As NATO allies with West Germany, Britain, and France seriously considered forming a balancing alliance,[112] but decided instead to deal with the threat of German power by strengthening its ties with Germany.

Similarly, the Soviet Union faced a great dilemma regarding both its withdrawal from East Europe and German reunification. After initially insisting that Germany leave NATO in return for Soviet acquiescence, Soviet leader Mikhail Gorbachev accepted the view that Russia would be safer with Germany restrained in NATO than unattached outside it. In more general terms, the Soviet withdrawal was predicated on the Soviet assessment that neither NATO nor Germany posed a threat to it. This assessment must partly reflect the fact that the European states were bound in a robust union of alliance that reduced the likelihood of attack at the same time that it aggregated Western strength.[113]

Much of the debate about the post-Cold War European political order has been about the rate and extent of binding as a way to forestall balancing. Binding is seen as a means to include parts of the former Soviet system into Western institutions. Advocates of rapid and narrow NATO extension to include the Visegrad countries of Poland, the Czech Republic, Slovakia, and Hungary argue that NATO membership will reduce the probability of conflicts between these countries. Similarly, advocates of expansion that would include Russia claim that a Russia tied to the West would be better than one balanced against it.

The Maastricht Treaty's commitment to European Monetary Union points to the prevalence of unit-level negarchies and binding practices and their ability to muffle the dynamics of balancing and hegemony. Germany is, in neorealist terms, a potential economic hegemon of Western Europe, but it has been a leader in creating the binding institutions of the European Union. Other European states have supported rather than resisted this goal, thus posing, as many have noted, an anomaly for neorealist theory. Yet West Germany, the most powerful state in Western Europe, also has a federal constitutional structure, with extensive separations and checks upon the central government. Because governmental authority is so disaggregated in Germany, it is easier to build European Union institutions. The establishment of a European currency union generally is seen as a major step in European integration, and Germany has been an active supporter of this process. Although the German economy is the strongest in Europe, German economic institutions are not organized as a hierarchical state, and the powerful Bundesbank is more insulated from the rest of the German political system than the American Federal Reserve System.[114] An explanation closely related to binding is Joseph Greico's hypothesis that other European states are seeking "opportunity voice" through monetary union.[115] This is possible because of the separation of the Bundesbank from the rest of the German governmental authorities.

Conclusions

Two general conclusions are suggested.

First, we should take more seriously the Philadelphian system as an alternative to the Westphalian system. Realists are unwarranted in

228

concluding that its brief life and the violence of its transformation into a national democratic and federal state indicate its intrinsically implausible character. The prerequisites for the creation of a Philadelphian system are more demanding than in the Westphalian order. Maintaining the constitution of sovereignty in the *Publius* formulation demanded an ethos of compromise and a toleration of diversity and central-state incapacity that is perpetually subject to stress and decay. The American republic depended upon a less extensive and less strenuous public virtue than did the city-state republics that had come before, but it did depend upon a degree of virtue. The viability of such an order cannot depend completely upon actors to spontaneously grasp its principles and norms in the course of their self-interested pursuits, but instead must have some mechanism to socialize and educate actors into its fundamentals.

It should be emphasized that the crisis of the Philadelphian Union was caused by the issue of slavery interacting with its structural and geopolitical elements. Of all the possible issues confronting the American Union, slavery and the contiguous geographical clustering of slave-holding states posed a challenge to which the order was uniquely vulnerable. The system of rounded power constraints justified by *Publius* presupposed the civic and republican character of the people and the polity. The extensive power constraint features of its political architecture left it particularly unsuited to produce such preconditions when they were absent and opposed by some substantial interest, as they were with slavery. Only the appeal to a democratic majority that is dedicated to making the liberal foundational principles of the polity genuinely universal within the system, and one willing and able to override basic constitutional constraints on power, could end slavery in the Union. Ironically, it was Calhoun's particular attachment to slavery that evoked a righteous democratic majority bent on establishing minimum liberal rights throughout the Union, which in turn destroyed his more general attachment to the Union's negative power constraint structures.

The second general conclusion that emerges concerns the roots and character of what realists refer to as American "idealism." A central theme of the rise of realism in the United States between the middle of the 1930s and the middle of the 1950s is that the indigenous American political tradition is naive about the realities of security and power, and had to be supplanted with the more realistic approach of realism, which was drawn from the Westphalian tradition of sovereign state-

Daniel Deudney

craft. By treating the early United States as a systemic alternative to the European model of organizing large political space, rather than simply as an odd unit-level variant in it, we have cast this realist contention into doubt. In doing so, we help reveal a much more extended lineage and more robust and rounded theoretical foundations for the distinctive American approach to international relations. The American preoccupation with human rights, political democracy, and international organization are facets of a strategy for achieving the full security of a particular type of sovereign. We are not faced with a choice between a realistic Westphalian approach and the idealistic and utopian American one, but rather a choice between two different configurations of authority and institutional structure.

From the perspective of the Philadelphian core, the theory and practice of Woodrow Wilson, commonly seen as the paradigmatic American liberal internationalist,[116] looks more liberal-democratic statist than Philadelphian. At home, Wilson opposed the checks and constraints of the Constitution of 1787, already in decay as a result of the Civil War, as impediments to national will and industrial modernization. Externally, Wilson's embrace of national self-determination made union in Europe much more difficult. The League of Nations championed by Wilson is clearly a descendent of the Union of 1787. Wilson was bound severely by practical circumstances, but the national democratic character of Wilson's vision of legitimate authority was intimately connected with his lack of an agenda to constitute a larger public as the basis for the architecture of interstate union. He was, in short, a variant of Webster at home, and of Calhoun abroad.

Oddly enough, the most ambitious and utopian of the liberal internationalists, the advocates of a World Federal State, are also still bound by the essential Westphalian typology of political order. Unlike Wilson, who was a domestic Webster, the world federalists are Websters on a world scale, positing the sovereignty of a nation of the earth, and insisting that this sovereign find expression in a democratic federal state. The world federalists looked to the founding of the American Constitution as a model for their world federation. But they conflated the founding process with the New Deal progressive state, erroneously concluding that the thirteen states joined to create a federal state, when in fact they only federated to erect an organized states' union. Ironically, the liberal internationalist image of the federal state as the only full alternative to anarchy reinforces the more essential realist claim about the universal applicability of the state form.

230

Notes

[1] Hinsley, F.H. 1986. *Sovereignty*. 2nd ed. Cambridge: Cambridge University Press.

[2] Rather than engage in another fruitless debate over the true meaning of the term "state", political science is advanced by distinguishing between the different forms of political order that have at different times been called states. In addition to the hier-state as a system of hierarchical authorities and structures, I distinguish the "real-state" as a mode of protection characterized by the centralized monopoly of violence capability in a particular territory.

[3] Bull, Hedley 1977. *The Anarchical Society*. New York: Columbia University Press.

[4] James, Alan 1986. *Sovereign Statehood*. London: Allen & Unwin.

[5] Most clearly in the distinction between "automatic" and "manual" balance of power. Inis, Claude 1962. *Power and International Relations*. New York: Random House, pp. 11–39.

[6] Forsyth, Murray 1981. *Unions of States*. Leicester University Press; and Elazar, Daniel (ed.) 1987. *Federalism as Grand Design*. Lanham, Md: University Press of America.

[7] For discussion, see Forsyth, Murray 1981. *Unions of States: The Theory and Practice of Confederation*. New York: Leichester University Press, pp. 79–85.

[8] On the American Civil War as a second founding, James McPherson notes: "Before 1861 the two words 'United States' were generally used as a plural noun: 'the United States' *are* a republic.' After 1865, the United States became a singular noun. The loose union of states became a nation [McPherson's emphasis]." 1991. "The Second American Revolution," in *Abraham Lincoln and the Second American Revolution*. New York: Oxford University Press, p. viii.

[9] Tyrrell, Ian 1991. "American Exceptionalism in an Age of International History," *American Historical Review* 95: 1031–55; Veysey, Laurence 1979. "The Autonomy of American History Reconsidered," *American Quarterly* 31: 455–77.

[10] Turner, Frederick Jackson 1932. *The Significance of Sections in American History*. New York: Henry Holt & Company, p. 316.

[11] An important exception to this general neglect is Peter Onuf and Nicholas Onuf 1993. *Federal Union, Modern World: The Law of Nations in an Age of Revolutions, 1776–1814*. Madison, Wis.: Madison House.

[12] Today, most liberal claims about popular sovereignty readily translate into claims about political democracy at the domestic level or claims about national self-determination as the basis for the establishment of another Westphalian sovereign in the society of state sovereigns. As such, liberal alternatives are seen as nothing more than a variation of how internal authorities in a Westphalian unit are constituted.

[13] For an astute analysis of the interaction of systemic and societal dimensions of the Westphalian system, see Buzan, Barry 1993. "From the International System to International Society: Structural Realism and Regime Theory Meet the English School," *International Organization* 47: 327–52.

[14] de Tocqueville, Alexis 1945. *Democracy in America* Part I. New York: Alfred A. Knopf, p. 59.

[15] Kelley, G.A. 1972. "Hegel's America," *Philosophy and Public Affairs* 2: 3–36; similarly, de Tocqueville observed "two governments, completely separate and almost independent ... [and] twenty-four small sovereign nations, whose agglomeration constitutes the body of the Union." de Tocqueville, Alexis 1945. *Democracy in America*, vol. II. New York: Alfred A. Knopf, p. 61

[16] Hinsley defines sovereignty as "the idea that there is a final and absolute authority in the political community." 1986. *Sovereignty*, p. 1. For competing concepts of sovereignty, see Onuf, Nicholas 1991. "Sovereignty: Outline of a Conceptual History," *Alternatives* 16: 425–46.

[17] Blackstone, William 1967. *Commentaries on the Laws of England* 4 vols. (1st ed. 1765–9). Oxford: Clarendon Press, pp. 156–7.

[18] Among the leading theorists of the hier-state, most notably Bodin and Hobbes, there is a vigorous conceptual insistence that sovereignty should reside within the state apparatus or in the head of state. They view the location of sovereignty in a body made up of many individuals rather than one or a few (in Hobbes's terms "one man or one council") as inimical to maintaining political order in practice. The division of sovereignty is a conceptual impossibility; its location in the people is in principle possible, but practically undesirable. Bodin, Jean 1967. *The Six Books of the Commonwealth* (M.J. Tooley, trans.). New York: Barnes & Noble.

[19] For the emergence and prevalence of claims of popular sovereignty in the British and American polities, see Morgan, Edmund S. 1988. *Inventing the People: The Rise of Popular Sovereignty in England and America.* New York: W.W. Norton; and Kammen, Michael 1988. *Sovereignty and Liberty: Constitutional Discourse in American Culture.* Madison: University of Wisconsin Press.

[20] Hamilton, Alexander, John Jay, and Madison, James, 1961. *The Federalist Papers*, no. 46, New York: New American Library, p. 294.

[21] For the centrality of security concerns, see *Federalist*, pp. 1–10, and Dietze, Gottfried 1960. "The Federalist as a Treatise on Peace and Security," in *The Federalist: A Classic on Federalism and Free Government* Part II. Baltimore: Johns Hopkins University Press, pp. 177–254.

[22] Montesquieu, Baron de 1948. *Spirit of the Laws* Book II, sec. 6. (Nugent trans.) New York: Hafner, p. 151.

[23] For more extended analysis of the relationship between the *Publius* sovereignty configuration, the security structures of the American Union, and the argument that this system embodied a distinct structural principle of negarchy, see Deudney, Daniel 1995. "The Philadelphian System: Sovereignty, Arms Control and Balance of Power in the American States-Union, ca-1787–1861," *International Organization* 49: 191–228.

[24] For a recent restatement on the state apparatus as protector and predator, see Tilly, Charles 1985. "War Making and State Making as Organized Crime," in Evans, Peter, Rueschemeyer, Dietrich, and Skopol, Theda (eds.) *Bringing the State Back In*. Cambridge: Cambridge University Press.

[25] *Federalist*, no. 51, p. 322.

[26] Hobbes, Thomas 1960. *Leviathan*. Oakeshot, Michael (ed.), Oxford: Basil Blackwell, p. 75.

[27] Locke, John 1960. *Second Treatise on Government*. Peter Laslett (ed.), Cambridge: Cambridge University Press, p. 405.

[28] Montesquieu, *Spirit*, p. 150.

[29] For pervasive fears of anarchy, see: Onuf, Peter 1987. "Anarchy and the Crisis of the Union," in Beltz, Herman, Hoffman, Ronald, and Albert, Peter (eds.) *To Form a More Perfect Union*. Charlottesville: University of Virginia Press.

[30] *Federalist*, no. 9, pp. 73 and 71.

[31] Slaughter, Thomas P. 1986. *The Whiskey Rebellion: Frontier Epilogue to the American Revolution*. New York: Oxford University Press.

[32] *Federalist*, no.6, p. 54. For fears of interstate American wars, see: Onuf, Peter 1983. *The Origins of the Federal Republic: Jurisdictional Controversies in the United States, 1775–1787*. Philadelphia: University of Pennsylvania Press.

[33] Main, Jackson Turner 1981. "The American States in the Revolutionary Era," in Hoffman, Ronald and Albert, Peter J. (eds.) *Arms and Independence: The Military Character of the American Revolution*. Charlottesville, Va.: The University Press of Virginia, pp. 1–30; and Jensen, Merrill 1940. *The Articles of Confederation*. Madison: University of Wisconsin Press.

[34] *Federalist*, no. 8, p. 67.

[35] Cress, Lawrence Delbert 1982. *Citizens in Arms: The Army and Militia in American Society to the War of 1812*. Chapel Hill: University of North Carolina Press, pp. 94–110; Kohn, Richard H. 1975. *Eagle and Sword: The Federalists and the Creation of the Military Establishment in America, 1783–1802*. New York: Free Press, pp. 40–90; and Riker, William 1957. *Soldiers of the States: The Role of the National Guard in American Democracy*. Washington: Public Affairs Institute.

[36] For fear of foreign incursion as a motive for Union, see Marks, Frederick W., III 1983. *Independence on Trial: Foreign Affairs and the Making of the Constitution*. Baton Rouge, La.: Louisiana State University Press.

[37] *Federalist*, no. 8, pp. 67–9.

[38] Storing, Herbert 1981. *What the Antifederalists Were For*. Chicago: University of Chicago Press.

[39] As Louis Henken observed: "Every grant to the President ... relating to foreign affairs, was in effect a derogation from Congressional power, eked out slowly, reluctantly, and not without limitations and safeguards." 1975. *Foreign Affairs and the Constitution*. New York: W.W. Norton, p. 33.

[40] Wormuth, Francis D. and Firmage, Edwin B. 1986. *To Chain the Dog of War: The War Power of Congress in History and Law*. Dallas: Southern Methodist University Press.

[41] "It is, indeed, the negative power which makes the constitution, and the positive which makes the government. The one is the power of acting, and the other the power of preventing or arresting action. The two, combined, make constitutional governments." Calhoun, John C. 1953. *A Disquisition on Government*. Indianapolis, Ind.: Bobbs-Merrill, p. 28.

[42] Of great importance was the practice of separating church and state and the role of Protestant Christianity in the construction of autonomous individuality.

[43] "The original, revolutionary-popular idea of patriotism was state-based rather than nationalist, since it related to the sovereign people itself, i.e. the state exercising power in its name. Ethnicity or other elements of historic continuity were irrelevant to the 'nation' in this sense, and language relevant only or chiefly on pragmatic grounds." Hobsbawm, Eric 1990. *Nations and Nationalism since 1870: Programme, Myth, Reality.* Cambridge: Cambridge University Press, p. 87.

[44] Kohn, Hans 1957. *American Nationalism.* New York: Collier Books; Curti, Merle 1946. *The Roots of American Loyalty.* New York: Columbia University Press.

[45] For the central role of liberty, see Kammen, Michael 1986. *Spheres of Liberty: Changing Perceptions of Liberty in American Culture.* Madison: University of Wisconsin.

[46] For republican symbolic culture, see Zelinsky, Wilbur 1988. *Nation into State: The Shifting Foundations of American Nationalism.* Chapel Hill: University of North Carolina Press; and Bodner, John 1992. "Public Memory in 19th-Century America: Background and Context," *Remaking America: Public Memory, Commemoration, and Patriotism in the 20th Century.* Princeton: Princeton University Press, chap. 2, pp. 21–40.

[47] MacPherson, C.P. 1962. *Possessive Individualism.* Oxford: Oxford University Press, pp. 47–51. MacPherson's two models are the liberal "possessive market society" and the illiberal "customary or status society."

[48] Simon, William H. 1991. "Social-Republican Property," *UCLA Law Review* 38: 1335–413.

[49] Taylor, John 1977. *Arator.* Indianapolis: Liberty Classics.

[50] Among the voluminous literature, two small pieces provide a good starting point: Savage, James D. 1994. "Corruption and Virtue at the Constitutional Convention," *Journal of Politics* 56: pp.174–86; and Euben, J. Peter 1989. "Corruption," in Ball, Terence, Farr, James and Hanson, Russell (eds.) *Political Innovation and Conceptual Change.* Cambridge: Cambridge University Press, pp. 220–46.

[51] Recent historical analysis by Gordon Wood and others of the transition from the republicanism of ancient and early modern city-states to the new American synthesis has emphasized that the American republic was based less upon civic virtue than upon the channeling of conflicting private interests by the architecture of regime, but that this entailed a less strenuous virtue rather than its complete elimination. See Wood, Gordon S. 1969. *The Creation of the American Republic.* New York: W.W. Norton.

[52] Wills, Garry 1984. *Cincinnatus: George Washington and the Enlightenment.* Garden City, N.Y.: Doubleday.

[53] For compromise as a constitutive norm, see Knupfer, Peter B. 1991. *The Union As It Is: Constitutional Unionism and Sectional Compromise, 1787–1861.* Chapel Hill: University of North Carolina Press.

[54] As the frontier closed, the widespread anxiety about American decadence and corruption stimulated the creation of "natural parks" where the strenuous and therefore disciplining encounter with raw nature could be reenacted in perpetuity.

[55] de Tocqueville, *Democracy*, vol. I, p. 178.

[56] For discussion of the Wyoming Valley and other similar conflicts, see Onuf, *Origins*, pp. 49–73; Meinig, 1986. *Atlantic America, 1492–1800*. New Haven, Conn.: Yale University Press, p. 290; and Morris, Richard B. 1983. *Forging the Union, 1781–1989*. New York: Harper & Row, pp. 222–3.

[57] A crucial feature of the resolution of conflicts between the states over frontier settlements was that the landowners from the losing side had their property rights guaranteed, even as their statehood changed.

[58] For descriptions, see Potter, David M. 1976. *The Impending Crisis: 1848–1861*. New York: Harper & Row. For the similarities with European Treaties, see: Turner, *Significance of Sections*, p. 88.

[59] Knupfer, *The Union As It Is*.

[60] Kammen, Michael 1986. *The Machine That Would Go of Itself: The Constitution in American Culture*. New York: Alfred A. Knopf.

[61] To "protect and maintain inviolate the three great and primary rights of personal security, personal liberty, and private property ... when actually violated or attacked" required courts, the right of petition and "the right of having and using arms for self-preservation and defense." Blackstone, *Commentaries*, pp. 136–40.

[62] Schwoerer, Lois G. 1974. *"No Standing Armies!" The Antiarmy Ideology in Seventeenth Century England*. Baltimore: Johns Hopkins University Press; Malcolm, Joyce Lee 1994. *To Keep and Bear Arms: The Origins of an Anglo-American Right*. Cambridge, Mass.: Harvard University Press; Halbrook, Stephen P. 1984. *That Every Man Be Armed: The Evolution of a Constitutional Right*. Albuquerque, N.M.: University of New Mexico Press.

[63] The recent debates over the Second Amendment have concerned establishing the founders' original intent, with regard to the question of personal gun control rather than the question of the original function of a well-regulated militia in the Union's security order. Contemporary defenders of an armed public fear the failure of policing to insure personal safety, while the founders wanted a counterweight against too much government policing.

[64] Calhoun, John C. 1992. *A Discourse on the Constitution of the Government of the United States* and *A Disquisition on Government, in Union and Liberty: The Political Philosophy of John C. Calhoun*. Ross Lence (ed.), Indianapolis: The Liberty Press.

[65] For discussion of Webster's position, see Forsyth, *Unions of States*, pp. 112–20.

[66] For the role of the great sectional spokesmen in articulating competing concepts of sovereignty and their relations to section interests, see Peterson, Merrill D. 1987. *The Great Triumvirate: Webster, Clay and Calhoun*. New York: Oxford University Press.

[67] For a succinct overview of the many controversies concerning the Kansas–Nebraska Act, see Potter, David 1976. *The Impending Crisis: 1848–1861.* New York: Harpers, chap. 7, pp. 145–76.

[68] Monaghan, James 1955. *Civil War on the Western Border, 1854–1865.* Boston: Little, Brown; and Rawley, James A. 1969. *Race and Politics: "Bleeding Kansas" and the Coming of the Civil War.* Philadelphia: Lippincott.

[69] Waltz, *Theory of International Politics*, pp. 124–7; Walt, Stephen M. 1987. *The Origins of Alliances.* Ithaca: Cornell University Press.

[70] Hiding "could take many forms: simply ignoring the threat or declaring neutrality in a general crisis, possibly approaching other states on one side or both sides of a quarrel to guarantee one's safety; trying to withdraw into isolation; assuming a purely defensive position in the hope that the storm would blow over; or, usually as a last resort, seeking protection from some other power or powers in exchange for diplomatic services, friendship, or non-military support, without joining that power or powers as an ally or committing itself to any use of force on its part." The second measure is binding, and the last bandwagoning. Schroeder, Paul 1994. "Historical Reality vs. Neorealist Theory," *International Security* 19: 101–48, at p. 117.

[71] "The perception of a threat from another power might lead a state to try either to form an alliance against that power, in order to meet the threat by capability-aggregation, or to ally with that power, in order to manage the threat through a *pactum de contrahendo*." Schroeder, Paul 1976. "Alliances, 1815–1945: Weapons of Power and Tools of Management," in Knorr, Klaus (ed.) *Historical Dimensions of National Security Problems.* Lawrence, Kan.: University of Kansas Press, pp. 227–62, pp. 257 and 231. Schroeder does not use the term "binding" to describe this foreign policy practice, and in his more recent writings this practice is not so salient or clearly distinguished as in the 1976 article.

[72] Hintze, Otto 1975. "The Preconditions of Representative Government in World History," in Gilbert, Felix (ed.) *The Historical Essays of Otto Hintze.* New York: Oxford University Press, pp. 302–56.

[73] Wolfers, Arnold and Martin, Laurence 1956. *The Anglo-American Tradition in Foreign Policy.* New Haven: Yale University Press, pp. i–xxvii.

[74] *Federalist*, no. 9, pp. 70–1; Gilbert, Felix 1961. *To the Farewell Address.* Princeton: Princeton University Press.

[75] Montesquieu, *Spirit* Book XVII, chap. 6, pp. 278–9; and Deudney, Daniel 1991. "The Natural Republic of Europe: The Geopolitics of a Balancer State-System, ca.1500–1900," paper presented at the International Studies Association, Vancouver, British Columbia.

[76] Among those who assign a central role to material division in constituting the European state system are: Kennedy, Paul 1987. *The Rise and Fall of the Great Powers.* New York: Random House, p. 17; Wesson, Robert 1978. *State Systems: International Pluralism, Politics and Culture.* New York: Free Press, p. 110.

[77] Buzan, Barry, Jones, Charles and Little, Richard 1993. *The Logic of Anarchy: Neorealism to Structural Realism.* New York: Columbia University Press.

[78] Realists commonly refer to the system-level structure that is stable in a situation of isolation as anarchy, but "nullarchy" is more appropriate because the system-level governance is impossible as well as absent.

[79] Gilbert, *To the Farewell Address*; and Varg, Paul A. 1963. *Foreign Policies of the Founding Fathers*. East Lansing: Michigan State University Press.

[80] For an astute analysis of the debates among Americans over relations with the European state system, see Lang, Daniel 1985. *Foreign Policy in the Early Republic: The Law of Nations and the Balance of Power*. Baton Rouge: Louisiana State University.

[81] Jessup, Philip C. and Deak, Francis 1935. *Neutrality: Its History, Economics, and Law*, vol. I, *The Origins*, New York: Columbia University Press.

[82] For American attitudes and uses of international law, see Lang, *Foreign Policy in the Early Republic*.

[83] For the relationship between the Monroe Doctrine and European diplomacy, see Watson, Adam 1984. "New States in the Americas," in Bull, Hedley and Watson, Adam *The Expansion of International Society*. New York: Oxford University Press; and May, Ernest R. 1975. *The Making of the Monroe Doctrine*. Cambridge, Mass: Harvard University Press.

[84] DeConde, Alexander 1966. *The Quasi-War: The Politics and Diplomacy of the Undeclared Naval War with France, 1797–1801*. New York: Charles Scribner's Sons.

[85] Stagg, J.C.A. 1983. *Mr. Madison's War: Politics, Diplomacy and Warfare in the Early American Republic, 1783–1830*. Princeton: Princeton University Press.

[86] Tucker, Robert W. and Hendrickson, David C. 1990. *Empire of Liberty: the Statecraft of Thomas Jefferson*. New York: Oxford University Press, particularly chap. 22, "Neutral Rights versus the Balance of Power."

[87] Cited in *ibid.*, p. 216.

[88] Dehio, Ludwig 1962. *The Precarious Balance*. New York: Alfred A. Knopf. Because the European balancing system depended upon mobilizing ever more resources from its flanks, it depended upon the unprecedented European expansion over the rest of the globe. This suggests that the European system depended upon a factor unlikely to be available in other balance-of-power systems.

[89] Higgonnet, Patrice 1968. "Origins of the Seven Years War," *Journal of Modern History* 40: 57–90.

[90] As de Tocqueville and others had predicted, America emerged as the greatest economic and military power (along with Russia).

[91] Betts, Raymond 1979. "Immense Dimensions: The Impact of the American West on the Late Nineteenth-Century European Thought About Expansion," *Western Historical Quarterly* 10: 100–25.

[92] Dehio, Ludwig 1960. *Germany and World Politics in the Twentieth Century*. New York: W.W. Norton.

[93] Coogan, John W. 1981. *The End of Neutrality: The United States, Britain, and Maritime Rights, 1899–1915*. Ithaca: Cornell University Press.

[94] Scott, James Brown 1920. *The United States of America: A Study in*

International Organization. Washington D.C.: Carnegie Endowment; and Knock, Thomas J. 1992. *To End All Wars: Woodrow Wilson and the Quest for a New World Order.* Oxford: Oxford University Press.

[95] Like many realists, Wilson was sloppy with his balancing terminology, but it seems clear that he understood his plan to rest upon a favorable distribution of power; balancing alliances would be replaced by an elaborate conflict resolution procedure and a binding union with a Constitution-like "solemn covenant." Buehrig, Edward H. 1955. *Woodrow Wilson and the Balance of Power.* Bloomington: University of Indiana Press.

[96] Bailey, Thomas A. 1945. *Woodrow Wilson and the Great Betrayal.* New York: Macmillan.

[97] Adler, Selig 1961. *The Isolationist Impulse.* New York: Collier.

[98] Carr, E.H. 1939. *The Twenty Years' Crisis.* London: Macmillan.

[99] Herwig, Holgar 1980. *The Politics of Frustration: The United States in German Strategic Planning, 1888–1941.* Boston: Little, Brown.

[100] Stein, Arthur A. "Domestic Constraints, Extended Deterrence, and the Incoherence of Grand Strategy: The United States, 1938–1950," in Rosecrance, Richard and Stein, Arthur A. (eds.) 1993. *The Domestic Basis of Grand Strategy.* Ithaca: Cornell University Press, pp. 96–123.

[101] For the Western system as a civic union and the limits of other liberal and realist theories to explain it, see Deudney, Daniel and Ikenberry, G. John 1993/1994. "The Logic of the West," *World Policy Journal* 10: 17–25.

[102] Wells, H.G. 1902. *Anticipations.* New York: Harper & Brothers.

[103] Steit, Clarence 1939. *Union Now: A Proposal for a Federal Union of the Democracies of the North Atlantic.* New York: Harper & Brothers; and 1961. *Freedom's Frontier: Atlantic Union Now.* New York: Harper & Brothers.

[104] Deutsch, Karl et al. 1957. *Political Community in the North Atlantic Area.* Princeton: Princeton University Press; and Adler, Emmanuel and Barnett, Michael 1994. "Pluralistic Security Communities: Past Present, Future," Working Paper Series on Regional Security, No.1, Madison: University of Wisconsin Press.

[105] Duffield, John S. 1994. "Explaining the Long Peace in Europe: the contributions of regional security regimes," *Review of International Studies* 20: 369–88.

[106] Lundstad, Geir 1990. *The American "Empire" and Other Studies of U.S. Foreign Policy in Comparative Perspective.* New York: Oxford University Press.

[107] Ruggie, John Gerard 1993. "Multilateralism: The Anatomy of an Institution," in Ruggie (ed.) *Multilateralism Matters.* New York: Columbia University Press, pp. 3–49.

[108] Burley, Anne-Marie 1992. "Law among Liberal States: Liberal Internationalism and the Act of State Doctrine," *Columbia Law Review* 92: 1907–96; and Slaughter, Anne-Marie 1995. "Neither Apology nor Utopia: International Law in a World of International States," *European Journal of International Law* 7: 100–52.

[109] The prerogatives of British sovereignty are intact, but the actual exercise

of British foreign and defense policy is intimately intertwined with that of the United States.

[110] Katzenstein, Peter 1987. *Policy and Politics in West Germany: The Growth of a Semi-Sovereign State.* Philadelphia: Temple University Press.

[111] Morgenthau, Hans 1967. *Politics among Nations* 4th ed. New York: Alfred A. Knopf, p. 498.

[112] Thatcher, Margaret 1993. *The Downing Street Years.* New York: Harper Collins, pp.796–9.

[113] For a more extended development of this point, see Deudney, Daniel and Ikenberry, G. John 1991–2. "The International Sources of Soviet Change," *International Security* 13: 74–118.

[114] Kennedy, Ellen 1991. *The Bundesbank: Germany's Central Bank in the International Monetary System.* London: Royal Institute of International Affairs/ Council on Foreign Relations.

[115] Greico, Joseph 1995. "The Maastricht Theory, Economic and Monetary Union and the Neo-Realist Research Programme," *Review of International Studies* 21: 21–40.

[116] Knock, Thomas J. 1992. *To End All Wars: Woodrow Wilson and the Quest for a New World Order.* Oxford and New York: Oxford University Press.

8   Hierarchy under anarchy: informal empire and the East German state

Alexander Wendt and Daniel Friedheim

States have sovereignty to the extent that they have exclusive authority over their territories. In the modern states system this authority is usually differentiated into internal and external sovereignty. This means that states have the ultimate authority within domestic society to make decisions even if the decisions are significantly constrained in practice by other domestic actors, and that states have the authority within international society to do as they please even if their actions are significantly constrained in practice by other states. To say that states are sovereign, in other words, is to say that they have certain *rights*, even if the exercise of those rights is constrained. Rights are not intrinsic, naturally given attributes, like the height or weight of an individual; they are conferred upon actors through a process of social recognition that constitutes particular kinds of identities. Rights are socially constructed. In the absence of recognition, a state might be able to achieve exclusive control by sheer force, but this is a very different and typically a more difficult matter than exercising rights. The recognition that constitutes states as sovereign comes from domestic and international society, both of which give permission to states to rule a particular space. In this chapter, we are interested primarily in the role of international society in this process.

We focus on external recognition because we are interested in situations in which state sovereignty coexists in relation to super-ordination, subordination, or hierarchy among states. That is, we focus on situations where some states are recognized as having a measure of de facto authority over others. Despite the juridical sovereignty of virtually every modern state, hierarchical political authority is also a pervasive phenomenon in international politics. Great Powers are widely acknowledged to have special prerogatives in their "spheres of

240

influence" to help "manage" the international system. These prerogatives are, of course, partly a function of superior material power and resources. But they also are recognized as legitimate by international society as a whole, which seems increasingly willing to sign off on Great Power interventions in other states, and, as we argue in this paper, by the subordinate states over whom this transnational authority is exercised. We are interested in the articulation of *competing* principles for distributing political authority in international politics. One principle does so on a basis of territorial exclusivity, and the other principle does so on a basis of hierarchical international governance.

The articulation of these competing principles takes place at the systemic rather than domestic level. Therefore, it is partly the task of "third image"[1] theories of world politics, which explain the structure and dynamics of interaction across territorial frontiers, to analyze it. Systemic theories cannot explain all of world politics, since much, if not most, of what actors do across frontiers is driven by domestic politics or leader psychology; these are the second and first "images," respectively. To the extent that world politics are caused by *inter*action, however, a distinctively systemic approach will be necessary.

How well these systemic theories play their part depends on how well their assumptions suit the reality they seek to explain. In the last two decades, systemic theorists have focused primarily on two agendas: showing whether distributions of power or international institutions are the principal systemic cause of interstate outcomes, *given* state identities and interests; and, to a lesser extent, showing whether systemic structures construct state identities and interests or merely constrain behavior, *given* a materialist definition of structure as a distribution of economic or military power. Work on these agendas has generated many insights, but both ignore an important possibility: that intersubjective structures at the systemic level might create state identities and interests. We believe it is precisely such a process that must be grasped to understand the articulation of competing principles for distributing political authority in contemporary international politics. In the spirit of advancing the third image project we explore this possibility, which has been relatively neglected by mainstream scholarship.

Hierarchical international governance structures come in various forms; in this paper, we focus on one known as "informal empire." We develop some general theoretical claims about this structure, and then illustrate it empirically with a case study of the relationship between the Soviet Union and the German Democratic Republic. Although in many respects this case is extreme, it also reveals very clearly the problems involved in combining sovereignty with more hierarchical ways of organizing global political space.

In the next section, we sketch an intellectual map of third image theorizing, showing how its different research programs characteristically approach a phenomenon like that of informal empire. We then develop our own, "constructivist," theory of informal empire, which focuses on the social construction of dominant and subordinate state actors by intersubjective structures at the systemic level. Finally, in the longest section, we illustrate this framework empirically by reference to the East German case.

Four sociologies of international politics

Systemic theory is often equated with neorealism, but in fact there are at least four ways to think in a structural way about the international system, and in effect four sociologies of international politics. In this section, we draw a map of these sociologies, and with it show how they approach informal empire.

Systemic theories are constituted partly by answers to two questions. One asks how much structures in the system are material or social. By "material," we refer to brute physical phenomena like natural resources and technological artifacts that exist independent of ideas (as in neorealism's "distribution of capabilities"). By "social," we refer to the shared ideas or common knowledge embodied in intersubjective phenomena like institutions and threat systems. Materialists believe material forces are the base of world politics, and shared ideas are at most a superstructure; anti-materialists (or "idealists" if this term is understood in a social, nonutopian sense) believe the basis of the international system is a shared knowledge structure, and that material forces are significant insofar as this structure gives them meaning.

The debate over this question is often muddied by two misunderstandings. First, it is not about the relative explanatory power of "power and interest" versus "ideas." It is about whether material forces can explain international politics *stripped of social (and thus ideational) content*. Idealists are not saying that states do not act on the basis of power and interest, but that this activity is contingent on the *social* structure in which states are embedded. In a conflictual system, power and interest matter, but what makes a system conflictual is an underlying structure of common knowledge. The threat posed to the United States by 500 British nuclear weapons, for example, is less than that posed by five North Korean weapons, because the British are friends and the North Koreans are not, and amity and enmity are social, not material, relations. In that sense it is "ideas all the way down." Second, this debate is also *not* about how much conflict exists in the system. Material forces may cause cooperation, and shared knowledge may cause conflict. Neorealists have helped confuse matters by treating conflictual systems as "realist" worlds. This conflates explanatory and descriptive issues and leads to the tautology that war makes realism true.[2] The rival hypothesis to constructivist idealism is not that world politics are mean and nasty, nor that states act on the basis of power and interest, but that material forces per se – that is, brute capabilities stripped of social content – determine the superstructure of the system.

The other question that divides systemic theories concerns the relationship between agency and structure. In particular it concerns the extent to which the properties of state agents – their identities, interests, and capabilities – are constructed by or endogenous to system structures rather than intrinsic to their nature.[3] Individualists at the systemic level argue that properties of state agents are given exogenously to the system (by human nature or domestic politics), and that systemic structures therefore function merely as constraints on behavior. Structuralists argue that these properties are in important part constructed by systemic structures.

One debate, then, is about what structures are made of. The other debate is about what explanatory difference they make. Despite the ontological and epistemological baggage that is often loaded onto these debates, we believe both should be seen ultimately as empirical questions.

The position that one takes on these debates will structure one's overall approach to systemic theory, and thus to informal empire. The two-dimensional space they define is occupied by four basic research programs; specific systemic theories are, in turn, expressions of these research programs.[4] We illustrate each of these programs with reference to a prominent systemic theory and the assumptions it brings to the study of informal empire.

Theories in the northwest quadrant combine a materialist definition of structure with a structuralist approach to agency. Neorealism in its structuralist mode belongs here, with its focus on the distribution of

System structure is social?

	Low (materialism)	High (idealism)
High (structuralism)	e.g. Dependency theory	e.g. Constructivism
Low (individualism)	e.g. Neorealism	e.g. Neoliberalism

States are constructed by system? appears to the left between the two rows.

Figure 8.1: Systemic structures

capabilities and its hypothesis about the production of "like units" by anarchic structure. Much of the literature on asymmetrical relationships in the international system, in turn, draws on some form of dependency theory.[5] This theory hypothesizes that material structures of economic exchange dominate the international system, and that these structures penetrate the territorial space nominally controlled by dependent states, helping to determine their character as opposed to merely constraining their behavior. Dependency theorists do not often talk of "informal empires," which are geopolitical rather than economic structures, but they do interpret the attributes of states as effects of transnational economic and class structures.

Theories in the southwest quadrant combine a materialist definition of structure with an individualist approach to state interests. Much of classical realism finds a place here, with its focus on material power and explanation of interests by human nature. And although neorealism has a structuralist mode, most neorealist scholarship is choice-theoretic (and thus individualistic) in character, neglecting the structuralist concern with the construction of interests.[6] Whether or not neorealism is properly located here, when we look at informal empire through this lens we tacitly presuppose the spatial integrity of state actors to the extent that it (this lens) treats their identities and interests as given exogenously to systemic structures. To that extent, rationalist methods attribute a *de facto sovereignty* to the state, in that the "state defines for itself how it will cope with its internal and external problems, including whether or not to seek assistance from others and in doing so to limit its freedom by making commitments to them."[7] Relations *among* states, therefore, will be inherently anarchic. States might be differently constrained behaviorally by their positions in the distribution of power, but rationalist methods do not treat states as constructed by systemic structures.

Like neoliberalism, theories in the southeast quadrant combine a more social view of structure, focusing in particular on international regimes, with an individualist view of agency. Regimes consist of norms, rules, and principles that constitute shared expectations among state actors, and in that sense regimes exist only in virtue of ideational phenomena. In common with much neorealist scholarship, however, neoliberalism is cast in rationalist terms. Institutions affect incentives for certain kinds of behavior, and this may generate novel predictions relative to the institution-poor models of neorealism, but they do not constitute the identities and interests of state actors. This not only attributes a de facto sovereignty to states (and thus anarchy to the states system), but it also dilutes the power of the institutionalist thesis, reducing regimes to "intervening variables" between material forces and outcomes.[8] As such, neoliberal theorizing about informal empire would probably tend toward a contractarian or "principal–agent" model, which reduces hierarchy to asymmetric exchange relationships between actors who are sovereign (or exogenously given) in the last instance.[9]

It is not possible in this chapter to develop, let alone critique, these rival approaches to informal empire. Our purpose has been only to suggest how different answers to two questions help define different systemic research programs on informal empire, and in so doing allow us to see certain phenomena and not others. Our discussion also points toward a relatively underdeveloped zone in the northeast quadrant of Figure 8.1. Many theories might fall in this space,[10] but they share two basic propositions: that the identities and interests of state actors are in important part constructed by structures in the international system, and that these structures are social rather than material. These two claims are the core of a social construction approach to international theory.

A constructivist model of informal empire

Informal empires are transnational structures of de facto political authority in which members are juridically sovereign states.[11] As such, they are constituted by a tension between two principles for structuring global political authority. In one principle, this authority is differentiated into mutually exclusive sovereign territorial units (constituting the system as an anarchy); in the other principle, this authority is differentiated functionally and asymmetrically across territorial frontiers (constituting the system as a hierarchy). This tension also calls attention to the two distinctive features of a constructivist approach. On the one hand, against realist materialism, the tension emphasizes that the issue in such structures is one of *authority*, an intersubjective concept that cannot be reduced to brute material power. And, against rationalist individualism, it emphasizes that *sovereign* authority is not an unproblematically given attribute of state identity. Since sovereignty is only one of many identities that a state actor can have, a first step in theorizing about informal empire is to disentangle states from sovereignty. We then show how the principles of sovereignty and hierarchy construct state actors in informal empire, and conclude with the contradictory behavioral dynamics that ensue.

The state as structure and as actor

The state is a structure of political authority in which there is a monopoly on the legitimate use of organized violence. As a structure, the state cannot *act* or *do* anything; it is the purposive organizational agents of governance, or state actors, that are embedded in structures of political authority which do things, have identities and interests, and so on.[12] In the formal organization of the Westphalian system these two concepts of state coincide spatially, since state actors are constituted as the sovereign centers of juridically distinct structures of political authority. This generates the "billiard ball" imagery of mainstream international relations theory, which assumes that state structures are exclusively controlled by, and thus conceptually subordinate to, distinct state actors. But such a one-to-one correspondence is not inevitable. The fact that the Soviet Union and East Germany shared a coercive monopoly in East German territory did not mean that East Germany was not a state actor any more than the emergence of a collective security regime in Western Europe makes France no longer a state actor. In these cases, state actors coexist in a transnational structure of political authority or "international state"[13] that is not anarchic.

Whether a states system is anarchic depends on states' relationships to each other, and this lies on a continuum that measures centralization of political authority. At one extreme, authority is mutually exclusive, relations are therefore anarchic, and agential and structural concepts of state coincide. In the absence of other constitutive principles, the relation between sovereign state actors will be of this form. In the middle of the continuum, relations are marked by internationalization in which authority is pooled or overlapped in a multilateral fashion, as in the European Union. At the other extreme are hierarchical relations in which the authority of one state actor is formally subordinate to that of another, as in the unitary, territorial state, or formal empire. Which of these patterns exists in a given case is an empirical question, and international relations scholars should therefore approach their mapping with an open mind.[14] Informal empire lies somewhere between the latter two – an international state with significant hierarchical elements – constituted as such by the articulation of principles of sovereignty and hierarchy. We describe these principles in this and the next section.

The constitution of the sovereign state

The concept of sovereignty is sometimes used to refer to a property of state actors, like "constitutional independence,"[15] and sometimes is used to refer to an institution of the states system as a whole. The two are in fact mutually constitutive but irreducible usages, and as such need to be differentiated clearly.

On the one hand, sovereignty refers to the possession by an actor or set of actors of exclusive authority over some domain of competence. Many types of actors can have this property. In the case of states it has referred historically to authority over a territory, although in principle it could apply to a specific issue. The fact that we say "exclusive" to describe this authority, however, reveals its inherently social quality, since that term implies a relation to other actors; it would be meaningless to say that Robinson Crusoe had sovereignty over his island. Sovereignty is about the social terms of individuality, not individuality per se, and in that sense it is an historically contingent social identity rather than an inherent quality of stateness. A similar intuition lies behind the suggestion that sovereignty confers upon states "territorial property rights,"[16] since rights have no meaning outside an intersubjective context.

The quality of being sovereign, then, presupposes an institutional framework in which it is recognized by others. "Recognition" is not meant here as formal diplomatic recognition, but as an effect of other

247

states' refusal to violate the exclusivity of one's territorial claims when the opportunity presents itself, in effect, a de facto permission from others to rule exclusively. The rules that structure this permission are, in turn, sometimes referred to as the "institution" of sovereignty. This institution divides political authority on a mutually exclusive, territorial basis to its members, constituting them as functionally equal actors in world politics. In so doing, it constitutes the states system as an anarchy, but one different from an anarchy that lacks sovereignty. In the latter there are no intersubjective constraints on interaction, and actors are free to conquer or destroy each other as they wish. Participation in a community of mutual recognition, in contrast, requires that actors refrain from such actions.[17]

In sum, the institution of sovereignty is produced and reproduced by state actors recognizing each other as sovereign, and to that extent it exists only by virtue of a social process. This reflects a mechanism of reflected appraisals at work. Actors learn to see themselves and thereby acquire social identities as a function of how others treat them. They then engage in practices of mutual recognition designed to confirm their identities, since it is through these that they give meaning to their existence and define who they are. In the case of sovereignty there are very few practices that states must engage in, and to that extent it is a very open-ended institution. But they have to avoid violating each other's sovereignty, and this refusal (or recognition) will be implicit in all of the practices that this open-ended institution makes possible. Given the reciprocal, live-and-let-live nature of sovereignty, the result is an assurance game in which each state recognizes the sovereignty of others as long as they reciprocate. The problem in this harmonious picture is that sovereignty is not the only principle constituting state actors.

The constitution of international hierarchy

In contrast to the institution of sovereignty, which today is global and singular, informal empires are regional and multiple. In the postwar period, the three principal informal empires have been those of the United States, the Soviet Union, and France, but there are other, more local examples as well. These hierarchical structures traverse the anarchic system constituted by the institution of sovereignty, and they articulate with the system in ways that give rise to characteristic dynamics of interaction, which we address in the next section. Here we examine the mechanisms by which these hierarchical structures are created and institutionalized, and we argue that they should be seen as intersubjective structures of authority rather than merely material structures of exchange.[18]

A necessary condition for informal empire is a distribution of military power so unequal that a more powerful state actor has the material capacity to provide security to a weaker one. The territorial rights distributed by the institution of sovereignty help constitute these capacities, and to that extent it is prior to informal empire. Sovereignty should not be seen as a given, first principle in the analysis of informal empire, however, since through its effects on state identities and interests informal empire helps create the conditions under which one state actor needs security assistance from another. This makes power disparities socially meaningful and compromises de facto sovereignty. After all, the vast majority of materially unequal dyads in the states system are not informal empires. In order to initiate an informal empire, a more powerful state must intervene in a weaker one with the object of creating a regime friendly to it. This can occur without the weak state's consent (as in the Soviet occupation of Eastern Europe in 1945), or with its consent (as in its intervention in Afghanistan).

The emerging hierarchical relationship is institutionalized in two ways that make it irreducible to underlying disparities in material power. The first is through the patron's provision of security assistance in exchange for influence over the client's national security behavior. Such assistance can be military, in the form of arms, arms technology, or training, or economic, in the form of foreign aid for security. In return, the client allows the patron some influence over what it does with this assistance, over its alliance partners, perhaps over domestic policy, and so on. As such, informal empire in part *is* an exchange relationship between juridically equal parties in which institutionalized norms and expectations structure behavior. A rationalist, principal–agent model, which concerns the behavior of exogenously given actors whose identities and interests are not affected by interaction, adequately captures this aspect of informal empire.

Nothing we say in the following passages questions the notion that unequal exchange relationships help constitute informal empires, or that they involve principal–agent problems. We do want to suggest, however, that the emergence of norms and expectations of behavior is only part of the story of how informal empires become institutionalized. Also important is the effect of unequal exchange on the identities and interests of the parties.

The exchange of security assistance for influence over time enables constellations of societal interests to control power in subordinate states that otherwise would not or would at least be forced to make significant concessions to competitors. The point of security assistance is to defend particular regimes against threats. Sometimes these threats are external, but often they are internal, posed by other contenders for state power. This is particularly true in the Third World, where many states are weak in the sense that the regimes that control them lack domestic legitimacy,[19] and it was also the case in the former Soviet bloc. Domestic weakness, however, is not a naturally given thing. It is perpetuated and even created by the external base of support provided by the patron, which enables clients to avoid implementing policies, let alone to reconfigure the constellation of societal interests controlling state power, that might solve legitimacy problems. To that extent, dominant state actors play a hegemonic role in defining what constitutes the security of subordinate states, which creates clients who have an "investment in subordination."[20]

Through a variety of mechanisms informal empire also has effects, perhaps less profound, on the identity and interests of dominant state actors. Clients may become actively involved as a form of lobbyist influencing the domestic politics of patrons.[21] In addition, by virtue of involvement with clients, constituencies within the patron may acquire internal institutional influence that they would not otherwise have had. Patrons may also become concerned about the credibility of their commitments such that they redefine their security interests; such concerns were one reason, for example, why intervention in South Vietnam was deemed in the US national interest. Finally, dominant state actors may develop narratives that justify their role to others and themselves (manifest destiny, white man's burden, and so on), and that affect national conceptions of self.[22] Informal empire is a codependency, even though it is hierarchical.

The unequal exchange relationships that underlie informal empire, then, create intersubjective understandings in terms of which identities and interests get defined. This is a deeper form of institutionalization than that revealed by an exchange-theoretic analysis alone, since it suggests *sui generis* forms of resistance to change. In particular, it creates state actors that depend for their existence as particular kinds of selves on continuing the relationship; in social psychological terms, one would say that the parties to informal empire internalize unequal opportunities and material capacities in new identities and interests that will continue to motivate their actions (at least for a time) even if the immediate incentives for, and constraints on, the original exchange are removed.[23] Through this process, patron–client exchange is transformed from a voluntary act by independently existing agents into a habitual practice in which dominant and subordinate state actors are effects.

The result is a hierarchical, transnational authority structure in which one state performs state-like functions in another; it constitutes a nonanarchic, non-Westphalian states system. An authority relationship is one in which there is a fusion of power and collective purpose.[24] It depends in the last instance on one actor's ability to impose its will on the other by force, yet "[r]esort to either positive incentives or coercive measures by a person in order to influence others is prima facie evidence that he does not have authority over them."[25] As such, authority rests on a normative arrangement involving the consent or recognition by the governed (in this case, subordinate state actors rather than society), which is irreducible to the material capacity to coerce. This consent expresses a "shared belief that it is legitimate for the superior ... to impose his will upon them and that it is illegitimate for them to refuse obedience."[26] The resulting "surrender of private judgment"[27] directly contravenes the kind of autonomous decision-making characteristic of sovereignty reflected in the quote from Waltz above on pp. 244–5 (see note 7). And in so doing this surrender of judgment institutes a functional division of labor between dominant and subordinate actors with regard to the provision and definition of political-military security. It is by virtue of this transnationalization of authority that an informal empire is an international "state;" and it is by virtue of its hegemonic character that this state is an "empire."[28]

The shared beliefs constituting informal empire will typically be embodied in an ideology. They will also typically be given legal-bureaucratic expression in various kinds of interorganizational links. The most important of these will be military, like the Warsaw Treaty Organization, which subordinated the operational and command structures of East European armies to that of the Soviet Union.[29] But interorganizational links might also develop between other governmental bureaucracies and, in the Soviet case, between the party organizations that control them (the Cominform). These links blur the boundaries between state actors' corporate bodies,[30] an integrative process that, were it not constrained by other constitutive principles, would culminate in the centralized territorial state or formal empire.

Through interorganizational links, informal empires begin to approach the type of authority structure that Weber designated "legal-bureaucratic." At the same time, however, states within informal empires remain formally independent by virtue of their participation in the institution of sovereignty, which gives them substantial organizational autonomy and an interest in resisting integration. This suggests that a better model for thinking about informal empires would be Weber's feudal authority. Like informal empire, the relation between lord and vassal was based on, but not reducible to, military power and security, and was at once contractual and hierarchical. It was contractual in the sense that its parties were formally free and juridically more or less equal actors who entered into an exchange of land and protection for military service; it was hierarchical in the sense that, even though the lord could not easily enforce his authority over the vassal, he could expect him to submit and fulfill his obligations.[31] The result is a decentralized structure of authority, but a structure of authority nonetheless that constitutes the identities and interests of its parties. Insofar as this analogy applies, it suggests that even though the relationship between members of an informal empire is anarchic in the legal-bureaucratic sense of authority, it is hierarchical in this other sense.[32] To that extent, the modern states system may have more structural similarity than is generally recognized with the heteronomous character of the medieval world.[33]

The dynamics of informal empire

The structural principles of sovereignty and hierarchy constitute multiple and potentially conflicting identities and interests within state actors in informal empire. The principle of sovereignty motivates them to mind their own business, to reduce dependency on each other, and to resist intervention; the principle of hierarchy motivates them to maintain and even deepen asymmetrical codependencies. This situation can generate substantial role conflict,[34] leading to a "push–pull" dynamic of interaction. This dynamic not only shapes the behavior of state actors, but it also reproduces their multiple identities and interests, which are at stake in each interaction.

More specifically, the structural tensions within informal empire suggest that the actions of dominant and subordinate state actors will be characterized by a contradictory mix of self-assertion and self-restraint "in which the limits of power and of response are ... reciprocally defined."[35] Subordinate state actors will periodically assert their autonomy, drawing on the resources of the institution of sovereignty to do so, while at the same time constraining themselves during these episodes to maintain their subordinate position. Conversely, dominant state actors will try to maintain their authority over clients, while constraining themselves in the use of force to do so, since this would constitute the breakdown of authority. By internalizing the contradictions between sovereignty and hierarchy in informal empire within their identities and interests, in other words, dominant and subordinate state actors can be expected to act in ways that strictly materialist and rationalist analyses would not predict.

The dynamics of informal empire concern not only the relationship between dominant and subordinate state actors, but also concern their joint relationship to societal actors in the subordinate state. In feudalism, after all, lord and vassal shared in the domination and exploitation of lower social strata like the serfs, who were not party to the feudal relation. In informal empire, the political-military dependence of subordinate on dominant state actors reduces their accountability to society, and, as such, undermines the authority relationship between state and society characteristic of the sovereign state. Subordinate state actors do not need to worry about domestic legitimacy as much as substantively sovereign states do, since they can depend on external coercive support, which enables them to reduce their compromises with, and if necessary repress, opposition groups in society. Indeed, the legitimacy they have to worry about may be more external than internal.[36] In effect, informal empire constitutes a subordinate state apparatus that is alienated from its society. This, in turn, may have the effect of creating at least latent nationalistic groups that might not otherwise exist in society, and setting in motion state–society conflicts that ultimately destroy a client state.

Hierarchy and sovereignty in the East German case

The purpose of this case study is to illustrate the framework of investigation proposed above, not to test it, and so no direct comparisons with rival hypotheses are made. The study is guided by propositions at two levels of theory. The hard core of a constructivist research program directs us to show how the identities and interests of state actors – and in the case of informal empire, specifically those related to security – are constructed through interaction with other state actors on the systemic level, and to show how intersubjective factors shape this process. In this case study, we are particularly interested in the construction of subordinate, as opposed to dominant, state interests. On a more superficial level of theory, we address the dynamics of self-constrained resistance and enforcement exhibited by state actors trying to negotiate the contradictions between sovereign and hierarchical principles, and the consequences of these efforts for the domestic legitimacy of subordinate states.

The formal sovereignty of the German Democratic Republic (GDR) was not widely recognized until 1972. The regime was led by lifelong communists, including veterans of Nazi jails or wartime exiles in the Soviet Union, who believed they belonged to a transnational Communist Party. Perhaps more than elsewhere in Eastern Europe, they remained loyal to their "anti-fascist liberators." Coupled with its weak domestic legitimacy, one might have expected the East German regime to have been reduced to utter servility. Yet, the GDR's very existence preserved costly Soviet wartime gains and guaranteed Germany's division, as its leaders often reminded their patrons. "It was of course true that the development of the GDR simultaneously secured the USSR's own influence," said General Secretary Erich Honecker as he resisted *perestroika* to the end.[37] GDR leaders repeatedly invoked theoretical sovereign rights in spite of a "near permanent anxiety about the USSR's ultimate intentions."[38] The result was a constant, unresolved tension between internationalist definitions of state security called for by Marxism-Leninism and more nationalist definitions inherent in the principle of sovereignty.

The parameters of the Soviet doctrine of "limited sovereignty" evolved at historical turning points, as new understandings or rules of the game served a prophylactic function until they were later misinterpreted by one side or the other.[39] We have divided the history of GDR–USSR relations into four phases. Each phase illustrates a shifting balance between the conflicting principles of hierarchy and sovereignty that characterize informal empire: 1949 to 1953, covering the constitution of informal empire; 1954 to 1961, culminating in construction of the Berlin Wall to consolidate that hierarchical relationship; 1962 to 1971, when the GDR explored the limits of its sovereignty; and 1972 to 1989, when lingering state–society conflict led to its collapse. Our discussion benefits from the flood of literature coming from archives opened since the GDR's collapse in 1989, which has filled in several blank spots in this history.

Constituting hierarchy, 1949 to 1953

Soviet dominance in the eastern part of Germany after World War II naturally reflected certain basic power realities. In April 1945, Stalin privately predicted, "whoever controls an area also erects his own social system there. Everyone imposes his own system as far as his army can reach. It cannot be otherwise."[40] This fact led to power-based tactics. Stalin believed the conditions for realizing socialism in the Soviet occupation zone did not permit erecting a full-fledged "People's Democracy," as in the rest of the Soviet informal empire in Eastern Europe, but only an "anti-fascist" front.[41] This belief produced the Socialist Unity Party (SED) from the forced merger of the resurrected Social-Democratic Party (SPD) and the Communist Party (KPD) on 22 April 1946. Given the explicitly democratic pledges in Stalin's Potsdam Agreement of August 1945 with Truman and Churchill, SED deputy leader Walter Ulbricht concluded that the new regime "must look democratic, but we must keep control in our hands."[42]

Just as important for the constitution of informal empire as the distribution of material power, however, was the way the Soviets had begun redefining German identity and security interests. The process began with the selection and socialization of KPD members during wartime exile in the USSR, where ruthless purges reduced the party leadership contenders to Stalinist *apparatchik* Ulbricht and national communist Anton Ackermann. The advancing Red Army returned those two and a handful of trusted cadré members to German soil on the same day Hitler committed suicide in his Berlin bunker. The Soviets continued to supervise the leadership selection process in Germany. They helped force Ackermann to recant his "separate German road to Socialism."[43] That handed de facto control of the party to Ulbricht, a Weimar Republic deputy in the Reichstag who had spent 1924 to 1927 and 1938 to 1945 in Moscow being socialized to the new conception of German security interests. It was not clear whether the postwar German government he was to help form would rule all of Germany or just a fragment, but he was determined to define its security strictly in terms of socialist internationalism.

These Soviet efforts to create a new German identity bore fruit even before the GDR was officially founded. In its first platform in 1946, the SED declared itself independent, granting the USSR no explicit hegemonic role in the socialist movement. But cultivation of a new German security identity bore fruit as the party soon acknowledged the USSR's "leading role." The Sovietization of the SED was completed when its leadership decided to transform it into a Leninist vanguard party and to create a politburo that did not reflect the old SPD's electoral strength. The works of Stalin and Lenin joined those of Marx and Engels as mandatory reading.

During the military occupation, the German communists lacked the most basic trappings of sovereignty. As one East German working for the Soviet occupation authorities (SMAD) reminded a frustrated party colleague, there was "a higher authority than your central secretariat."[44] That higher authority vetoed Ulbricht's initial plans to stage show trials of prominent Nazis, and it did not invite the SED to the September 1947 founding of the Cominform.[45]

The Soviets began consolidating their relationship with the nascent subordinate state by demonstrating their willingness to intervene. Since Germany was an occupied country, however, that demonstration precipitated an international crisis and ended in apparent failure. The land and water blockade of the western three sectors of Berlin from June 1948 to May 1949, which the Soviets and East Germans introduced cautiously and blamed on unstated "technical difficulties," was triggered by the sovereignty issue of control over the currency. It exploited the Allied failure to have extracted written guarantees of surface access to the divided city, which lay deep inside the Soviet zone, but it ultimately foundered on the written guarantee of access by air. An eleven-month-long Anglo-American airlift employed war surplus aircraft, new radar technology, and construction of a third Berlin airport to deliver 1.4 million metric tons of food and coal at the cost of seventy-four lives. The blockade failed to deter the Allies from unifying the administration of their zones into "trizonia," in part because they wanted to avoid "a more colonial type of government."[46] Despite that appearance of failure, the first Berlin crisis established the Soviet willingness to intervene in the zone that soon became the GDR.

Stalin had met secretly with SED leaders in July 1947, but only after a last-minute trip to Moscow in September 1949 did they obtain his permission to found the GDR. Their letter to Stalin requested his "opinion on the timing and procedure of forming a government and its composition," to which the Soviets responded by approving the new state, postponing democratic elections, and ratifying two dozen top appointments.[47]

After its founding on 7 October, which was two months after the

Federal Republic of Germany (FRG) was forged out of "trizonia," the GDR continued to endure a heavy reparations burden. As authorized in the Potsdam agreements, the Soviets exported whole factories and operated many large industrial firms as "Soviet Joint Stock Companies." The almost one-quarter of East German industrial production diverted to the USSR this way exacerbated economic grievances that would plague the state throughout its forty-year existence.

In August 1950, the SED purged politburo members who had spent their wartime exile outside the USSR, including the editor of the official party newspaper, *Neues Deutschland*. The party followed Stalin's lead after the notorious "Doctor's Plot" and dutifully purged its highest-ranking Jewish members, including one politburo member whose crime was to have spent his exile in France.[48] And the Soviet commitment to the continued existence of the GDR still was open to question. Under the terms of the "Stalin Notes" of early 1952, which proposed a reunified but neutral Germany, the SED almost certainly would have been reduced to a minor party.[49] But the new "socialist state on German soil" was no puppet. It soon initiated independent decisions, some of which would require another Soviet intervention.

Even as he proclaimed the slogan "To learn from the Soviet Union means learning to win," Ulbricht was defying Soviet warnings not to force a quick transition to socialism. Using his single labor union, he began cutting workers' pay rates by increasing their minimum work quotas. By July 1952, a party congress announced the beginning of "the construction of Socialism." The ensuing "intensification of the class struggle" meant that work quotas were raised again. Supervisors who fell short of production quotas were tried as saboteurs; food shortages followed the collectivization of all remaining private farms; ration cards were limited to workers in socialized firms. Coupled with the initial remilitarization of a war-weary population, these pressures created a wave of emigration that reached 331,390 in 1953, the year that Stalin's death made reform possible. The party knew it was imposing goals to which workers were "opposed."[50] A struggle between state and society was underway in the GDR, and it would take Soviet intervention to protect the party from the people.

At first, the Soviets had tolerated Ulbricht's policy of Sovietization, but KGB chairman Lavrenti Beria soon warned Ulbricht to slow down his drive. At a presidium (politburo) meeting on 27 May, a decision was reached to require Ulbricht to abandon the policy. Ulbricht responded with a renewed Stalin personality-cult campaign and scheduled the next work quota increase for 1 June. Beria backed Ulbricht's rivals, *Neues Deutschland* editor Rudolf Herrnstadt, and secret police (abbreviated from the German, *Staatssicherheitsdienst* as *Stasi*) chief Wilhelm Zaisser, who forced Ulbricht to back down and adopt a post-Stalinist new course. Ulbricht nonetheless defiantly retained the work-quota increase, which was enough to inspire workers to go on strike against a "workers' state" for the first time in history.

The uprising of 17 June 1953 actually began on 15 June when construction workers walked off showcase project sites in East Berlin. As the politburo debated the Soviet-prescribed moderation in its policy the next day, workers laid siege to the Council of Ministers building, demanding that the new work quotas be rescinded and declaring a general strike for the following day. The strike on 17 June spread to 300 localities and by official count involved 7 percent of the workforce. Political demands were added, police headquarters ransacked, and political prisoners released. Soviet High Commissioner General Vladimir Semenov declared martial law, took over the paramilitary police, and deployed his own tanks to restore order. By 24 June, when the last of the first wave of strikes ended, at least 6,325 strikers had been arrested.[51] The state of emergency declared in 167 localities could not be lifted until early July, however, due to a second wave of strikes. Officially, the SED blamed the uprising on "imperialist" agents.

The particularly intense interparty relations during this episode illustrate the ill-defined boundaries between states in informal empire. In May, the Soviets summoned Ulbricht to Moscow and told him to abandon the fast track to socialism. To ensure his obedience, Soviet Commissioner Semonov began attending SED politburo meetings, where he announced that his orders were to "actively participate." He instructed the politburo to publish its new policy in an unprecedented "communiqué," warning it strongly against delay by stating, "In two weeks you might no longer have a state left."[52] At 10 a.m. on 17 June, Semenov ordered the entire politburo to his office at the Karlshorst compound in East Berlin, which forced its members to drive through throngs of striking workers. At noon he informed them that Moscow had decided to deploy its tanks. One hour later the Soviet deputy defense minister arrived to oversee operations. Ulbricht agreed to stay at Karlshorst overnight.

Since Moscow had already considered replacing Ulbricht, his demise now seemed certain. His rivals on the politburo staged a showdown during their 7 July meeting. Only two of thirteen members (including future successor Honecker) stood by their neo-Stalinist leader, two abstained, and a clear majority of nine opposed him. That same night, Ulbricht flew to Moscow to learn his fate. But the Soviets had changed their minds and Beria was arrested as a spy the next day. Ulbricht returned from Moscow not to resign, but to purge his rivals. He survived in part because 17 June had shown that the regime was too weak to survive change, but the Soviet about-face also was due to the simultaneous struggle over Stalin's succession then raging inside the Kremlin.[53] The parallel power struggles produced parallel purges. Beria was ousted as Khrushchev began to consolidate his control in the USSR, and Herrnstadt and Zaisser were ousted as Ulbricht consolidated his in the GDR.[54] SED leaders did not need a high commissioner to enforce their loyalty. Zaisser confided to fellow purge victim Herrnstadt that he would not defend himself from the trumped-up ideological charges, because "that could damage the Soviet Union."[55]

Out of the GDR's near collapse, and the simultaneous intraparty power struggles, tacit new rules of the game governing the hierarchical relationship emerged. Chief among these was that the Soviets would use their troops if necessary to rescue the regime from its people. All dissent would be blamed on foreign provocateurs. More concretely, the Soviets announced in August that they would stop collecting war reparations. They also agreed to write off some debts and extend credits for the first time. The National People's Army was formed, the People's Police were allowed to carry arms, and the *Stasi* secret police were reorganized and expanded. After the Berlin Foreign Ministers' Conference of 1954 failed to block West German integration into the North Atlantic Treaty Organization (NATO), the Soviets also renounced some of their occupation privileges and declared the GDR to be sovereign. They signed a bilateral treaty in 1954 that legalized the continued stationing of Soviet troops in East Germany. The GDR also attained full membership in the Warsaw Pact once the West integrated the Federal Republic of Germany into NATO in 1955. The GDR's newfound sovereignty was not to come at the expense of its steadfast loyalty, as was suggested by a new youth initiation ceremony (*Jugendweihe*), in which teenagers personally pledged, "as a true patriot, to deepen my constant friendship with the Soviet Union."[56] A hierarchical relationship composed of formal sovereignty and de facto hierarchy had been constituted.

Consolidating sovereignty, 1954 to 1961

The second Berlin crisis, from the first Soviet ultimatum in 1958 to the Berlin Wall and US–Soviet tank face-off in 1961, demonstrates the importance of controlling territory even for limited sovereignty. The decisionmaking process during the crisis illustrates the influence a materially weak client may exercise over a patron's policies. Despite the GDR's striking lack of material leverage against the Soviets, and despite fundamentally divergent interests – GDR sovereignty over the city would threaten Soviet rights as an occupying power – the subordinate GDR obtained support for policies that would enable it to consolidate control over its society. The literally concrete form of the compromise, a ring of "inward-facing fortifications"[57] around West Berlin, also exacerbated the conflict between the consolidated state and the captive society.

Beginning in May 1952, the GDR had begun fortifying its border with the FRG, but Berlin remained open and exploited by dissatisfied East Germans who used it more and more to leave the country. In a November 1958 ultimatum to the US, Britain, and France, Khrushchev threatened to settle for an abbreviated bilateral treaty with the GDR in six months if the Allies continued to reject a full four-power peace treaty. A separate Soviet–East German deal abrogating the Potsdam agreements could have cast doubt on the international legal status of the Allied troop presence in Berlin, but this attempt to consummate East German sovereignty proved to be a bluff.

Not only the international legal status of Berlin, but also the GDR's struggle with its society, remained unresolved. A second collectivization drive that began in 1959 caused another food shortage and another surge of emigration. One in six Germans living in the Soviet Occupation Zone in 1945 had fled west by 1959. The steady population loss caused economic and political uncertainties that motivated Ulbricht to propose a unilateral compromise short of a peace treaty.

Ulbricht needed Soviet support for his plan to seal off West Berlin, but the Soviets withheld this at the March 1961 Warsaw Pact summit. Khrushchev only renewed the lapsed ultimatum in June 1961 at his Vienna summit with US President John F. Kennedy. Ulbricht continued to lobby the Soviets, cynically increasing the pressure on them through actions that aggravated his own situation.[58] His announcement that East Germans commuting to work in West Berlin would need to find other jobs, as well as the disingenuous promise that "nobody intends to build a wall," seemed calculated to increase the panicky flow of refugees out of the GDR. Privately Ulbricht warned the Soviet ambassador that leaving borders open would trigger an "explosion" and the GDR could "collapse."[59] After Kennedy began to signal his determination to preserve the status quo only in West Berlin, the Soviet ambassador in East Berlin notified Ulbricht he could begin secret preparations for sealing the border. The Warsaw Pact then sanctioned Ulbricht's plans in a Moscow summit from 3 to 5 August.

What the GDR called an "anti-fascist protection wall" was erected beginning the evening of 13 to 14 August 1961, first as barbed wire, then as a twelve-foot-high cinder block wall and patrolled no-man's land. For the first time, GDR planners knew how large their workforce would be the following quarter. From 1949 to August 1961, the number of people who left the GDR totaled 2.7 million; from then through 1977, it amounted to only 177,000. Society was forced to reach an accommodation with the state. And Western allies "undertook fewer countermeasures than was expected," Ulbricht could report to Khrushchev.[60] They were content to preserve their presence in West Berlin and to uphold the principle of acknowledging only Soviet authority in East Berlin.

The dynamics of international politics within an informal empire precipitated a military showdown before the crisis ended. With the apparent support of Soviet hard-liners, East German police demanded that Allied civilian diplomats acknowledge East German authority by displaying identification at border crossings. Armed US soldiers escorted a diplomat into East Berlin on 22 October; US tanks took up position at the central Checkpoint Charlie crossing point; then Soviet politburo hard-liners appear to have allowed the Soviet commandant to move tanks into position on 26 October. The tank face-off lasted until Soviet hard-liners scaled down Khrushchev's dominance during the simultaneous Soviet party congress that ended on 28 October. Ulbricht's alliance with hard-liners in Moscow and the Soviet military command in East Berlin did not keep alive his hopes for a definitive peace treaty. It did demonstrate how well he could exploit the dynamics of informal empire to exercise influence.[61]

But East German influence on the USSR had its limits. The Soviets signed their first Treaty of Friendship and Cooperation with the GDR in 1964 and Khrushchev quietly dropped his threat to sign a separate peace treaty. The wall also symbolized the enduring failure to manufacture consent in civil society. A small trickle of refugees never dried up, however harsh the border regime was. As the conflict between state and society festered, the destructiveness of the wall could be measured in the 244 East Germans who died trying to cross it.[62]

The limits of sovereignty, 1962 to 1971

Ulbricht explored the possibilities for autonomy until the Soviets exercised their hierarchical authority to replace him. Almost as soon as the Berlin Wall had made it possible, Ulbricht launched in 1963 economic reforms modeled on Khrushchev's. Although a new trade treaty with the USSR signed in 1964 formalized such unfavorable export requirements and prices that the East German economics minister committed suicide, Ulbricht soon announced that the GDR had finished "building socialism." In 1967, he arrogated to himself the ideological license to reclassify the GDR as a "developed societal system of socialism," no longer a country merely making a slow transition to communism.

Partly emboldened by short-run economic success, as growth outpaced the USSR and the rest of the informal empire from 1964 to 1967, the GDR led the charge to crush Czechoslovakian communist leader Alexander Dubcek's Prague Spring reforms. After Dubcek's Action Program appeared in April 1968, Ulbricht became the first Warsaw Pact member to call openly for intervention. Although the two East German army units that were moved to the Czech border did not participate in the invasion on 20 August, army and secret-police squads participated in reconnaissance beforehand and mop-up afterwards. Ulbricht sought intervention so strongly partly in an attempt to derail Brezhnev's first steps toward détente with the FRG, which he believed could threaten the GDR's existence.

The East German rationale for advocating Soviet intervention in Czechoslovakia anticipated the tacit rules of the game governing mutual security interests that became the Brezhnev Doctrine. To bolster Warsaw Pact "solidarity," Ulbricht had begun calling as early as the February 1968 Pact summit in Bucharest for renewed "socialist internationalism," denouncing "nationalistic tendencies," and rhetorically demoting Czechoslovakia to an "outpost of socialism." He had ridiculed Czech claims to national autonomy as "babble."[63] Three years later, Ulbricht fell victim to the same logic of socialist solidarity when he continued to resist the new Soviet policy of détente and normalization of relations with the FRG. His resignation under pressure in 1971 came while the Soviets were negotiating for greater recognition of East German sovereignty from the FRG and the West, an irony that illustrates the paradox of a dominant state asserting de facto control even while defending its subordinate's sovereignty.

New documents about Ulbricht's fall also offer evidence about USSR–GDR interparty relations. Brezhnev had secretly designated Honecker as Ulbricht's successor in 1970. Honecker had been instructed during a one-on-one meeting to keep a close watch on Ulbricht and report back to the Kremlin at least once every two days. "I say to you in all candor, he will not be able to govern without taking us into account," Brezhnev had promised. "We have troops there, after all."[64] The Soviet move helped produce a politburo voting majority against Ulbricht by December. Honecker repeatedly sought the Soviet ambassador's assistance. He and his supporters in the politburo and Central Committee secretly wrote Brezhnev on 21 January, 1971 to complain that Ulbricht considered himself "on a par with Marx, Engels, and Lenin" and to suggest he be instructed to resign.[65] Why and when the Soviets decided to oblige this German request is the story of Ulbricht pushing the limits of sovereignty under informal empire too far.

The domestic sources of Ulbricht's fall included East German politburo resentment of his domineering neo-Stalinist style and difficulties sustaining the high level of economic development established after building the wall.[66] Internationally, the combination of a new Social Democratic government in the FRG and the Soviet policy of détente produced a bilateral USSR–FRG Renunciation of Force Treaty in August 1970 that did not recognize the GDR de jure. The Soviets, who had given up in February demanding de jure recognition, stopped insisting the FRG promise to negotiate with the GDR. They also accepted a side letter reasserting the FRG's goal of reunification. The German–German détente implied by Soviet détente policies threatened a central tenet of the GDR's claim to legitimacy. The claim was that only an aggressive capitalist front blocked peace and eventual reunification. With the advent of détente, a new formula was necessary. Ulbricht began casting GDR legitimacy in terms of separate nationhood for the first time, officially redesignating the GDR "a socialist German national state." The weakness of this ersatz nationalism would emerge clearly in 1989.

Ulbricht dug in his heels on the follow-up Berlin accord between all four occupying powers; the FRG had linked the accord's negotiation to ratification of the USSR–FRG bilateral treaty. The GDR disrupted travel to West Berlin, which, in the context of the USSR's new desire to reduce confrontation, ensured that the Soviets paid attention, too. The distance between Soviet and East German positions on Berlin remained large. Brezhnev conceded to the West that separate Berlin "interests" were at stake, despite the GDR's longstanding claim to the whole city. The Soviets agreed to isolate the issue of Berlin's legal status to speed agreement on the West's access rights. Eventually, the diplomatic pirouettes around the contested interpretation of GDR sovereignty ended with the West German promise to negotiate an agreement with "the same binding force customary between states."[67]

The prospective Berlin Treaty, and a third treaty between the GDR and the FRG, were so important to both the dominant and the subordinate states' understandings of their security interests that Ulbricht spent five weeks discussing the issue in Moscow, from 9 February to 15 March 1971. His de facto demand to control the pace of détente himself was so unacceptable that the Soviets finally agreed to help depose him. They used the leadership consultations link to signal the change. In April, Honecker led an official delegation to the USSR without Ulbricht. On 3 May 1971, after the Soviets had abruptly canceled his next scheduled Moscow consultations, Ulbricht announced his resignation as party leader. When Ulbricht died in 1973 no foreign dignitaries attended his funeral. He had pursued to its limit the motive for resisting external control inherent in sovereignty under hierarchy.

Honecker's more loyal policies included cooperating with negotiation of the Four-Power Berlin Treaty, which opened the GDR for the first time since the wall's construction to large numbers of visitors from the West. He reiterated Ulbricht's demands for an exchange of ambassadors and other attributes of de jure recognition, but immediately dropped them when Brezhnev insisted. The trio of treaties that initiated the era of détente was then completed with the signing in December of a GDR–FRG Basic Treaty, in which the two Germanies agreed to exchange Permanent Representatives, respect each other's independence, and cooperate on many mundane issues. A dominant state's policy change had forced its subordinate to adopt unwanted policies and change its leader.

International recognition, new thinking, and collapse, 1971 to 1989

Now that the new GDR leadership had defined its security interests in terms of Soviet-led détente, it received diplomatic recognition from more than a hundred states by 1972. West Germany never granted full diplomatic recognition, always calling its envoy in East Berlin a Permanent Representative, and putting "inner-German" policy under the purview of the chancellor's office, rather than the foreign ministry. But the United Nations admitted the two Germanies simultaneously in 1973, and the GDR signed the Helsinki Final Act in 1977. Honecker discovered other benefits in détente, earning trade credits for easing travel and communication restrictions and selling 33,755 political prisoners for more than $1 billion.[68] Honecker also tried to use détente to help ameliorate his continuing domestic legitimacy problem. Casting himself as one leader of a socialist international peace campaign was popular. The GDR jettisoned the ideological innovations by Ulbricht that had displeased the Soviets and shifted economic priority from rapid industrialization to consumer goods production, reducing shortages of housing, food, and durable goods. Honecker searched less successfully for ways to limit the threat that increased exposure to the West posed to societal compliance.

A revised Friendship Treaty in 1975 formalized the GDR's socialist "international duty," and loyalty to the USSR remained a Honecker theme. In 1979, he wrote that "the closer the friendship with the Soviet Union, the better socialism in one's own country."[69] Loyalty meant embracing détente. In fact, East German theorists took the logic of détente further than its Soviet originators had. Ideas foreshadowing what would later become New Thinking came out of the GDR's Institute for International Relations. It suggested that socialist states should focus on reducing the military factor in international relations and cooperate with all countries to help solve global problems, such as energy and the environment.[70]

But détente also posed an undeniable threat by removing an important legitimizing "enemy image" (*Feindbild*). To limit the risk that the world would seem safe enough for German reunification at the GDR's expense, Honecker decided to counterbalance inter-German cooperation in the name of détente with a strict policy of "delimitation" (*Abgrenzung*). Ideological vigilance was increased; the *Stasi* was expanded; elementary schools initiated compulsory military training; and more than one million citizens suddenly found themselves banned from the new opportunities for travel to the West since they were labeled "carriers of state secrets." Eventually the regime resurrected and tried to co-opt the images of German historical figures such as Prussia's Frederick the Great and Martin Luther.

At the end of the 1970s, though, Brezhnev abruptly abandoned détente. The sharpening confrontation with NATO and the United States inspired a renewed Soviet emphasis on unity and ideological orthodoxy. The cohesion of the Soviet informal empire in Eastern Europe became a practical requirement for realizing policies such as the Los Angeles Olympics boycott. And the Intermediate-range Nuclear Forces (INF) debate focused each alliance directly on the Germanies, as the new conservative majority in the West German Bundestag accepted US Pershing missiles and the Soviets threatened to install more SS-20s in the GDR.

Honecker exploited the room for maneuver created by the succession struggles in the Kremlin, following Brezhnev's and Andropov's deaths, to cultivate renewed possibilities for autonomy. Even before the invasion of Afghanistan in 1979, the GDR had declined a Soviet request in 1977 to forego its "back door" into the European Community, through which the FRG exempted GDR products from duties.[71] The initial Soviet deployment of SS-20 missiles in 1982 so jeopardized the GDR's peace strategy that even a loyalist like Honecker openly challenged his patron. When NATO counter-deployed Pershing missiles, and the Soviets walked out of SALT negotiations in Geneva, he called even Soviet missiles "the devil's tool." The GDR made gestures of continued détente, like dismantling the automatic firing devices it had installed along the border with the FRG and quadrupling officially-sanctioned emigration. Honecker also convinced Andropov to replace a domineering Soviet ambassador with a more compliant one, who recalled that, "Andropov called me up and said, 'We need an ambassador in the GDR, not a governor.' "[72]

An unprecedentedly open ideological debate raged about whether GDR national interest might diverge from Soviet policy. Official theorists wrote that the ideology of socialist internationalism in no way excluded the pursuit of national interests. *Neues Deutschland* republished a Hungarian official's statement that national interests could be subordinated to socialist unity only "in an extraordinary situation."[73] The Soviets published a hard-line Czech rebuttal: "fundamental socialist interests" should not be sacrificed for "momentary national advantage."[74] The SED foreign policy journal *Horizont* nonetheless called differences of opinion "natural" in a "voluntary community of equal and independent parties."[75]

In this contentious ideological atmosphere, the Soviets drew the line on East German sovereignty at Honecker's proposed first visit to the

FRG. Chancellor Helmut Kohl had invited him at Andropov's funeral in February 1984, and Konstantin Chernenko had twice approved, but Honecker canceled the visit at the last minute in September. Soviet foreign minister Andrei Gromyko ironically praised his demonstration of "socialist internationalism in action."[76]

Interparty relations, which routinely had served the dominant state's interests in the past, now contributed to the subordinate state's autonomy. The confusion that had been evident in the Soviet response to the rise of Solidarity in Poland in 1980 to 1981 spanned the entire period between Brezhnev's death and the beginning of the Chernenko era. In contrast, Honecker's position was secure and he could exploit a divided Kremlin. The Soviet leadership struggle ended only in 1985. Mikhail Gorbachev consolidated his control and began to turn Soviet foreign policy not back to détente, which Honecker would have embraced, but in the radical direction of a New Thinking no longer based on socialist internationalism.

Suddenly the Soviets began scaling down their sponsorship of the subordinate states in Eastern Europe in order to save money and promote lucrative new ties to the West. New Soviet foreign minister Eduard Shevardnadze granted "respect for full sovereignty" and considered members of the informal empire "completely free to choose their own path."[77] Because Soviet troops in Eastern Europe had "proved to be unbearably costly," he advocated opening "a credit line of trust" by "convincing the world of the absence of a Soviet threat."[78] But precisely because they were no longer willing to intervene, the Soviets ironically had set the GDR free to *not* redefine its own interest.

The GDR continued to depend on internal and external protection derived from its subordinate position in the Soviet informal empire. Yet the opportunities it had found to exercise limited autonomy under hierarchy generated a false sense of security. New Thinking stimulated unprecedented East German criticism of the Soviet Union despite the GDR's stake in its subordinate status. Unwilling to risk liberalization on the Soviet model of *glasnost*, the GDR ended up with enough autonomy to spark a "peaceful revolution" instead. The connection between New Thinking and "the German question" was direct. What Honecker later called a decision to sacrifice the GDR was not immediately apparent. Although Shevardnadze claimed, "After April 1985, the possibility of military intervention was completely ruled out,"[79] Honecker only perceived the implications of the policy change in 1987.[80] The West, of course, was tardier still.

267

Escalating societal discontent spawned open dissent, but Honecker could still resist the reforms his patron advocated but did not dictate. While Gorbachev reiterated the "absolute priority of cooperative links between fraternal countries," he also proclaimed their independence.[81] One East German politburo member mocked, "Just because your neighbor changes the wallpaper in his house does not mean you must do so as well."[82] In 1988 Gorbachev rejected "force and interference in internal affairs"[83] and Honecker walked out of the Soviet pavilion at an East German trade fair when New Thinking was mentioned. An official Soviet think tank referred to "the Brezhnev Doctrine of limited sovereignty now being eliminated," and the GDR banned the widely read German-language Soviet journal devoted to Gorbachev's reforms, *Sputnik*.[84] By April 1989 a frank Soviet policy memo catalogued the implications of New Thinking for the GDR, criticized Honecker's "ideological primitivism," declared that the GDR had lost its economic competition with the FRG, and concluded that "one cannot conceive of a common European home without overcoming the division of Germany."[85] The Soviets did not fully abandon their client – with Gorbachev pledging his commitment to Honecker "personally"[86] – but they clearly expected to see change. Honecker resisted this to the end, which came quickly.

In September 1989, as the opening of the Hungarian border with Austria generated a flood of East German refugees, the Soviets gave up working through Honecker. Expecting financial credits from the FRG, the Hungarians had abrogated their consular agreement with the GDR.[87] The SED regime began to pay for its failure to manufacture consent in society as the lingering state–society struggle erupted into the first demonstrations since 1953. As the opposition movement, New Forum, organized, special trains transported hundreds of East Germans who had sought refuge in the West German embassy in Prague back across the GDR to the West. It was during this precarious moment that Gorbachev issued his last warning: "Life punishes those who act too late," during fortieth anniversary festivities on 7 October.[88] Security forces suddenly stopped using attack dogs, tear gas, and water cannons to break up demonstrations. The protest crowds then mushroomed to sizes of 100,000 and more.

Throughout this ferment the hierarchical organizational links of informal empire remained intact. Relatively young East German polit- buro members Egon Krenz and Günter Schabowski kept Soviet ambas- sador Vyacheslav Kochemasov closely informed as they deposed

Honecker and declared a vaguely reformist policy "turnabout" (*Wende*) in mid-October. Krenz then consulted Gorbachev in Moscow before appointing Hans Modrow, a more serious advocate of *perestroika* and *glasnost*, as prime minister. On 9 November, ambassador Kochemasov conveyed Moscow's "green light" for looser travel regulations but not, it seems, for the last-minute gamble to completely open the wall.[89] Krenz cabled Gorbachev that large crowds at border-crossing points had forced his hand, thereby confusing cause with effect.[90] A Soviet emissary may have brokered his resignation, which came after just fifty-five days in office. The Soviets continued to influence the East German democratic transition under Modrow from November 1989 to the election in March 1990. Perhaps ironically, New Thinking was implemented through the interparty organizational links of informal empire.

Soviet influence became much less direct under the democratic government of lawyer Lothar de Maizière. But even when the Germanies agreed after the March election to monetary union, which had the effect of compromising East German sovereignty irreversibly, New Thinking never extended to reunification negotiations. Until the Soviets dropped their demand in July 1990 that a unified Germany be neutral, de Maizière had resisted allowing a democratic GDR to become "a buffer zone."[91] GDR–USSR relations in the era of New Thinking demonstrate that even though it is possible for dominant and subordinate states in an informal empire to redefine their security interests, the process can be protracted and may, under some circumstances, jeopardize the hierarchical relationship itself. In the fall of 1989, after repeatedly exploiting its limited sovereignty, the GDR finally secured sufficient autonomy to collapse, *almost* entirely on its own.

Conclusion

This chapter operates at two levels. On the one hand, it focuses on the articulation of two different principles for distributing political authority in international politics, one sovereign/anarchical and the other hierarchical. The process that underlies this articulation is one of producing and reproducing competing conceptions of states' rights or social competencies, which exist by virtue of recognition at the international level. These competencies constitute different modes of subjectivity or identity in international politics, which, despite their apparent contradictions, form a remarkably coherent structure of transnational authority. On the other hand, thinking about the constitution of political authority forces us to question traditional ways of thinking about the third-image project, which has been dominated by rationalism and materialism.

Insofar as the articulation of sovereignty with more hierarchical principles of governance is about constituting the boundaries of sovereign identity, a rationalist approach that accords privilege to that identity cannot give us a full picture of what's going on in informal empire. Certainly the Soviet and East German states made rational choices under constraints, engaged in exchange relationships, and encountered principal–agent problems, all as rationalism would predict. But as an exclusive basis for systemic theory such an approach is problematic, since an important part of what was going on in the system was the ongoing negotiation of each actor's identity. The existence of certain identities was very much at stake during interaction, often poignantly so, and as such they were not, in fact, exogenously given. As an empirical claim about the world, therefore, this rationalist assumption would seem to be mistaken, even if it is useful for certain purposes. The structure of informal empire constructs certain kinds of subjects; it does not merely constrain the behavior of preexisting subjects.

Given that the articulation of sovereignty with hierarchy is about constituting authority rather than simply domination, a materialist approach that sees only material capability also cannot give us a full picture of what's going on. Certainly the foundation of this system was unequal material power. The significance of this was shown when the Soviets withdrew support in 1989. Yet the distribution of material capabilities tells us little about the purposes that the Soviet–East German relationship served, or the rules, norms, and expectations that governed its dynamics – in short, how the system worked. East German leaders at times showed surprising independence from the Soviets, due to their participation, albeit incomplete, in the institution of sovereignty. At other times, they showed surprising deference to Soviet ideas and desires, a willingness to surrender private judgment more characteristic of an authority relationship. These features of the Soviet–East German system cannot be explained in terms of big billiard balls pushing around smaller ones. Instead, we need to know what intersubjective meanings state actors made of material inequalities, which is a fundamentally social process.

270

The East German case is exceptional. Few states in the contemporary international system have been as thoroughly and deeply dependent on a single Great Power, although many live in varying degrees with such dependence. However, it is representative in a larger sense of processes in international politics to which virtually all states are subject: processes by which identities and interests are constructed by intersubjective dynamics at the systemic level. The materialist and rationalist models that dominate mainstream international relations theory have many strengths, but an analysis of such processes is not one of them. For this we need a constructivist research program in which their investigation is part of the hard core.

Notes

For helpful comments on previous drafts the authors would like to thank Mike Barnett, Mlada Bukovansky, Mark Laffey, A. James McAdams, John Odell, Walter Süss, Nina Tannenwald, Henry Turner, Celeste Wallander, Jutta Weldes, members of the Sovereignty Project, and four anonymous referees. Friedheim also thanks the Berlin Program for Advanced German and European Studies, which supported his field research. This chapter is an earlier version of an article published under the same title in *International Organization* in Fall 1995.

[1] Waltz, Kenneth 1959. *Man, the State, and War*. New York: Columbia University Press.

[2] See, for example, Mearsheimer, John 1994–1995. "The False Promise of International Institutions," *International Security* 19: 5–49, and for a response, see Wendt, Alexander 1995. "Constructing International Politics," *International Security* 20: 71–81.

[3] See, for example, Wendt, Alexander 1987. "The Agent–Structure Problem in International Relations Theory," *International Organization* 41: 335–70; Dessler, David 1989. "What's at Stake in the Agent–Structure Debate?" *International Organization* 43: 441–74; and Buzan, Barry et al. 1993. *The Logic of Anarchy*. New York: Columbia University Press.

[4] For a more extensive development of this map see Wendt, Alexander Forthcoming. *Social Theory of International Politics*. New York: Cambridge University Press, chap. 1.

[5] For applications to the East European case see, for example, Zimmerman, William 1978. "Dependency Theory and the Soviet–East European Hierarchical Regional System," *Slavic Review* 37: 604–21, and Bunce, Valerie 1985. "The Empire Strikes Back: The Evolution of the Eastern Bloc from a Soviet Asset to a Soviet Liability," *International Organization* 39: 1–46.

[6] The reason for this may lie in the "production of like units" argument, which makes processes of identity and interest-formation seem uninteresting. For individualist interpretations of neorealism see Ashley, Richard 1984. "The

Poverty of Neorealism," *International Organization* 38: 225–86, and Wendt, "The Agent–Structure Problem."

[7] Waltz, Kenneth 1979. *Theory of International Politics*. Reading: Addison-Wesley, p. 96.

[8] Krasner, Stephen 1983. "Regimes and the Limits of Realism: Regimes as Autonomous Variables," in Krasner, Stephen (ed.) *International Regimes*. Ithaca: Cornell University Press, pp. 355–68.

[9] For a good overview of such models see Moe, Terry 1984. "The New Economics of Organization," *American Journal of Political Science* 28: 739–77.

[10] Among them are neo-Gramscian theories, the world-society paradigm of John Meyer, poststructuralist theories, and arguably the English School of Hedley Bull. See Wendt, *Social Theory of International Politics*.

[11] This definition is specific to the Westphalian states system; there may be other systems lacking the institution of sovereignty but containing informal empires, but these would involve somewhat different principles and dynamics than the ones we address here.

[12] On the distinction between state-as-actor and state-as-structure see Benjamin, Roger and Duvall, Raymond 1985. "The Capitalist State in Context," in Benjamin, R. and Elkin, S. (eds.) *The Democratic State*. Lawrence: University of Kansas Press.

[13] On the concept of an "international state" see Wendt, Alexander 1994. "Collective Identity Formation and the International State," *American Political Science Review* 88: 384–96, and the citations therein.

[14] See Milner, Helen 1991. "The Assumption of Anarchy in International Relations Theory," *Review of International Studies* 17: 67–85; and Ferguson, Yale and Mansbach, Richard 1991. "Between Celebration and Despair: Constructive Suggestions for Future International Theory," *International Studies Quarterly* 35: 363–86.

[15] See James, Alan 1986. *Sovereign Statehood*. London: Allen & Unwin.

[16] See Ruggie, John 1983. "Continuity and Transformation in the World Polity: Toward a Neorealist Synthesis," *World Politics* 35: 261–85; and Kratochwil, Friedrich 1989. *Rules, Norms, and Decisions*. Cambridge: Cambridge University Press.

[17] On the difference this makes see Jackson, Robert and Rosberg, Carl 1982. "Why Africa's Weak States Persist: The Empirical and the Juridical in Statehood," *World Politics* 35: 1–24, and Strang, David 1991. "Anomaly and Commonplace in European Expansion: Realist and Institutionalist Accounts," *International Organization* 46: 143–62.

[18] For an earlier version of this argument see Wendt, Alexander and Barnett, Michael 1993. "Dependent State Formation and Third World Militarization," *Review of International Studies* 19: 321–47. Among existing theoretical treatments of dominant–subordinate state relations ours is closest to that of Robinson, Ronald 1986. "The Eccentric Idea of Imperialism, With or Without Empire," in Mommsen, Wolfgang and Osterhammel, Jürgen (eds.) *Imperialism and After*. London: Allen & Unwin, pp. 267–89, and Ikenberry, John and Kupchan,

Charles 1990. "Socialization and Hegemonic Power," *International Organization* 44: 283–316. A classic formulation of our argument in the East European context is Brzezinski, Zbigniew 1967. *The Soviet Bloc*. Cambridge, Mass.: Harvard University Press.

[19] On the concept of weak states see Buzan, Barry 1991. *People, States, and Fear*. Boulder: Lynne Rienner.

[20] Fave, Richard Della 1986. "The Dialectics of Legitimation and Counter-norms," *Sociological Perspectives* 29: 441.

[21] On the lobbyist analogy see Naimark, Norman 1989. "Soviet–GDR Relations: An Historical Overview," *Bundesinstitut für ostwissenschaftliche und internationale Studien* 51: 8.

[22] On the general problems of legitimizing domination see Merelman, Richard 1986. "Domination, Self-Justification, and Self-Doubt: Some Social-Psychological Considerations," *Journal of Politics* 48: 276–300.

[23] On this effect see, for example, Wolf, Charlotte 1986. "Legitimation of Oppression: Response and Reflexivity," *Symbolic Interaction* 9: 217–34, and England, Paula and Browne, Irene 1992. "Internalization and Constraint in Women's Subordination," in Agger, Ben (ed.) *Current Perspectives in Social Theory*. Greenwich: JAI Press, pp. 97–123.

[24] See Blau, Peter 1963. "Critical Remarks on Weber's Theory of Authority," *American Political Science Review* 57: 305–16; and Ruggie, John 1983. "International Regimes, Transactions, and Change: Embedded Liberalism in the Postwar Economic Order," in Krasner, *International Regimes*, pp. 195–232.

[25] Blau, "Critical Remarks," p. 307.

[26] Ibid., p. 307.

[27] Lukes, Steven 1991. "Power and Authority," in his *Moral Conflict and Politics*. Oxford: Clarendon Press, p. 95.

[28] It is in virtue of this authoritative or state-like character that we prefer the language of "informal empire" to "spheres of influence," which is the more traditional way to describe such relationships, even though in many respects our argument is similar. On spheres of influence in world politics see, for example, Keal, Paul 1983. *Unspoken Rules and Superpower Dominance*. New York: St. Martin's Press; and Triska, Jan (ed.) 1986. *Dominant Powers and Subordinate States*. Durham: Duke University Press.

[29] For an empirical study of such subordination see Barany, Zoltan 1991. "Soviet Control of the Hungarian Military under Stalin," *Journal of Strategic Studies* 14: 148–64.

[30] On this point more generally see Geser, Hans 1992. "Towards an Interaction Theory of Organizational Actors," *Organization Studies* 13: 429–51. One thinks here of the incorporation of Algeria into Metropolitan France in the 1950s.

[31] For a good discussion of this relationship see Poggi, Gianfranco 1988. "Max Weber's Conceptual Portrait of Feudalism," *British Journal of Sociology* 39: 211–27.

[32] The principal previous use of this analogy in international relations

Alexander Wendt and Daniel Friedheim

scholarship is by Johan Galtung in 1971. "A Structural Theory of Imperialism," *Journal of Peace Research* 8: 81–109.

³³ Cf. Ruggie, "Continuity and Transformation in the World Polity."

³⁴ For a good discussion of role conflict in international relations see Barnett, Michael 1993. "Institutions, Roles, and Disorder: The Case of the Arab States System," *International Studies Quarterly* 37: 271–96.

³⁵ Wolf, "Legitimation of Oppression," p. 225.

³⁶ On this point see Zimmerman, William 1972. "Hierarchical Regional Systems and the Politics of System Boundaries," *International Organization* 26: 26.

³⁷ Andert, Reinhold and Herzberg, Wolfgang 1990. *Der Sturz: Honecker im Kreuzverhör.* Berlin: Weimar, p. 62.

³⁸ Sodaro, Michael 1990. *Moscow, Germany, and the West: From Khrushchev to Gorbachev.* Ithaca: Cornell University Press, p. 9.

³⁹ Jones, Robert 1989. *The Soviet Concept of "Limited Sovereignty" from Lenin to Gorbachev.* New York: St. Martin's Press, pp. 143, 175.

⁴⁰ Djilas, Milovan 1962. *Conversations with Stalin.* New York: Harcourt, Brace & World, p. 114.

⁴¹ Documents recently located in German archives show that Stalin told SED leaders on 18 December 1948 that "the situation cannot be compared" because there was "still no unified state." Staritz, Dietrich 1991. "Die SED, Stalin, und die Gründung der DDR," *Das Parlament* 41: B7.

⁴² As he told Leonhard, Wolfgang 1979/1957. *Child of the Revolution.* London: Link Inks, p. 303.

⁴³ Contrast Ackermann, Anton 1946. "Gibt es einen besonderen deutschen Weg zum Sozialismus?" *Einheit* 1: 22 passim; and Ackermann, 1948. "Über den einzig möglichen Weg zum Sozialismus," *Neues Deutschland.*

⁴⁴ Leonhard, *Child of the Revolution*, pp. 362–3.

⁴⁵ Naimark, Norman M. 1994. "'To know everything and to report everything worth knowing': Building the East German Police State, 1945–49," Cold War International History Project (hereinafter CWIHP), Working Paper 10, Washington, D.C.: Woodrow Wilson Center, p. 10.

⁴⁶ See the memoirs of American occupation commander Gen. Clay, Lucius 1950. *Decision in Germany.* Westport, Conn.: Greenwood, p. 179.

⁴⁷ "Brief der SED-Führung an J.W. Stalin," presented September 17, 1949 and "Vorschläge des Politburos an den P[artei] V[orstand] ..." received September 27, 1949. Staritz, "Die SED, Stalin, und die Grundung der DDR," B9.

⁴⁸ He was Franz Dahlem. Richter, James 1993. "Re-examining Soviet Policy Towards Germany in 1953," *Europe–Asia Studies* 45: 676.

⁴⁹ Deputy Foreign Minister Andrei Gromyko had proposed playing the nationalism card to stop NATO's formation. See Wettig, Gerhard 1993. "Die Deutschland-Note vom 10.März 1952 auf der Basis diplomatischer Akten des russischen Außenministeriums: Die Hypothese des Wieder-vereinigungsange-bots," *Deutschland Archiv* 26: 795.

[50] Internal survey conducted February–March 1953, as quoted in Loth, Wilfried 1994. *Stalins unbeliebtes Kind*. Berlin: Rowohlt, p. 196.

[51] These figures are based on newly available Stasi reports. See Mitter, Armin 1991. "Die Ereignisse im Juni und Juli 1953," *Das Parlament*, B32–3.

[52] As quoted in Herrnstadt, Rudolf 1990. *Das Herrnstadt Dokument, das Politbüro der SED und die Geschichte des 17.Juni 1953*. Berlin: Rowohlt, p. 74.

[53] See Baras, Victor 1975. "Beria's Fall and Ulbricht's Survival," *Soviet Studies* 27: 380.

[54] Beria's rivals accused him of being too willing to abandon the GDR; Andrei Gromyko quotes him having said: "The GDR? What is the GDR worth? It's not even a real state. It is kept alive only by Soviet troops, even if we call it the German Democratic Republic." 1989. *Memories*. London: Hutchinson, p. 318.

[55] Herrnstadt, *Dokument*, pp. 149, 163.

[56] Rytlewski, Ralf 1984. "Politik in der DDR als Ritual: Das Beispiel der Jugendweihe," *DDR-Report* 12: 717.

[57] Turner, Henry 1992. *Germany from Partition to Reunification*. New Haven: Yale University Press, p. 89.

[58] His influence on Soviet policy "actually increased as the stability of the . . . regime weakened," concludes Harrison, Hope 1993. "Ulbricht and the Concrete Rose: New Archival Evidence on the Dynamics of Soviet–East German Relations and the Berlin Crisis," CWIHP, Working Paper 5, p. 20.

[59] See then Soviet Embassy translator Kvitzinsky, Yuli 1993. *Vor dem Sturm* [Before the Storm]. Frankfurt: Siedler, p. 179.

[60] Letter dated 15 September, as quoted in Harrison, "Concrete Rose," p. 52.

[61] Robert Slusser identifies Ulbricht's hard-line allies in the Soviet politburo as Mikhail Suslov and Frol Kozlov, and chronicles the party congress in 1973. *The Berlin Crisis of 1961: Soviet–American Relations & the Struggle for Power in the Kremlin*. Baltimore: Johns Hopkins University Press, pp. 355–8, 377–80, 440–1.

[62] According to the "Arbeitsgemeinschaft 13. August" [13th of August Working Group], 507 citizens also died trying to cross East German land and sea frontiers. See *Tagesspiegel* (12 August 1994).

[63] McAdams, A. James 1985. *East Germany and Détente: Building Authority after the Wall*. Cambridge: Cambridge University, pp. 84, 90–1.

[64] See the former party archives in Berlin, "Protokoll einer Unterredung zwischen L.I. Breschnew und Erich Honecker" (28 July 1970), Document 5, Arbeitsprotokoll 8, Politbüro (1989), Stiftung Archiv der Parteien und Massenorganisationen der DDR (hereinafter SAPMO): J IV 2/2A/3196.

[65] "Brief an Breschnew" (21 January 1971), Document 17, ibid.

[66] Naumann, Gerhard and Trümpler, Eckhard 1990. *Von Ulbricht zu Honecker: 1970, ein Krisenjahr der DDR*. Berlin: Dietz, p. 35 passim.

[67] And the statement that the treaty was signed only "after consultation and agreement with the government of the GDR." The language in the USSR–FRG bilateral treaty was: "respect for the independence and autonomy of each of

the two states in matters concerning their internal competency within their respective borders." Moreton, Edwina 1978. *East Germany and the Warsaw Alliance*. Boulder: Westview, pp. 191, 151.

[68] Payments totaled 3.5 billion Deutche Marks, according to the West German official in charge of the secret program. See Rehlinger, Ludwig 1991. *Freikauf, Die Geschäfte der DDR mit politisch Verfolgten, 1963–1989*. Frankfurt: Ullstein, p. 247.

[69] As quoted in Gedmin, Jeffrey 1992. *The Hidden Hand: Gorbachev and the Collapse of East Germany*. Washington, D.C.: American Enterprise Institute, p. 29.

[70] See Sodaro, *Moscow, Germany, and the West*, pp. 302–4.

[71] The "Protocol on German Internal Trade and Connected Problems" attached to the original Treaty of Rome. See Pinder, John 1991. *The EC and Eastern Europe*. London: Pinter, p. 9.

[72] Kochemasov, Vyacheslav 1992. "'Schmeichelei und Unterwürfigkeit': Moskaus Ex-Botschafter in der DDR ... über Erich Honecker," *Der Spiegel* 47: 148–9. He replaced Abrasimov.

[73] 1984. "The Reciprocal Effect of National and International Interests," *Tarsadalmi Szemle*, as quoted in Asmus, Ronald 1985. "Dialectics of Détente and Discord," *Orbis* 28: 754.

[74] 1984. "The National and the International Policy of the CPCS," *Rude Pravo*, ibid.

[75] Neubert, Harald 1984. "The Actual Tasks of Communists," ibid., p. 758.

[76] During the GDR's 35th Anniversary celebrations in Berlin, 7 October 1984, ibid., p. 765.

[77] Shevardnadze, Eduard 1991. *The Future Belongs to Freedom*. London: Sinclair-Stevenson, p. 124.

[78] Ibid., pp. xvi, 58–9.

[79] Ibid., p. 121.

[80] Based on reporting by East German ambassador König that the "common European home" would be built at the GDR's expense. *Der Sturz*, p. 21.

[81] As quoted in Gedmin, *Hidden Hand*, p. 12.

[82] Kurt Hager in *Neues Deutschland* (10 April 1987), p. 3.

[83] As quoted in Gedmin, *Hidden Hand*, p. 20.

[84] Ibid., p. 21.

[85] Vyacheslav Dashichev, as reprinted in *Der Spiegel* (5 February 1990), pp. 50–1.

[86] Or so Honecker claimed in his report on a trip to Moscow from 27 June to 1 July 1989. See 1989. *Beschlußprotokolle des Politbüros* SAPMO: JIV 2/2/2235.

[87] Gyula Horn calls himself "the Hungarian Foreign Minister who opened the Iron Curtain" in his 1991. *Freiheit, die ich meine*. Hamburg: Hoffmann & Campe, p. 308.

[88] "Stenografische Niederschrift," Gorbachev meeting with SED politburo in Berlin (7 October 1989), SAPMO: JIV/971.

[89] The best summary of recent findings about the mysterious decision to

open the wall unconditionally is Maximytschew, Igor and Hertle, Hans-Hermann 1994. "Die Maueröffnung," *Deutschland Archiv* 27: 1148 passim.

[90] Cable dated 10 November 1989, SAPMO: IV 2/1/704: 83–4.

[91] As quoted in Menges, Constantine 1991. *The Future of Germany and the Atlantic Alliance*. Washington, D.C.: American Enterprise Institute, pp. 103–4.

**Reconstructing the analysis of
sovereignty: concluding reflections
and directions for future research**

Cynthia Weber and Thomas J. Biersteker

Social construction links identity with practice. The practices that
interest us in this volume are those that construct and deconstruct
territorial states and international systems, as well as organize relations
among these different entities. The identity of the territorial state is not
given, but is constituted through complex, overlapping, and often
contradictory practices. Numerous practices participate in the social
construction of a territorial state as sovereign, including the stabilization of state boundaries, the recognition of territorial states as sovereign, and the conferring of rights onto sovereign states.

As Alexander Murphy notes in Chapter 4, p. 119, "the survival and
success of sovereignty as an organizing principle of the modern state
system has much to do with its territorial underpinnings." But territorial boundaries are not the only ones that require stabilization. The
chapters by Michael Barnett and Daniel Deudney suggest that territorial boundaries do not always coincide with spheres of authority.
The boundaries between pan-Arabism and territorial nationalism
(Barnett) or between Westphalian and Philadelphian authority systems
(Deudney) are not straightforward, but require constant attention and
negotiation to make them appear as if they are.

Roxanne Doty suggests in Chapter 5, p. 122, that state boundaries
are not just a function of territory or authority relations. Rather, they
 are also "a function of a state's ... ability ... to impose fixed and stable
meanings about who belongs and who does not belong to the nation."
This is important because, as Doty's chapter illustrates, national
identities are unstable, not only in war zones and Third World
countries, but also in seemingly stable nation-states like Great Britain.
For Doty, debates about immigration policy are the very practices that
help refine the definition of the boundary between *inside* and *outside*.

278

As these authors argue, constructing the identity of a territorial state entails the construction and reconstruction of a stabilized *inside* (a population organized into a nation) that is clearly delineated from the *outside* (alternative organizations of this population and other populations). The construction of the inside versus the outside of a territorial state is a function of both the internal process of nation-building (as Barnett and Deudney argue), which may be, as Doty suggests on p. 122 of her chapter, "a function of a state's discursive authority" and of external practices of recognition.

As we argued in Chapter 1, recognizing a territorial state as sovereign is often viewed as the "social" part of social construction. David Strang's chapter alerts us to an often-neglected dimension of external recognition – that the meaning of social recognition is itself socially constructed. Strang argues on p. 45, Chapter 2, that recognition depends upon "broad understandings of the cultural features that states share." He notes that sovereignty has historically been denied to those deemed "uncivilized" (as it was during the age of imperialism), to republicans (as it was during the Napoleanic wars), or to socialist revolutionaries (as it was at the beginning of the twentieth century).

Social recognition of a territorial state as *sovereign* constitutes a particular identity that enjoys certain rights, "even if the exercise of those rights is constrained," as Alexander Wendt and Daniel Friedheim suggest in Chapter 8, p. 240. These rights themselves are a product of contestation and negotiation, and are therefore an integral part of identity construction. Even though rights that help to ensure the viability of sovereign territorial states (such as a right to international independence and a right to claim absolute authority within its domain) traditionally have been central to the identity of sovereign states, they may fall short of enabling a state to "realize sovereignty." Naeem Inayatullah underscores this point in Chapter 3, when he broadens the scope of the analysis of sovereignty to include international political economy issues. One right that Inayatullah argues should be included among the rights of sovereign states is a right to wealth. Without this right, Inayatullah believes states cannot be constituted as fully sovereign, that is, able to maintain independence, autonomy, or authority.

On reflection, one of the most striking conclusions that emerges from these chapters is the observation that while state sovereignty is important, it is only one among several competing organizing principles for

279

state relations in the international system. As Wendt and Friedheim suggest, sovereignty is only one of many identities that a state actor can take on. Indeed, every author in this collection identifies and elaborates on at least one important alternative to state sovereignty.

Inayatullah, Wendt and Friedheim, and Deudney all focus on authority relations as the basis for alternative ways of thinking about state relations in the international system. For Wendt and Friedheim, the hierarchy associated with informal empire suggests a different way of distributing political authority in international politics. While sovereignty distributes political authority on the basis of territorial exclusivity, informal empire – described by Wendt and Friedheim on p. 245 as "transnational structures of de facto political authority in which members are juridically sovereign states" – does so on the basis of hierarchical international governance.

For Inayatullah, the international division of labor provides an equally compelling alternative organizing principle. It, too, is based on a hierarchy – in this instance a hierarchy of wealth – and has associated with it detailed roles and functions for different states in a cohesive, integrated international economy.

For Deudney, writing in Chapter 7, p. 191, systems that "are constituted without exclusive sovereignty within the units and are amalgamated with other similar units in ways that go beyond instrumental alliance or confederation" provide important alternatives to Westphalian state sovereignty. He identifies a great many different political orders of this sort that have existed on the periphery of the Westphalian system, including the Hanseatic League, the Swiss Confederation, the Holy Roman Empire, the Iroquois Federation, the Concert of Europe, the early United States, and possibly, the emerging European Union. His analysis of the Philadelphian states-union of the early United States provides not only an alternative to state sovereignty, but also what he describes on p. 230 as the "extended lineage and more robust and rounded theoretical foundations for the distinctive American approach to international relations." It is an approach that encompasses America's longstanding concern with human rights, the spread of political democracy, and reliance on international organizations. For Deudney, this peculiarly American approach to international relations is not idealistic and utopian, but it reflects, as he suggests on page 000, "a choice between two different configurations of authority and institutional structure."

The identification of alternatives to state sovereignty is not based on differences in authority relations alone. Doty, Strang, and Barnett elaborate on the presence of competing identities that suggest alternatives to state sovereignty. For Doty, the identity associated with a Commonwealth discourse challenged the exclusionary, nationalist discourse associated with a narrow conception of state sovereignty. For Strang, non-Western conceptions of sovereignty and identity constitute important alternatives. Similarly, Barnett elaborates extensively on the alternative identity presented by pan-Arab nationalism. He contends in Chapter 6, p. 148, that pan-Arab nationalism – based on the claim "that the Arab state's authority derives not from its citizens, but from the Arab nation that envelops its borders" – clashed directly with Westphalian ideas of territorial exclusivity during the postcolonial period. Arab nationalists urged greater integration to erase the colonially derived territorial boundaries, as he writes on p. 149, "to bring them into line with the state and the nation."

Murphy contends in Chapter 4, p. 84, that "[s]ince no set of discrete territorial units – no matter how configured – can accommodate existing social, political, and economic arrangements, we need to consider the possibility of a multilayered and not strictly hierarchical approach to governance in which the territorial notions that undergird decisionmaking more closely reflect the different spatial structures in which issues and problems arise." He finds evidence for this emergent multilayered approach to governance in the contemporary European Union.

Thus, whether they base their argument on alternative authority relations, identities, or territorial conceptions, each of the authors in this volume identifies at least one significant alternative to state sovereignty. Many also make the important ancillary point that although these alternatives exist, they coexist simultaneously with state sovereignty and should not be conceptualized as mutually exclusive of it. Sometimes they coexist uneasily with state sovereignty, while at other times they exist in harmonious ambiguity.

With his emphasis on competing identities, Barnett contends that state sovereignty and pan-Arabism coexisted in uneasy and often conflictual ways. Barnett explains on p. 175 of Chapter 6 that "Arab states were embedded in overlapping international and regional societies that undermined their sovereignty, offered rival behavioral expectations and standards of legitimacy, and weighed heavily on their foreign policy." While state sovereignty appears to have prevailed in the recent past, it continues to coexist uneasily with elements of contemporary pan-Arabism and Islamic conceptions of identity that have gained force throughout the region.

For Wendt and Friedheim, sovereignty and hierarchy not only coexisted, but they both participated in the construction of state actors in informal empire. In a sense, the sovereignty of the German Democratic Republic was made possible, in part, because of its relationship in the informal empire of the former Soviet Union. Inayatullah makes a similar point when he describes state sovereignty and the international division of labor as complementary for juridical sovereignty, but not for actual sovereignty, where wealth is a prerequisite. He writes on p. 52 of Chapter 3, "[t]he constructed nature of weak or quasi- states can be revealed by clarifying the separable but not separate workings of both sovereignty and the division of labor, not only as opposing but also complementary principles that contribute to the constitution of a state." Thus, while alternative ways of organizing state relations in the international system often coexist, it would be misleading to imply that one consistently or characteristically "wins out" over another.

One final point that emerges from the chapters is the observation that the social construction of sovereignty is a constant, ongoing process. As Barnett suggests in Chapter 6, p. 176, "Arab leaders must continually work to reproduce the state's sovereignty." In his view, some of the recent disappointments associated with statist ideologies have contributed to the conditions in which alternative ethnic and religious identities have reemerged to challenge state sovereignty. Doty agrees with Barnett when she writes on p. 143 of Chapter 5 that "the social construction of sovereignty is always in process, and is a never completed project." With reference to the construction of national identity, she maintains that a people is always presumed and simultaneously in the process of formation.

The conclusions contained in this volume have important implications for traditional interpretations of state sovereignty offered by realists, rationalists, and materialists. In Chapter 7, Deudney moves beyond a realist frame of analysis to the point of subverting it. Deudney accomplishes this by identifying foreign policy practices such as *hiding* (pursuing isolation or neutrality) and *binding* (alliance formation) as alternatives to Westphalian, realist balancing practices. He contends that these different practices reinforce different configurations of sovereignty when he writes on p. 214 that "[b]alancing is congenial *with and reinforces a salient state sovereignty, while hiding and binding are uncongenial and subversive to it."*

In Chapter 8, Alexander Wendt and Daniel Friedheim make similar arguments concerning systems analysis. They argue that a social constructivist approach challenges "third-image" explanations of international politics. Wendt and Friedheim's analysis of Soviet–East German relations as informal empire illuminates aspects of their relationship that are missed by rationalist and materialist explanations. While a rationalist explanation offers a system-based theory, it takes state actors as given, thus neglecting how each actor's identity is negotiated in relations of informal empire. In contrast, Wendt and Friedheim argue on p. 270 of Chapter 8 that a materialist explanation – thanks to its predominant focus on material capabilities of state actors – "tells us little about the purposes that the Soviet–East German relationship served, or the rules, norms, and expectations that governed its dynamics – in short, how the system worked." They conclude on p. 270 that one cannot explain the independence and deference the German Democratic Republic showed the Soviets without knowing "what intersubjective meanings state actors made of material inequalities, which is a fundamentally social process."

Overall, the authors in this volume suggest several different avenues for future research, some that should be avoided and some that should be pursued.

Many point to the danger of dehistoricizing sovereignty, either by freezing its meaning through definitions or by relying on narrow understandings of history. Sovereignty is not an ontological problem that can be defined away. Rather, as Doty argues in Chapter 5, the questions raised by the practices of sovereignty elicit responses that attempt to fix the meanings of sovereignty and the identities that go by that name. As Murphy reminds us in Chapter 4, there is nothing fixed or undialectic about state sovereignty and its territorial basis. As he argues on p. 110, "To conclude ... that we are indefinitely imprisoned within the current political-territorial order ... is as dubious as to assume that territory and politics are about to be entirely uncoupled." Instead, we must resist the impulse to participate in fixing the meaning and the history of sovereignty through definitional practices and must instead treat "the current political map" as problematic. To do otherwise is to universalize one set of meanings and one history of sovereignty to the entire globe.

This point comes out most clearly in the chapters by Strang and

Inayatullah. Strang argues in Chapter 2, p. 23, that an international order based on recognition "is crucial only within the Westphalian conception." Furthermore, his work documents both the existence of non-Western conceptions of sovereignty and their active delegitimation by Western powers. Inayatullah links this process of delegitimation to the organization of the global economy. Examining the historical context of the world political economy, Inayatullah suggests, reveals the historical construction of the incapacities and weaknesses of Third World states. A universalized definition of state sovereignty would gloss over the very practices that are vital to the identity construction of colonial territories and postcolonial states.

The tendency by international relations theorists to dehistoricize understandings of state sovereignty is linked to a positivist desire to know precisely where we have been in history and when we are moving to a new historical era. But, as Murphy reminds us on p. 109 of Chapter 4, "If the history of state-territorial ideas and practices tells us anything, it is that changes in arrangements and understandings occur, but that no one era represents a radical break with the preceding era." This means that just as there was no clear break point at Westphalia from the non-sovereign to the sovereign, there is not going to be a single break point at which we see an unambiguous shift from sovereignty to non-sovereignty, regardless of how definitionally constrained our understandings of state sovereignty become.

With this in mind, then, there is little to gain from research efforts that define away the rich historical contents and changing practices that are often labeled state sovereignty. Indeed, there is much to be lost from such an exercise. What forms should a social constructivist research program take? The authors in this volume suggest many avenues for future research.

Among the promises of constructivism, Deudney argues on p. 192 of Chapter 7, is its openness "to variation in the forms of authority, sovereign or otherwise, and the social practices that constitute political order." Deudney advocates an analysis of the republican underpinnings of the Philadelphian states-union as a way of transcending the limitations of Westphalian models and understanding the social structures that exist between anarchy and hierarchy.

Furthermore, we must investigate the effects of a Westphalian model of authority. Doty makes this point in Chapter 5, p. 142, when she argues that an understanding of British state sovereignty as an externally recognized right to exercise final authority over its affairs "presumes the very things that *were* in doubt: the internal and external divide and the differentiation of the inside from the outside of the British nation-state." As researchers, we must remain open to possible variations and interrogate practices that try to fix the meanings of sovereignty and the identities constituted in part through practices associated with sovereignty.

This suggests that we should not treat state sovereignty as unproblematic and should not begin with pre-given conceptualizations of sovereign states. As Murphy argues on p. 103 of Chapter 4, "the modern territorial order pervades so much of our lives that we rarely even think about its role in shaping our spatial [political, cultural, and economic] imaginations." Mindful of this, we must ask how and why this is the case and what are the effects of an unproblematic treatment of state sovereignty.

We have suggested that one reason why sovereignty is treated unproblematically by international relations theorists is because the current social construction of state sovereignty is so exclusionary. As a focus of ongoing social constructivist research, we must continue to weave into our understandings of international relations forgotten histories of colonial territories and postcolonial states (Strang, Inayatullah, Murphy, Doty); neglected structures of the global political economy (Inayatullah), the Philadelphian states-union (Deudney), or hierarchies like informal empire (Wendt and Friedheim); and non-Western cultural configurations of sovereignty (Strang, Barnett). Once incorporated, these forgotten dimensions of international relations will continue to challenge our understandings of both sovereignty and the process of state-building. Critically evaluated through social constructivist lenses, neither set of practices – of sovereignty or of state-building – can be regarded as exclusively internal or external (Barnett, Doty, Inayatullah).

The result of this research program is to question understandings of the sovereign territorial state by questioning each of its components – territory, population, authority, and recognition – and the practices that constitute, delineate, and organize each of these components individually and collectively.

Social construction provides us with an approach that enables us to investigate how and why Westphalian state sovereignty is privileged in international relations theory and practice. Most important, it gives us a basis for self-consciously recognizing when we are reproducing the practices that constrain the meanings of sovereignty and privileging those understandings to the exclusion of others.

Note

For variety, the authors' names appear in reverse alphabetical order. The contributions of both authors, however, is equal.

Index

absolutism, 85, 86, 95
actors, 156, 159, 160, 171, 245
  and state sovereignty, 247–8
  states as, 246–7
  subordinate, 251
  transnational, 6–8
  see also agency
Afghanistan, 27, 37, 249, 266
Africa, 24, 26, 27, 29, 76, 125, 130
  cultural understandings of, 32
  imperialism in, 34, 35–6, 38, 44
  see also non-Western states
agency, 8, 10, 11, 76
  and environment, 156
  principal–agent model, 249, 270
  social construction of, 12
  and sovereignty, 13
  and structure, 243
  see also actors
'altercasting', 76
American Union, 191–2, 200–2
  admittance of states to, 208, 211–12
  binding practices in, 214
  centralized powers of, 203–4
  and Civil War, 209–12
  external threats to, 202–3
  fear of democracy in, 201
  law and constitution, 207–9
  popular arms control, 209
  popular sovereignty in, 195, 197–8
  see also Philadelphian system; United
    States
anarchy, 190, 192, 198–9, 200, 204, 205, 215,
  217
  in Arab system, 175
  of international systems, 5, 98
  and sovereign state system, 88, 248
  and state structures, 246–7
  in system theory, 194, 218, 244, 245

Andropov, Y., 266, 267
anticolonialism, 160–1
  see also colonialism
anti-immigrant discourse, 137–40
  see also British Commonwealth
    immigration
Arab–Israeli war (1967), 157, 165, 167
Arab Maghrebi Union, 169
Arab states system, 16
  absence of order in, 153–5
  changes in, 171–4
  conflicts within, 165, 168
  contradictions in, 174–5
  institutional framework of, 152–60
  integration and fragmentation in, 166,
    167
  interstate interactions, 166–71
  leadership of, 173–4
  realist accounts of, 157–8
  regional order in, 149, 151–2, 157–60
  role of nationalism in, 148–52, 154–5,
    158, 162, 164, 165, 169, 170
  sense of identity in, 170
  sovereignty in, 149–51, 160–2, 163–6,
    169, 171–4, 175–6
  state and nation in, 150–1, 177–8
  state formation in, 163–6
  summit meetings, 173
  unity talks, 172–3
  see also non-Western states; Middle East;
    pan-Arabism
arms, 249
  control, 209
Ashley, Richard, 123
Asia, 24, 27, 29, 125, 130
  cultural understandings of, 32
  imperialism in, 35, 38, 44
  see also British Commonwealth
    immigration; non-Western states